MW00668702

Biblical Studies

The
New Testament
Witness *to* Christ
& His Kingdom

The Messiah Announced

. . . .

The Messiah Opposed

. . . .

The Messiah Revealed

. . . .

The Messiah Vindicated

This curriculum is the result of thousands of hours of work by The Urban Ministry Institute (TUMI) and should not be reproduced without their express permission. TUMI supports all who wish to use these materials for the advance of God's Kingdom, and affordable licensing to reproduce them is available. Please confirm with your instructor that this book is properly licensed. For more information on TUMI and our licensing program, visit *www.tumi.org* and *www.tumi.org/license*.

Contents

1

2

3

4

About the Instructor

Rev. Dr. Don L. Davis is the Executive Director of The Urban Ministry Institute and a Senior Vice President of World Impact. He attended Wheaton College and Wheaton Graduate School, and graduated summa cum laude in both his B.A. (1988) and M.A. (1989) degrees, in Biblical Studies and Systematic Theology, respectively. He earned his Ph.D. in Religion (Theology and Ethics) from the University of Iowa School of Religion.

As the Institute's Executive Director and World Impact's Senior Vice President, he oversees the training of urban missionaries, church planters, and city pastors, and facilitates training opportunities for urban Christian workers in evangelism, church growth, and pioneer missions. He also leads the Institute's extensive distance learning programs and facilitates leadership development efforts for organizations and denominations like Prison Fellowship, the Evangelical Free Church of America, and the Church of God in Christ.

A recipient of numerous teaching and academic awards, Dr. Davis has served as professor and faculty at a number of fine academic institutions, having lectured and taught courses in religion, theology, philosophy, and biblical studies at schools such as Wheaton College, St. Ambrose University, the Houston Graduate School of Theology, the University of Iowa School of Religion, the Robert E. Webber Institute of Worship Studies. He has authored a number of books, curricula, and study materials to equip urban leaders, including *The Capstone Curriculum*, TUMI's premiere sixteen-module distance education seminary instruction, *Sacred Roots: A Primer on Retrieving the Great Tradition*, which focuses on how urban churches can be renewed through a rediscovery of the historic orthodox faith, and *Black and Human: Rediscovering King as a Resource for Black Theology and Ethics*. Dr. Davis has participated in academic lectureships such as the Staley Lecture series, renewal conferences like the Promise Keepers rallies, and theological consortiums like the University of Virginia Lived Theology Project Series. He received the Distinguished Alumni Fellow Award from the University of Iowa College of Liberal Arts and Sciences in 2009. Dr. Davis is also a member of the Society of Biblical Literature, and the American Academy of Religion.

Introduction to the Module

Greetings, in the strong name of Jesus Christ!

There can be no question that the most critical and important subject to master in the life of a Christian leader is the actual person and teachings of Jesus of Nazareth. No other subject is as significant or controversial as the meaning of his life and ministry. This module is designed to introduce you to a "life of Jesus" survey that concentrates on the historical accounts in the Gospels, beginning at the announcement of his birth to his ascension after his death at Calvary. No other study can yield a greater intellectual and spiritual harvest than a concentrated focus upon the historical facts surrounding Jesus' life, ministry, passion, death, resurrection, and ascension. Jesus of Nazareth is Messiah and Lord of all!

Our first lesson, *The Messiah Announced*, will concentrate on a brief first look at the critical perspectives and processes associated with a profitable study of the life of Christ. We'll then proceed to look at the birth, infancy, and childhood narratives of the Messiah. We will see that the New Testament reveals in the Gospel accounts of the Apostles that Jesus of Nazareth is the Messiah who fulfills the promise of God for salvation, redemption, and revelation. We will also look carefully at the one chosen by God to announce Messiah's ministry, John the Baptist, attending both the baptism of Jesus, and his temptation in the wilderness. We end our first lesson by considering two important incidents concerning Jesus' announcement of his Messiahship: his inaugural sermon at Nazareth, and his first public miracle attesting his Messiahship at the wedding at Cana.

In our second lesson, *The Messiah Opposed*, we begin by looking at the historical context which surrounded Jesus at the time of his appearing in his public ministry. We will survey the nature of Rome's domination of the first century world, and see how the different Jewish sects and parties responded to Rome and to Jesus. We will look at the Sadducees, Pharisees, Essenes, Zealots, and Herodians. In the second segment of this lesson we will explore the Jewish concept of the Kingdom of God at the time of Jesus. We'll see how the nation of Israel, oppressed by political powers, believed that when Messiah came, the Kingdom of God would come in power, restoring the material universe and saving humankind from the control of Satan. Of course, Jesus proclaimed the Kingdom present, and demonstrated its reality in his healings and exorcisms, revealing the Kingdom's presence in his own person and ministry.

Lesson three deals with *The Messiah Revealed*, which aims to understand that in the person of Jesus, the promised Messiah is powerfully revealed through his perfect life and character, his masterful leadership of the Apostles, and his submissive sonship to his Father. Jesus' Messiahship is made plain through his prophetic teaching ministry, as well as in the mighty demonstrations of power, both in signs and wonders (miracles) and dramatic encounter with spiritual demons. Here we will also briefly consider the suffering and death of Jesus (i.e., his Passion). His death provides us with a clear revelation of the promised Messiah. We will also consider Peter's confession of Jesus' true identity, accompanied by Jesus' prediction of his death, and his resolve to go toward Jerusalem. We will look at Jesus' triumphal entry into Jerusalem, his final week encountering the Jewish leaders, and his Passover with the disciples. Finally, we will look at the events surrounding his crucifixion and death, his agony in prayer in the Garden to his burial after his death on the cross. Undoubtedly, Jesus' suffering and death give strong and undeniable testimony of his identity as the Son of God, as God's anointed Christ, the one who can reassert God's right to rule over his creation and over all humankind.

Finally, lesson four discusses *The Messiah Vindicated*. This lesson considers both the significance of the resurrection of Messiah Jesus, and its importance in our theology, faith, and ministry. Once we consider the evidence for the resurrection, we will then survey the various appearances of Jesus, beginning with his resurrection at the tomb up until his appearance to the Apostles at the Sea of Galilee. Nothing provides a clearer witness to the vindication of the Messianic identity of Jesus Christ than this one unequivocal fact: Jesus Christ has been raised from the dead.

We will close this module with a critical study of the Great Commission as a continuing vindication of Jesus' identity as Messiah, and the importance of this commission as it relates both to the fulfillment of prophecy as well as to global mission. For forty days after his resurrection, Jesus demonstrated its truthfulness to the Apostles, and gave his promise to send them the Holy Spirit to fulfill that commission. We close our study of the life of Jesus with a look at the Ascension, the final historical sign which gives evidence of Jesus' vindication as Messiah. Jesus of Nazareth is the Messiah of God.

Again, there can be little doubt that the depth of our ministry and leadership can proceed no further than the depth of our knowledge of Jesus Christ, the Messiah of God and Lord of all. Therefore, may our God and Father provide you with both the hunger, passion, and discipline to master the life and ministry of Jesus. In so doing, you will be able to be his disciple and make disciples of Jesus in your church, in your ministry, and wherever else God may lead.

Take his yoke upon yourself, and learn of him–this is the key to godly servant leadership in Christ.

"For me to live is Christ, and to die is gain."

- Rev. Dr. Don L. Davis

Course Requirements

Required Books and Materials

- Bible (for the purposes of this course, your Bible should be a translation [ex. NIV, NASB, RSV, KJV, NKJV, etc.], and not a paraphrase [ex. The Living Bible, The Message]).

- Each Capstone module has assigned textbooks which are read and discussed throughout the course. We encourage you to read, reflect upon, and respond to these with your professors, mentors, and fellow learners. Because of the fluid availability of the texts (e.g., books going out of print), we maintain our *official* Capstone Required Textbook list on our website. Please visit *www.tumi.org/books* to obtain the current listing of this module's texts.

- Paper and pen for taking notes and completing in-class assignments.

Suggested Readings

- Demarest, Bruce A. *Jesus Christ: The God-Man.* Eugene: Wipf and Stock Publishers, 2004

- Hunter, Archibald M. *The Work and Words of Jesus*, rev. ed. Philadelphia: The Westminster Press, 1973.

Summary of Grade Categories and Weights

Attendance & Class Participation	30%	90 pts
Quizzes	10%	30 pts
Memory Verses	15%	45 pts
Exegetical Project	15%	45 pts
Ministry Project.	10%	30 pts
Readings and Homework Assignments.	10%	30 pts
Final Exam	10%	30 pts
Total:	100%	300 pts

Grade Requirements

Attendance at each class session is a course requirement. Absences will affect your grade. If an absence cannot be avoided, please let the Mentor know in advance. If you miss a class it is your responsibility to find out the assignments you missed, and to talk with the Mentor about turning in late work. Much of the learning associated with this course takes place through discussion. Therefore, your active involvement will be sought and expected in every class session.

Every class will begin with a short quiz over the basic ideas from the last lesson. The best way to prepare for the quiz is to review the Student Workbook material and class notes taken during the last lesson.

The memorized Word is a central priority for your life and ministry as a believer and leader in the Church of Jesus Christ. There are relatively few verses, but they are significant in their content. Each class session you will be expected to recite (orally or in writing) the assigned verses to your Mentor.

The Scriptures are God's potent instrument to equip the man or woman of God for every work of ministry he calls them to (2 Tim. 3.16-17). In order to complete the requirements for this course you must select a passage and do an inductive Bible study (i.e., an exegetical study) upon it. The study will have to be five pages in length (double-spaced, typed or neatly hand written) and deal with a significant event or subject related to the life and ministry of Jesus Christ as recorded in the Gospels. Our desire and hope is that you will be able to draw from the text rich truths regarding the person and work of Jesus Christ, and be able to make practical application to your own life as well as those to whom you minister. As you go through the course, be open to finding an extended passage (roughly 4-9 verses) on a subject you would like to study more intensely. The details of the project are covered on pages 10-11, and will be discussed in the introductory session of this course.

Ministry Project

Our expectation is that all students will apply their learning practically in their lives and in their ministry responsibilities. The student will be responsible for developing a ministry project that combines principles learned with practical ministry. The details of this project are covered on page 12, and will be discussed in the introductory session of the course.

Class and Homework Assignments

Classwork and homework of various types may be given during class by your Mentor or be written in your Student Workbook. If you have any question about what is required by these or when they are due, please ask your Mentor.

Readings

It is important that the student read the assigned readings from the text and from the Scriptures in order to be prepared for class discussion. Please turn in the "Reading Completion Sheet" from your Student Workbook on a weekly basis. There will be an option to receive extra credit for extended readings.

Take-Home Final Exam

At the end of the course, your Mentor will give you a final exam (closed book) to be completed at home. You will be asked a question that helps you reflect on what you have learned in the course and how it affects the way you think about or practice ministry. Your Mentor will give you due dates and other information when the Final Exam is handed out.

Grading

The following grades will be given in this class at the end of the session, and placed on each student's record:

A - Superior work	D - Passing work
B - Excellent work	F - Unsatisfactory work
C - Satisfactory work	I - Incomplete

Letter grades with appropriate pluses and minuses will be given for each final grade, and grade points for your grade will be factored into your overall grade point average. Unexcused late work or failure to turn in assignments will affect your grade, so please plan ahead, and communicate conflicts with your instructor.

Exegetical Project

As a part of your participation in the Capstone *New Testament Witness to Christ and His Kingdom* module of study, you will be required to do an exegesis (inductive study) on one of the following passages:

❑ Matthew 12.22-30   ❑ Luke 4.16-30

❑ Matthew 16.13-23   ❑ John 11.1-46

❑ Mark 2.1-12   ❑ Luke 24.36-48

❑ Luke 4.1-13   ❑ Acts 1.1-11

The purpose of this exegetical project is to give you an opportunity to do a detailed study of a major passage on an aspect or event in the life of Jesus of Nazareth. The above list represents a variety of teachings and happenings of Jesus Christ, and your study should concentrate on explaining the meaning of the text in light of his mission and ministry. As you select and study one of the above texts (or a text which you and your Mentor agree upon which may not be on the list), our hope is that you will come to understand better the significance of our Lord's life and ministry. Further, we hope that you will also be able to relate its meaning directly to your own personal walk of discipleship, as well as to the leadership role God has given to you currently in your church and ministry.

This is a Bible study project, and, in order to do *exegesis*, you must be committed to understand the meaning of the passage in its own setting. Once you know what it meant, you can then draw out principles that apply to all of us, and then relate those principles to life. A simple three step process can guide you in your personal study of the Bible passage:

1. What was *God saying to the people in the text's original situation*?

2. What principle(s) does *the text teach that is true for all people everywhere*, including today?

3. What is *the Holy Spirit asking me to do with this principle here, today*, in my life and ministry?

Once you have answered these questions in your personal study, you are then ready to write out your insights for your *paper assignment*.

Here is a *sample outline* for your paper:

1. List out what you believe is *the main theme or idea* of the text you selected.

2. *Summarize the meaning* of the passage (you may do this in two or three paragraphs, or, if you prefer, by writing a short verse-by-verse commentary on the passage).

3. *Outline one to three key principles or insights* this text provides on the New Testament witness to Christ.

4. Tell how one, some, or all of the principles may relate to *one or more* of the following:

a. Your personal spirituality and walk with Christ

b. Your life and ministry in your local church

c. Situations or challenges in your community and general society

As an aid or guide, please feel free to read the course texts and/or commentaries, and integrate insights from them into your work. Make sure that you give credit to whom credit is due if you borrow or build upon someone else's insights. Use in-the-text references, footnotes, or endnotes. Any way you choose to cite your references will be acceptable, as long as you 1) use only one way consistently throughout your paper, and 2) indicate where you are using someone else's ideas, and are giving them credit for it. (For more information, see *Documenting Your Work: A Guide to Help You Give Credit Where Credit Is Due* in the Appendix.)

Make certain that your exegetical project, when turned in meets the following standards:

- It is legibly written or typed.

- It is a study of one of the passages above.

- It is turned in on time (not late).

- It is 5 pages in length.

- It follows the outline given above, clearly laid out for the reader to follow.

- It shows how the passage relates to life and ministry today.

Do not let these instructions intimidate you; this is a Bible study project! All you need to show in this paper is that you *studied* the passage, *summarized* its meaning, *drew out* a few key principles from it, and *related* them to your own life and ministry.

Grading

The exegetical project is worth 45 points, and represents 15% of your overall grade, so make certain that you make your project an excellent and informative study of the Word.

Ministry Project

God the Holy Spirit has supplied us with the Holy Scriptures in order that we may be transformed into the very image of Jesus Christ, to the glory of God the Father. God's Word is living and active, cutting to the very heart of our innermost thoughts (Heb. 4.12). James the Apostle commands us to be doers of the Word, not hearers only, deceiving ourselves. The Word must be engaged and obeyed, not merely studied and discussed. Neglecting this discipline, he suggests, is analogous to a person viewing our natural face in a mirror and then forgetting who we are, and are meant to be. In every case, the doer of the Word of God will be blessed in what he or she does (James 1.22-25).

Our sincere desire is that your study of the Word of God will transform your life and ministry. This occurs when you apply your learning practically, correlate your learning with real experiences and needs in your personal life, and connect it to your ministry in and through your church. Therefore, a key part of completing this module will be for you to design a ministry project to help you share some of the insights you have learned from this course with others.

Your requirement for this module is to take some insights and/or principles you have gleaned from your study of this module, *New Testament Witness to Christ and His Kingdom*, and share this teaching in a life or ministry setting with others. Of course, many ways exist for you to fulfill this requirement for this module. For instance, you may choose to conduct a brief study of your insights with an individual, or a Sunday School class, youth or adult group or Bible study, in a sermon, or even at some ministry opportunity. Concentrate on sharing insights from class with your audience. (Of course, you may choose to share insights from your Exegetical Project in this module with them.)

Feel free to be flexible in your project. Make it creative and open-ended. At the beginning of the course, you should decide on a context in which you will share your insights, and share that with your instructor. Plan ahead and avoid the last minute rush in selecting and carrying out your project.

After you have carried out your plan, write and turn in to your Mentor a one-page summary or evaluation of your time of sharing. A sample outline of your Ministry Project summary is as follows:

1. Your name

2. The place where you shared, and the audience with whom you shared

3. A brief summary of how your time went, how you felt, and how they responded

4. What you learned from the time

The Ministry Project is worth 30 points and represents 10% of your overall grade, so make certain to share your insights with confidence and make your summary clear.

Purpose

Planning and Summary

Grading

LESSON
1

The Messiah Announced

page 243 📖 *1*

Lesson Objectives

Welcome in the strong name of Jesus Christ! After your reading, study, discussion, and application of the materials in this lesson, you will be able to:

page 243 📖 *2*

- Explain the critical perspectives and processes associated with a profitable study of the life of Christ.

- Give an outline of the key stories associated with the Birth narratives, infancy, and childhood of Jesus.

- Defend the idea that the New Testament reveals in the Gospel accounts of the Apostles the person of Jesus of Nazareth, who is the Messiah who fulfills the promise of God for salvation, redemption, and revelation.

- Provide a concise explanation of the ministry of John the Baptist as the one chosen by God to announce Messiah's ministry to the nation of Israel.

- Describe the temptation of Jesus in the wilderness, as well as his calling of his disciples, and two important incidents concerning the announcement of the Messiah: his public announcement of his Messiahship at Nazareth, and his first public miracle attesting his Messiahship at the wedding at Cana.

Devotion

Joy to the World, the Lord Is Come

page 244 📖 *3*

Read Isaiah 9.6-7. Can we enjoy the Christmas spirit all through the year, every month and week, every single day of the year? It is not only possible, but, for the disciple of Jesus, it is important to cultivate this spirit every single day. The celebration of Christmas is associated with the First Advent (coming) of Messiah Jesus at his birth. On the Church calendar, it is celebrated formally as a part of the Christian liturgy, with formal celebration, special worship services, and the ancient and contemporary carols, hymns, and songs we are so familiar with. While this celebration is appropriate and important, the season itself often is bogged down with the trappings of commercialism and greed. Christmas itself easily becomes associated with the giving of gifts, classic films and office parties, and ornaments and the trappings of the holiday season. The Christ of Christmas becomes regulated to a nativity scene in the church foyers of the land.

Actually, the idea of Messiah coming to earth, and the Christian confession that Jesus of Nazareth is the Messiah of God is reason for unbroken praise and unending joy. The actual claim being made in the New Testament is that the person of Jesus is the fulfillment of God's intent to send to us a Lord and Savior who would make things right, defeat the devil, overcome our sin, eventually overcome all the effects of the curse and restore the universe to God's perfect reign. The story of the coming of Jesus into the world fits in with the theology of the great hymn writer Isaac Watts who wrote so eloquently in the first lines of his well-known Christmas carol, "Joy to the world; the Lord is come! Let earth receive her King! Let every heart prepare him room, and heaven and nature sing." This song resonates with the ancient word of prophecy that Isaiah bellowed in Israel seven centuries before our Lord was born: A King would come from David's line who would reign and establish righteousness and justice forever through the zeal of the LORD of hosts. Amazingly, we now know that Jesus of Nazareth, the supposed son of Joseph the carpenter of Nazareth, is the Messiah, the one of whom Isaiah and the prophets all spoke. The promise of God has been fulfilled, and the Kingdom has come in his person.

What is the right response to this amazing proclamation? Joy. Unbroken, unashamed, unbounded. Christians must joyfully proclaim and express the remarkable truth that the promise of God, that ancient word of hope believed on by his people for generations, has now been fulfilled in the humble birth of a lowly child in a stable. While Jesus for some may only mean a religious symbol or a chance to receive a gift, for those of us who believe he himself is the Lord of all, the future King of the earth, the Son of the Living God. He has come, and we belong to him by faith. Christmas as a spirit need never die as long as we understand who this Jesus truly is: the very Lord of all, come to earth, to deliver his own from sin and death. "Joy to the world, the Lord is come. Let earth receive her King. Let every heart prepare him room, and heaven and nature sing."

After reciting and/or singing the Nicene Creed (located in the Appendix), pray the following prayer:

Nicene Creed and Prayer

> *Almighty God, heavenly King who sent your Son into the world when he took our nature upon him and was born in the stable at Bethlehem: Accept our praise, and grant that as we have been born again in him so he may evermore live in us and reign on earth as he reigns in heaven with you and the Holy Spirit now and for ever.*

~ The Church of the Province of South Africa.
Minister's Book for Use With the Holy Eucharist and Morning and Evening Prayer.
Braamfontein: Publishing Department of the Church of the Province of South Africa. p. 23

Quiz	No quiz this lesson
Scripture Memorization Review	No Scripture memorization this lesson
Assignments Due	No assignments due this lesson

Is Reverend Moon the Real Messiah?

page 245 📖 *4*

The followers of the Rev. Sung Yung Moon believe him to be the Messiah of God in the earth. He is worshiped, acknowledged as the Lord's representative, and understood to be the fulfillment of the ancient prophecies regarding the Lord's anointed Messiah. While many have rejected his claim that he is the Messiah, many thousands have embraced his claim and given their allegiance and unqualified support to him. If someone were to ask you your opinion about Rev. Moon or others who claimed to be the Messiah, how would you complete the following statement. "We know that Rev. Moon or others who claim to be Messiah must be impostors, for the real Messiah, according to the Scriptures will be one who . . ."

Messianic Prophecy: Not to Be Taken Lightly

At a recent lecture in the religion department at a State university, one of your youth group leaders heard a statement that has caused her great angst and doubt. In reading an essay on the nature of prophecy in the Bible, the visiting religion professor stated, "We know that the Scriptures that are usually given in support of the Messiah's coming are not true in our modern, scientific sense of that term, nor can these prophecies be found to agree with the facts of history, as we call it. Prophecies in the Bible are usually written after the fact; in other words, writers and commentators wrote about events after they had already occurred, and then wrote them as if they had not happened yet." How would you answer your students questions about the reliability of Messianic prophecy in the Bible?

Could Jesus Have Sinned?

In a lively Sunday School class on the book of Mark, a student raises their hand and asks a question regarding the nature of Jesus' humanity. In discussing the temptation of Jesus in the wilderness, the student asks, "If Jesus was a human being, just like us in every way except that he did not commit any sin– does that mean that he could not have sinned in the wilderness? And if he could not have sinned, was he really tempted at all?" How would you attempt to answer the student's question concerning Jesus's ability to say "Yes!" or "No!" to temptation?

The Messiah Announced

Segment 1: Jesus' Birth and Childhood

Rev. Dr. Don L. Davis

In studying the life and person of Jesus Christ, we must understand the importance of prophecy as a witness to the true identity of the Messiah. The concept of Messiah is central to the understanding of the Old Testament, the key to the promise to Abraham, and the renewal of that covenant through Isaac and Jacob, through Judah and David, and finally to the history of Mary, Joseph, and Jesus of Nazareth. A diligent study of the Scriptures should lead the seeker to an awareness of the historical climate and conditions that occurred prior to Jesus' birth and childhood, and how those conditions and events affected his early years in Israel.

Our objective for this segment, *Jesus' Birth and Childhood*, is to enable you to see that:

- The study of Messiah is rooted in the Old Testament's motif of promise and fulfillment through God's covenant promise with Abraham, and through him to Isaac, Jacob, Judah, and David.

- The historical climate and conditions around the time of Messiah's coming were critical to his arrival in the world.

- The birth and infancy narratives of Jesus provide key insight into the person and work of Jesus, both in terms of his identity and his purpose in coming to earth as God's anointed Messiah.

- The New Testament reveals in the Gospel accounts of the Apostles that the person of Jesus of Nazareth is the Messiah, the one chosen and anointed by God to fulfill his promise for salvation, redemption, and revelation.

Summary of
Segment 1

I. Prolegomena, Part 1: Critical Perspectives in the Study of the Life of Christ

    A. Messiah's coming in Messianic prophecy: promise and fulfillment motif in the Old Testament

        1. *Protoevangelium*: Gen. 3.15

        2. Messiah as warrior and restorer

        3. Messiah as prophet, priest, and king

            a. The prophet like Moses, Deut. 18.15-19

            b. The priest like Melchizedek, Gen. 14.18-20 with Heb. 7.17-21

            c. The king like David, 2 Sam. 7.4-17

    B. The life of Christ should be seen in light of the Abrahamic Covenant.

        1. Gen. 12.1-3

        2. Gen. 15.5-6

        3. Gen. 17.4-8

1

C. The Messiah was prophesied to come from the tribe of Judah, Gen. 49.10.

D. The Messiah was to come from the family of David.

    1. 2 Sam. 7.16

    2. Ps. 89.34-36

II. Prolegomena, Part 2: Critical Procedures for a Productive Life of Christ Study

A. Make a commitment to be thorough and rigorous: be a workman of the Word of the Lord, 2 Tim. 2.15.

B. Focus on Scripture: the New Testament provides an authoritative, accurate, and spiritually moving account of the life of Christ.

    1. John 5.39-40

    2. Matt. 5.17-18

    3. Luke 24.44-48

C. Integrate your study around the Kingdom of God, Mark 1.14-15.

D. Be aware of the historical climate around the time of Messiah Jesus' coming.

(Erich Sauer, *The Dawn of World Redemption*. Grand Rapids, Michigan: Eerdmans Publishing, 1951, p. 176.)

1. A time of *world centralization* (commerce within the empire itself, political organization, overall governmental and military oversight)

2. A time of *world cultural unity* (Graeco-Roman influence, koine Greek used as the universal business language)

3. A time of *world trade and intercourse* (interaction and inter-connection among provinces in terms of finance, commerce, trade among representative cultures, nations, and peoples)

4. A time of *world peace* (the conquest of Rome of the then-known world)

5. A time of *world demoralization* (varying degrees of Roman oppression, as well as varying degrees of national allegiance to Rome)

6. A time of *world mingling of religions* (great diversity of religious belief and spiritual practice)

E. Distinguish between having a comprehensive treatment of Jesus' life in the Gospels but not an exhaustive one.

page 245 📖 *5*

F. Make discipleship your purpose in studying the life of Christ, Matt. 28.19.

1. Being a disciple of Jesus yourself (not merely to have a factual knowledge of the life of Christ), John 8.31-32

2. Making disciples in the context of the Church, Eph. 4.9-16

New Testament Witness to Jesus Christ: The Birth Narratives and the Childhood of the Messiah

I. The Birth Narratives of Jesus the Messiah

A. The historical accuracy of the Gospels

1. Luke's opening, Luke 1.1-4

2. Differences in the Gospel accounts

a. Mark's abrupt opening, Mark 1.1-3

b. Matthew and Luke: the birth of Messiah

c. John the Apostle: the pre-existent Word of God, John 1.1-3

B. Luke's historical situating of Jesus's birth, Luke 2.1-7

1. Where: in Palestine, in Judea, at the city of David (Bethlehem)

2. When: during the time of Caesar Augustus, when Quirinius was governor of Syria, v. 1-2

3. What details

    a. Joseph went up from Galilee, from the city of Nazareth, v. 4.

    b. To Judea, to the city of David, "Bethlehem," v. 4

    c. Global census: Joseph and his betrothed went to be registered.

    d. Jesus is born during the journey.

C. Critical birth narratives

1. Zacharias and Elizabeth: the promise of Messiah's forerunner, Luke 1.5-25

2. Mary and Joseph: the promise of Messiah

    a. The promise to Mary, Luke 1.28-35

    b. Joseph's dilemma and its resolution, Matt. 1.18-25

3. The *Magnificat*: Mary's visit to Elizabeth, Luke 1.39-56

4. The birth of John the Baptist, Luke 1.57-80

5. The birth of Messiah

   a. Announcement to the shepherds, Luke 2.1-20 (Luke 2.10-14)

   b. Anonymity to the world: God reveals Messiah to the poor and unimportant.

6. Presentation at the Temple: Jesus' infancy

   a. Luke 2.21-24

   b. Lev. 12.1-8

7. Visit of the Magi, Matt. 2.1-12

   a. Wise men from the east, Matt. 2.1-2

   b. Worship of the Messiah and avoidance of Herod, Matt. 2.10-12

II. The Childhood of Jesus of Nazareth

A. Selective portraits: the Holy Spirit's revelation of Jesus

   1. Concise

2. Particular

3. Significant

B. Flight into Egypt: fleeing the wrath of Herod, Matt. 2.13-23

    1. The Magi's caution, 2.13

    2. Jesus' flight into Egypt, cf. Hos. 11.1

    3. Herod's death and the return of Joseph and his family to Palestine

C. Jesus as an adolescent: teaching the elders in the Temple of Jerusalem, Luke 2.39b-52

    1. Spiritual fervency

    2. Messianic identity

    3. Perfect character (which grew more and more from childhood into adolescence), Luke 2.40

    4. Growth into manhood, Luke 2.51-52

Conclusion

» A profitable study of the life of Christ demands an understanding of the critical perspectives and processes associated with Messianic study and the Bible.

» Jesus of Nazareth is the Messiah, as testified in the Gospel accounts of his birth, infancy, and childhood.

Please take as much time as you have available to answer these and other questions that the video brought out. Any profitable study of the Bible's teaching on the Messiah will go forward with a clear awareness of both the theological and historical issues associated with his coming. Be clear and concise in your answers, and where possible, support with Scripture!

Segue 1

Student Questions and Response

page 246 📖 *6*

1. How does the Old Testament motif of *promise and fulfillment* help us to understand the importance of connecting the coming of Messiah to the prophecies of the Old Testament?

2. How does the coming of Messiah relate to the promise given to Abraham, Isaac, and Jacob? How does it relate to the promise given to Judah and to David?

3. Why is it important to base your understanding of the Messiah on the *Old Testament Scriptures*? Explain.

4. How does the idea of the Kingdom of God connect with our study of the Messiah?

5. What ought we to believe regarding the *historical accuracy* of the Gospels regarding the birth stories of Jesus?

6. What are some of the key insights we learn from a study of the birth and infancy stories of Jesus in the New Testament? What are some of the ways in which these stories identify Jesus of Nazareth in relationship to the promise of the Messiah?

7. In your opinion, why don't the Gospels provide us with a "blow-by-blow" commentary on all the various episodes in the early life of Jesus? Explain your answer.

8. Describe the events and purpose surrounding the flight of Mary and Joseph to Egypt. What prompted this change of plans, and when did they return to Palestine?

9. What do we learn about the personality and calling of Jesus from the incident of teaching the elders in the Temple at Jerusalem? How does Jesus describe himself in this episode?

10. In Luke's accounts of Jesus' upbringing, what do we learn about the growth of the young boy Jesus into manhood?

The Messiah Announced

Segment 2: John the Baptist and the Baptism in the Desert

Rev. Dr. Don L. Davis

Summary of Segment 2

page 247 📖 7

John the Baptist is the forerunner and messenger of the Messiah, who announced his coming and prepared his way by preaching a message of repentance and faith to the nation of Israel. As the fulfillment of the Old Testament prophecy of Messiah's coming, John served as a witness to Jesus, announcing his presence, and baptizing Jesus in accordance with Jesus' unqualified identification with sinners in all things. Jesus was recognized as the Messiah at his baptism, and was led into the wilderness where he endured and triumphed over Satan's temptations. Jesus announced himself as Messiah to his hometown synagogue in Nazareth, to his initial followers early in his ministry, and through his miracle at Cana of Galilee.

Our objective for this segment, *John the Baptist and the Baptism in the Desert*, is to enable you to see that:

*   John the Baptist was the forerunner and witness of the Messiah, chosen by God to provide witness to Jesus' arrival and prepare the nation of Israel for his coming.

*   Jesus' baptism reveals his complete identification with sinners, as well as God's validation of Jesus as his Son on whom the Holy Spirit rested.

- Jesus' temptation in the wilderness demonstrated his ongoing conflict with Satan, and his endurance and triumph over the devil's temptations and attacks.

- Jesus inaugurated his ministry by selecting some early followers after his baptism, and announcing his Messianic identity through two important incidents: his public announcement of his Messiahship at Nazareth, and his first public miracle attesting his Messiahship at the wedding at Cana.

I. John the Baptist

Video Segment 2
Outline

A. The biblical citations

   1. Matt. 3.1-12

   2. Mark 1.2-8

   3. Luke 3.1-20

   4. John 1.19-28

B. The forerunner of the Messiah: Old Testament prophecy and its New Testament fulfillment in John

   1. The messenger who clears the way before Messiah, Mal. 3.1

   2. He would instruct the people, Mal. 2.7.

3. He would come in the spirit and power of Elijah, Mal. 4.5.

4. Prophecies were given at his birth, Luke 1.76.

5. Jesus acknowledges John as the messenger of the covenant.

    a. Matt. 11.10-11

    b. Mark 1.2-3

    c. Luke 7.26-28

C. His striking manner and appearance, Matt. 3.4

    1. Matt. 11.8

    2. Mark 1.6

    3. Luke 1.17

D. His relationship to Jesus

    1. As a witness

        a. John 5.33

b. John 1.6-7

c. Acts 19.4

2. As one who preceded the Messiah's coming, and who would recede after he announced his presence, John 3.28-30

3. As he who rehearsed and announced the presence of Messiah and his work, Matt. 3.11-12

II. The Baptism of Jesus

A. Biblical citations

1. Matt. 3.13-17

2. Mark 1.9-11

3. Luke 3.21-23

4. John 1.29-34

B. Baptism as a sign of *repentance*

1. Luke 3.3 cf. Acts 19.4

2. Indication of the acknowledged penitence of the one who is baptized (i.e., of the desire to change one's ways and so reorder one's life back in sync with the ways of the Lord)

3. Baptism was *defacto* unimportant and unnecessary for Jesus.

   a. Jesus was the Lamb commissioned to take the world's sin away, John 1.36.

   b. He committed no sin; there was no need for him to repent.

   c. John felt the need to be baptized by Jesus, Matt. 3.13-14.

C. The baptism of Jesus Christ: "it is fitting for us to fulfill all righteousness," Matt. 3.15.

   1. Baptized (submerged) within the Jordan

   2. The heavens open, the Spirit of God descends like a dove.

   3. The Father's voice: Matt. 3.17

D. The significance of Jesus' baptism

   1. Fulfilling the righteousness of God

2. Confirmation of Jesus' place and identity to John the Baptist, John 1.31-34

3. Jesus' relationship to the Holy Spirit: unbounded filling of the Holy Spirit

   a. Isa. 61.1

   b. John 3.34

4. Jesus' relationship to the Father: unqualified pleasure, Matt. 12.18

III. The Temptation of Jesus

A. Biblical citations

   1. Matt. 4.1-11

   2. Mark 1.12-13

   3. Luke 4.1-13

B. The nature of the temptation

   1. Jesus is truly tempted: Heb. 2.17-18; 4.15-16.

a. Grueling forty-day fast in the desert

b. The devil's timing in the temptation

c. Not mere formality; authentic temptation of his person

2. Demonic casting of doubt on the sonship of Jesus Christ

    a. *If you are the Son of God, command these stones to be made bread.*

        (1) Solicited Jesus to abuse of power

        (2) Jesus' reply: Deut. 8.3

    b. *If you are the Son of God, throw yourself down.*

        (1) Taken to Jerusalem, placed on a pinnacle of the Temple; solicited an unnecessary test of God's promise (quoted Ps. 91.11-12)

        (2) Jesus' reply: Deut. 6.16

3. Demonic suggestion of greed: *All these* [i.e., the kingdoms of the world and the glory of them] *I will give you, if you will fall down and worship me*, v. 9.

    a. The offer of personal glory and power

    b. Jesus' reply: Deut. 6.13-14

4. The resolution of the temptation episode

    a. The devil's departure for a more opportune time for the next round of struggle, Luke 4.13

    b. Angelic support given to Jesus (a token of the Father's care and oversight to Messiah)

      (1) Mark 1.13

      (2) Matt. 4.11

      (3) Cf. Matt. 26.53; 1 Tim. 3.16; Luke 22.43

C. Significance of the temptation

1. Jesus identifies with us for he has been tempted as we have.

    a. Heb. 4.15-16

    b. Heb. 2.18

2. The devil is a liar (lies and deception are his most effective and cunning tactical approach and weapon), John 8.44.

3. We do spiritual battle with the enemy through our handling of (quoting and use of) the Holy Scriptures, Eph. 6.16-17.

IV. The Announcement of Messiah

    A. The disciples following the baptism: earliest disciples of Jesus

        1. Early followers of Jesus after the baptism, John 1.35-51

            a. John's announcement of Jesus as the one whom he came to bear witness about, John 1.36ff.

            b. Introduction of some of John's followers who become disciples of Jesus

        2. The Two (John and Andrew), John 1.40

        3. Peter (Simon), John 1.41

        4. Philip, John 1.43-44

        5. Nathaniel, John 1.45-50

    B. The declaration of his calling: announcement of his Messiahship at Nazareth, Luke 4.16-21

        1. Jesus' public announcement in his own hometown, Nazareth

        2. Makes the announcement in the synagogue (place of worship of Yahweh)

3. Quotation of Isaiah 61

    a. Announces himself as the Servant of Yahweh

    b. Declares his unqualified ministry to the poor and the broken

    c. Draws attention to his role and relationship to the Holy Scriptures: "Today this Scripture has been fulfilled in your hearing," v. 21 (cf. Matt. 5.17-18)

C. The display of his glory: the miracle at Cana of Galilee, John 2.1-12

    1. Occurred several days after his baptism and conversation with his early followers (a wedding feast in Cana of Galilee)

    2. Mary, the mother of Jesus, was in attendance.

    3. Mary's petition and Jesus' reply: "My hour"

    4. Miracle called a "sign" (verse 11)

        a. Sign of his power and authority: the Son of Man is Lord.

        b. Manifestation of his glory (i.e., his divine majesty and position)

        c. Food for faith ("and his disciples believed in him," v. 11)

5. After this miracle, Jesus spent some time in Capernaum, a significant place and center of his future ministry, John 2.12.

Conclusion

» John the Baptist was God's chosen forerunner to announce Messiah's ministry.

» Jesus' Messianic identity was demonstrated through his baptism by John, and his temptation by the devil in the wilderness.

» Jesus of Nazareth began his public ministry as Messiah by gathering some early disciples, and announcing his Messiahship at his hometown synagogue in Nazareth and through his first miracle at Cana.

Segue 2

Student Questions and Response

The following questions were designed to help you review the material in the second video segment. These events associated with the early Messianic announcement of Jesus are pivotal in understanding Jesus' unique ministry in Israel. Be clear and concise in your answers, and where possible, support with Scripture!

1. How does the Old Testament depict the coming of the forerunner of Messiah in its prophetic descriptions and predictions?

2. How and where did Jesus acknowledge that John the Baptist was the fulfillment of these Old Testament references regarding the one who would "prepare the way of the Lord"?

3. What was striking about the manner and appearance of John, and how does the New Testament describe precisely his relationship to Jesus?

4. What occurred at the baptism of Jesus that gives evidence that indeed Jesus of Nazareth is the Messiah of God?

5. If Jesus did not commit sin, then why was he baptized at all?

6. What do we learn about the relationship of Jesus to Satan in the temptation in the wilderness? Could Jesus have actually given in to the devil's temptations, and committed sin against God, either in the wilderness or at any other time of his life? Explain.

7. What do you find especially significant in Jesus' choice of Isaiah 61 as the text to announce to the nation that he in fact was the promised Messiah?

8. How do Jesus' very earliest followers understand him to be? How do they describe him and his purpose in the world?

9. In what way does the miracle at Cana of Galilee reveal the glory of Jesus as the Messiah of God? According to John, what conclusions and interpretations do the disciples draw from this remarkable display of miracle working power there?

CONNECTION

This lesson focuses upon the critical concepts and events associated with the initial announcement and presentation of Messiah, Jesus of Nazareth, in his birth, infancy and childhood. It also highlights critical truths connected with his baptism, his temptation in the wilderness, and the subsequent presentation of himself to the nation Israel, beginning in the synagogue at his hometown in Nazareth and his first miracle at Cana of Galilee.

Summary of Key Concepts

page 248 📖 *8*

- ↪ The New Testament reveals in the Gospel accounts of the Apostles the person of Jesus of Nazareth, who is the Messiah who fulfills the promise of God for salvation, redemption, and revelation.

- ↪ The study of Messiah is rooted in the Old Testament's motif of *promise* and *fulfillment* through God's covenant promise with Abraham, and through him to Isaac, Jacob, Judah, and David.

- ↪ Jesus appeared in the world at a critical time of world centralization, unity, trade, and change. The historical climate and conditions around the time of Messiah's coming were critical to his arrival in the world.

- ↪ The birth and infancy narratives of Jesus provide key insight into both the person and work of Jesus, both in terms of his identity and his purpose in coming to earth as God's anointed Messiah.

- ↪ John the Baptist was the forerunner and witness of the Messiah, chosen by God to provide witness to Jesus' arrival and prepare the nation of Israel for his coming.

☞ Jesus' baptism reveals his complete identification with sinners, as well as God's validation of Jesus as his Son on whom the Holy Spirit rested.

☞ Jesus' temptation in the wilderness demonstrated Jesus' ongoing conflict with Satan, and his endurance and triumph over the devil's temptations and attacks.

☞ Jesus inaugurated his ministry by selecting some early followers after his baptism, and announcing his Messianic identity through two important incidents: his public announcement of his Messiahship at Nazareth, and his first public miracle attesting his Messiahship at the wedding at Cana.

Student Application and Implications

page 249 📖 *9*

Now is the time for you to discuss with your fellow students your questions about this first lesson in *The New Testament Witness to Christ and His Kingdom* module, *The Messiah Announced*. The information covered in this lesson focuses on the events and issues associated with Jesus' arrival as Messiah into the world, physically as Mary's baby, and later as the growing adolescent of Joseph and Mary, and finally as the Messiah announced by John to the nation. Grasping the importance of Jesus' announcement as Messiah can aid you greatly as you continue your study of his ministry, and in your effort to fully comprehend the meaning of Jesus' person as well as his work in the world. As you review this lesson, what particular questions have come up that you are curious about, that demand your further consideration? Maybe some of the questions below might help you form your own, more specific and critical questions.

* Why did Jesus of Nazareth come into the world at the time and moment that he did?

* Why wasn't Jesus immediately recognized by the nation to be its long-awaited Messiah and conquering King who was destined to rule on David's throne? Why did so many find the announcement of Jesus troublesome and annoying? Explain your answer.

* Did Jesus *become* Messiah at the baptism, or was he merely *recognized* to be so there? Explain.

* Considering the fact that Jesus was in every way just like we are, was it possible for Jesus to sin at all, either during the Temptation or at any other time of his life? How so or how not?

* How does the announcement of Jesus as Messiah reveal his calling to engage the powers of the enemy as Lord and Savior?

* What does the lowliness and humility of the life of Jesus of Nazareth reveal to us about the nature of God, of Messiah, and of all true spirituality? Explain your answer carefully.

* What kind of images do the stories of Jesus' birth, infancy, and childhood, give us about the person and work of Jesus? What do we learn about his parents, and the place where he lived and grew up.

* The call of Jesus to the disciples provides a clear snapshot into the nature of his claim to lordship. What lessons do we learn about following Jesus from the encounters Jesus had with his disciples early in his public ministry.

* Keeping the first miracle at Cana in mind, what do you think about the role that miracles will play in announcing the identity of Jesus of Nazareth as Messiah? Explain.

CASE STUDIES

Can Jesus Really Understand Where I'm At?

Many today believe that although Jesus is described as a human being, one who experienced in the full the same condition that all human beings endure, he cannot really feel what we do. After all, Jesus never knew what it meant to fail, to feel guilty over sins committed, to have to reconcile with others because of wrong, or overcome the power of condemnation and remorse for wrongs done. How would you counsel an individual who asserted that Jesus could not understand where they were at because he simply didn't experience the "dark side" of human life. Is it possible for Jesus to sympathize with our weaknesses, even though he never sinned against God in thought, word, or deed?

A Confusing Doctrine

In discussing the identity of Jesus of Nazareth with a Muslim friend at work, you are struck by their inability to comprehend the doctrine that Jesus of Nazareth was both a human being and the Son of God. In expressing their difficulty in grasping the truth of this, the Muslim colleague says, "I find this to be one of the most troubling and confusing concepts in all of Christian theology. I know that it makes much sense to you and other Christians, but, as a Muslim, I simply cannot understand how you can suggest that the God of heaven became a man, was born of a woman, grew up, learned language and did chores, and endured the lowly, difficult realm of life that all human beings do. I find your view of Jesus an ambitious but confusing doctrine. Could you explain to me, as simply as possible, how you believe Jesus to be the Son of God, and yet fully a human being, too?" How would you answer his question?

A Kingdom Postponed

 In sharing your insights in your studies with a fellow seminarian, you are challenged with an idea regarding the nature of the coming of Messiah, and the coming of the Kingdom. The Christian friend agrees with the idea that Jesus of Nazareth is the fulfillment of the Old Testament prophecies regarding the coming of the Messiah, but he rejects the idea that the Kingdom of God has in any way arrived with him. Their theological opinion, *dispensationalism*, suggests that Jesus came and made the kingdom *offer* to Israel, but they rejected his offer, crucified the Messiah, and the Kingdom was postponed. Now, instead, the age of the Church has dawned, and the promise of the Kingdom will not emerge again until the Second Coming of Jesus where he will fulfill his kingdom promise in full. How would you answer this claim that Jesus' announcement of his Messiahship and *the Kingdom* are different? In your opinion, has the Kingdom of God come, in any way, in the first coming of Jesus, and if so, how?

Restatement of the Lesson's Thesis

A profitable study of the life of Christ demands a devout and studious spirit, and an awareness of the critical perspectives and processes associated with his first coming. The announcement of Jesus coming as Messiah is connected with the key New Testament stories of the birth, infancy, and childhood of Jesus. The New Testament Gospel accounts reveal that the person of Jesus of Nazareth is the Messiah who fulfills the promise of God for salvation, redemption, and revelation. John the Baptist is God's chosen messenger to announce Messiah's ministry to the nation of Israel. Jesus' identity as Messiah is announced through his baptism, his temptation in the wilderness, his calling of his disciples, and two important incidents concerning the announcement of the Messiah at the synagogue in Nazareth and the wedding at Cana.

If you are interested in pursuing some of the ideas of *The Messiah Announced*, you might want to give these books a try:

Beasley-Murray, G. R. *Jesus and the Kingdom of God*. Grand Rapids: Eerdmans, 1986.

Ladd, George Eldon. *The Presence of the Future*. Rev. ed. Grand Rapids: Eerdmans, 1974.

Resources and
Bibliographies

Now you want to explore the practical ministry connections that the teaching regarding the announcement of Jesus' Messianic ministry may have for you in your life and ministry setting. In reviewing all the different issues associated with Jesus' arrival and appearance to the world, which particular issues stand out to you as those which you need to be thinking and praying about for this next week and period? In surveying some of the critical concerns highlighted in this lesson, which one in particular does the Holy Spirit suggest requires your further meditation, study, and application? Is there a particular person or ministry situation that comes to mind when you reflect on the meaning of the announcement of Messiah? Allow time to leisurely review this material for the express purpose of listening to the Lord through it, seeing what ideas, issues, or insights he wants you to apply, pursue, and study further.

Ministry Connections

Pray to the Lord with thanksgiving for the reality that his ancient promise of a Messiah has been fulfilled in the person of Jesus of Nazareth. God reveals himself to be one of absolute trustworthiness and faithfulness in the keeping of his prophetic covenant to Abraham and the patriarchs, to David as King, and to his people for a Deliverer and Savior. Undoubtedly, there are areas you face today where you need to confidently cling to the faithful promise of God for fulfillment. Allow the Holy Spirit to direct you to those areas and concerns that require the Lord's faithful intervention and answer, and have others pray for these needs and areas as the Lord leads. The God who was faithful to reveal his Son to us in the fullness of time is likewise faithful to work in the lives of those who cling to him in faith.

Counseling and Prayer

> ◣ **ASSIGNMENTS**

Scripture Memory

John 1.14-18

Reading Assignment

To prepare for class, please visit *www.tumi.org/books* to find next week's reading assignment, or ask your mentor.

Other Assignments

page 249 📖 *10*

Please be aware that you will be quizzed on the content (the video content) of this lesson next week. Make sure that you spend good time reviewing the key concepts of the lesson in your notes. Focus especially on the lesson's main ideas, and read the assigned reading, and be sure to summarize your reading assignment briefly, with no more than a paragraph or two for each. Give in your own words your best understanding of what you think was the main point in each of the readings. Do not be overly concerned about giving detail; simply write out what you consider to be the main point discussed in that section of the book. Please bring these summaries to class next week. (Please see the *Reading Completion Sheet* at the end of this lesson.)

Looking Forward to the Next Lesson

Having looked carefully at the events surrounding the announcing of Messiah at the beginning of Jesus' ministry, our next lesson will focus upon the various texts within the New Testament that testify of the different kinds of opposition that Jesus of Nazareth attracted as he fulfilled his role as the promised Messiah of God. In both spiritual and social realms, Messiah Jesus was opposed in his role as God's anointed Savior of the world.

Name _____

Date _____

For each assigned reading, write a brief summary (one or two paragraphs) of the author's main point. (For additional readings, use the back of this sheet.)

Reading 1

Title and Author: _____ Pages _____

Reading 2

Title and Author: _____ Pages _____

LESSON

2

The Messiah Opposed

page 251 📖 1

Lesson Objectives

page 254 📖 2

Welcome in the strong name of Jesus Christ! After your reading, study, discussion, and application of the materials in this lesson, you will be able to:

- Explain the historical context which surrounded Jesus at the time of his appearing in his public ministry, including the various details which defined Rome's domination of the world and their relationship to Jesus' contemporaries.

- Describe the way in which the various groups in Israel at the time of Jesus reacted differently to the Roman occupation, and show how these reactions of the different Jewish sects and parties largely determined their response to Jesus.

- Give a brief overview of the Sadducees, Pharisees, Essenes, Zealots, and Herodians, their response to the Roman occupation, and their corresponding reaction to the ministry of Jesus.

- Detail the Jewish concept of the Kingdom of God at the time of Jesus, influenced as it was by their oppression from political powers, including their belief that the Kingdom of God would come in power, restoring the material universe and saving humankind from the control of Satan.

- Defend the biblical evidence that supports the idea that Jesus proclaimed the Kingdom present, and demonstrated its reality in his person, and works of healings and exorcisms.

Devotion

The Servant and His Lord

page 254 📖 3

Read John 15.18-26. Can a disciple of Jesus maneuver through this world without experiencing the kind of rejection, persecution, and tribulation known and experienced by our Lord? Was our Lord's experience sui generis (utterly unique) to him, or must all of his own also experience a level of the world's hatred and rejection, even as he did?

One of Jesus' favorite sayings was the familiar word, "Truly, truly, I say to you, a servant is not greater than his master; nor is a messenger greater than the one who sent him" (John 13.16 [ESV]). *A servant is not greater than his master, nor is the one who is sent greater than the one who sent him.* Jesus, the truly great and sovereign Master of all, endured the persecution and hatred of the ungodly and hardhearted, and his obvious word in our devotional text is that if the world hated him, they will hate us as well. No genuine disciple of Jesus can go through this world without scars, with no opposition, operating gloriously scot-free; we all must experience the rejection and opposition of God's enemies. We have to fight, we will be opposed, even hated, for the sake of Christ. We need not marvel at this, however. Jesus himself, our Lord and Master, was rejected and hated and we, because of our union with him, will experience the same. God will grant to those who belong to Christ the same grace that he received, which enabled our Lord to endure such hateful treatment and abuse for the sake of the Father.

Always remember, as you endure troubles and trials, tribulation, hatred, and hardship, that our Lord endured the same, and will help us to persevere till the end.

After reciting and/or singing the Nicene Creed (located in the Appendix), pray the following prayer:

Nicene Creed and Prayer

> *Almighty God, whose blessed Son was led by the Spirit to be tempted by Satan: Come quickly to help us who are assaulted by many temptations; and, as you know the weaknesses of each of us, let each one find you mighty to save; through Jesus Christ your Son our Lord, who lives and reigns with you and the Holy Spirit, one God, now and for ever. Amen.*

~ Episcopal Church. **The Book of Common Prayer and Administrations of the Sacraments and Other Rites and Ceremonies of the Church, Together with the Psalter or Psalms of David.** New York: The Church Hymnal Corporation, 1979. p. 218

Put away your notes, gather up your thoughts and reflections, and take the quiz for Lesson 1, *The Messiah Announced.*

Quiz

Review with a partner, write out and/or recite the text for last class session's assigned memory verse: John 1.14-18.

Scripture Memorization Review

Turn in your summary of the reading assignment for last week, that is, your brief response and explanation of the main points that the authors were seeking to make in the assigned reading (Reading Completion Sheet).

Assignments Due

Is the Health-Wealth Gospel Heretical?

page 256 4

Many now proclaim a gospel which promises ease, comfort, and blessing in the face of a world becoming increasingly violent, vicious, and unjust. The heart of this gospel is the belief that the death of Jesus won for the believer a triumphant victory which touches every area of life without stain or admixture of trouble or trial. If our faith is firm, if our confession is clear, and our affirmation of the Word of God steadfast, we will receive the health and wealth of the Lord, the blessings which come to those whose faith remains unwavering and strong. This lifestyle of blessing and victory is indicative of saving faith; those who cling to God are assured of a level of blessing and grace that will not diminish, as long as their faith remains resolute. What do you believe about this "gospel?" Is it biblical, extreme, or even heretical?

A Question for the City: Kinds of Misery

It appears in the urban neighborhoods of today that many people suffer daily in misery. Some go without housing and food, without shelter and clothing, without the bare necessities of life and health. Many are victims of abuse and violence, and many live daily in loneliness and despair. What is the role of misery in the Christian life? Why do terrible things happen to some of the best people, and some of the most wicked and unjust people appear to live problem-free lives? Are there different kinds of misery; is there a kind of misery and opposition that actually leads to godliness and growth, or are all versions of misery expressions of sin and the enemy's hatred of God's people?

Blame the Right One

Who is precisely to blame for the opposition and hatred that oftentimes occurs in the life of those who belong to Jesus? While it is entirely obvious to see that Jesus suffered opposition from various quarters due not to himself but to the evil intentions of his enemies, can the same be said of us? Do we as disciples of Jesus experience opposition because we are associated with him, or do we sometimes experience opposition due to our own sinfulness and ungodly reactions to others? If that is true, then how can we tell *when* we are receiving persecution because of *our allegiance to Jesus*, and when we are receiving persecution due *to our own sinful behavior in this world*?

The Messiah Opposed

Segment 1: Opposition by His Contemporaries

Rev. Dr. Don L. Davis

CONTENT

By analyzing the historical context of the Roman world at the time of Jesus' public ministry, we can better comprehend the reaction of the groups that made up his contemporaries. In looking at the Sadducees, Pharisees, Essenes, Zealots, and Herodians, we can see Jewish groups who each responded differently to the Roman occupation, and through their position, determined to relate uniquely to the Messianic ministry of Jesus.

Summary of Segment 1

Our objective for this segment, *Opposition by His Contemporaries*, is to enable you to see that:

- The historical context of the Roman empire was the main environment affecting the various Jewish groups which surrounded Jesus at the time of his appearing in his public ministry.

- Groups responded to Jesus based upon the position they took juxtaposed to their understanding of Rome's domination of the world.

- The contemporaries of Jesus all reacted differently to the Roman occupation, and these reactions of the different Jewish sects and parties largely determined how these groups responded to Jesus.

- The most significant groups which reacted to Jesus during his public ministry are the Sadducees, Pharisees, Essenes, Zealots, and Herodians. Because each of these groups responded differently to the Roman occupation, they therefore reacted differently to the Messianic ministry of Jesus.

I. The Historical Context (milieu) of Jesus' Life: the Context of the Roman World

Video Segment 1 Outline

(Erich Sauer. *The Dawn of World Redemption*. Grand Rapids, Michigan: Eerdmans Publishing, 1951. p. 176.)

A. A time of *world centralization* (commerce within the empire itself, political organization, overall governmental and military oversight)

B. A time of *world cultural unity* (Graeco-Roman influence, koine Greek used as the universal business language)

    1. Thin coating of cultural uniformity

    2. "*Lingua Franca:*" Greek as the language of commerce and business

        a. Aramaic spoken in Palestine; Hebrew was used in rabbinic circles.

        b. Most ordinary folk in Galilee would have probably known Greek.

C. A time of *world trade and intercourse* (interaction and inter-connection among provinces in terms of finance, commerce, trade among representative cultures, nations, and peoples)

    1. Much prosperity in Rome; huge number of slaves (great difference between aristocrats and slaves)

    2. Sea lanes with important ports (Alexandria, Black Sea, Carthage, etc.)

    3. Land routes (famous for building roads)

D. A time of *world peace* (the conquest of Rome of the then-known world)

1. *Pax Romana* = the peace of Rome (ruled most of the world)

2. Tension within Palestine whether to obey Roman authority or not

3. Tensions between strong central government and strong local rule

   a. Emperor who ruled the entire empire for life with absolute power

   b. Province rule: senatorial and imperial provinces ("legates"); Quirinius was *legate* of Syria

E. A time of *world demoralization* (varying degrees of Roman oppression, as well as varying degrees of national allegiance to Rome)

   1. Dramatic differences between the have and have-nots

   2. No sense of hope for change in some provinces which retained their own fierce national and religious allegiances (Israel)

   3. Roman rule for 60 years before Jesus was born

      a. Brought benefits but was terribly unpopular in Palestine

      b. Oppressive system of taxation on the occupied country

         (1) Unofficial scam game of the collaborators ("tax collectors" or "publicans")

(2) Tax collectors were a feared and hated group, viewed as traitors of the nation and friends of the oppressors.

4. Political domination and oppression was the chief cause of resentment of Israel population (did not line up with their identity as God's people).

F. A time of *world mingling of religions* (great diversity of religious beliefs and spiritual practices)

1. Emperor worship was popular, but did not preempt other local god worship.

2. Eastern religions poured into the empire (centers of Egypt, Syria, Phrygia in Turkey).

3. Astrology, the occult, and philosophies were diverse, odd, filled with much superstition and magic.

page 256 📖 5

II. The Contemporaries of Jesus: Jewish Reactions to Jesus

A. The Sadducees (associated with the priests, who with the lay "elders" exercised leadership over the Jews under Roman domination): *leaders under Rome*

1. Materialistic party among the Jews of Jesus' time, associated with the priests, Acts 5.17

2. Denied the resurrection and the existence of angels and spirits

a. Matt. 22.23

b. Acts 4.1-2

c. Acts 23.6-8

3. Along with the Pharisees, demanded signs from Jesus, Matt. 16.1

4. The high priestly family was in close connection with them, Acts 4.1ff; Acts 5.17-18.

B. Pharisees (experts in the law and its rigorous application to everyday life): *keepers of the Jewish tradition*

1. General data

    a. Said to be around 6,000 of them at the time of Jesus, the only sizeable group to survive the revolt of 70 A.D.

    b. Modern Judaism follows the pharisaical tradition.

    c. Accepted the writings of the Old Testament; believed in the resurrection, angels, and the reality of spirits, Acts 23.8

2. A sect of the Jews who were expert in the knowledge and strict observance of the Mosaic law

a. Acts 15.5

b. Phil. 3.5

3. They possessed a great zeal for the tradition of the elders.

a. Mark 7.3

b. Mark 7.5-8

c. Gal. 1.14

4. Were outwardly pious and moral in their observance of their own traditions, oftentimes in a self-righteous and greedy manner

a. Luke 18.11-12

b. Phil. 3.5-6

c. Luke 16.14-15

d. Luke 20.47

e. Luke 16.14

5. Were active in their proselytizing of others to their practices, and willing to persecute the unconverted

   a. Matt. 23.15

   b. Acts 9.1-2

6. Were generally opposed to Jesus

   a. Rejected John's baptism, Luke 7.29-30

   b. Early on in Jesus' public ministry, they sought to have Jesus arrested, John 11.57.

   c. Couldn't stand Jesus' association with sinners, Luke 15.1-2

   d. Known for placing conformity to ritual over love for people, Matt. 15.1-14

   e. Ascribed the works of Jesus' deliverance to Satan

      (1) Matt. 9.34

      (2) Matt. 12.24

7. Reserved his most pronounced teaching against them, Matt. 23.1-33

   a. Called them serpents, a generation of vipers, Matt. 23.33

b. Called them hypocrites and blind guides, compared them to white sepulchers, cf. Matt. 23.27

    c. Associated them with those who earlier killed and tortured the prophets of old, Matt. 23.29-33

C. Essenes (withdrew from all political and social connection to Israel and Rome in monastic lifestyle): *withdrawal into monastic lifestyle*

    1. From the Greek, *Essenoi* (not mentioned explicitly in the Bible, but represented a social response to the Roman rule)

    2. Sources for information about them: Philo (first half of the 1st Century A.D.); Pliny (his writings around 77 A.D.); Josephus (writings of the period around 75-94 A.D. for his writings), Hippolytus (3rd Century A.D.)

    3. Some debate as to the accuracy of these sayings regarding the Essenes who lived during the period of Herod the Great (37 B.C.- 4 A.D.).

    4. Broke away from mainline Judaism probably around 100-140 B.C.

    5. They were devoted to live a life of *asceticism* (disciplined, simple life withdrawn from larger social and political worlds).

        a. No luxury items; avoided all unnecessary social and economic contacts with those outside their groups

     b. Centered their lives on prayer, hard work, and study of Scripture

     c. Maintained strict laws of obedience

  6. They lived in community around the Mediterranean Sea (Qumran) (property held in common, worshiped and studied Scripture together, common meals).

  7. Held a *dialectic* view of the world (i.e., they believed everyone was either "*children of the light*" or "*children of darkness*")

  8. Believed strongly in a two kingdoms kind of theology, expected Messiah to return and destroy the children of darkness and bring victory to the children of the light

D. Zealots (a group that advocated insurrection and rebellion against the Roman occupation of Israel): *defenders of the theocracy*

  1. From the Greek *zelot*, "zealous one"; New Testament zelotes

  2. Radically opposed to Roman rule on the ground of its interference with "theocracy" (i.e., the rule of God) over the nation of Israel; they were militant nationalists

  3. Were loyal to Jewish customs and laws

  4. Were apocalyptical in their vision (*apocalypse* = unveiling)

a. Were pessimistic about the present age

b. Were not opposed to insurrection and armed rebellion against the occupation of Israel by Roman officials

c. Felt that things would inevitably change, and very soon

5. Simon the Cananaean (one of the Twelve) was a member of the Zealot party.

a. Mark 3.18

b. Luke 6.15

c. Acts 1.13

E. Herodians (members of a Jewish party who favored the rule of Herod and his dynasty): *collaborators with the enemy*

1. Believed it was right to pay homage to a ruler (i.e., Herod) who might be able through collaboration to bring to the nation the advantages of friendship with Rome

2. Opposed Jesus early in Galilee, with an attempt to take his life, Mark 3.6

a. Viewed Jesus as a threat to the peace of Israel

b. Jesus was a magnet for opposition among weird groups which disagreed with each other.

3. Opposed Jesus later in Jerusalem; with the Pharisees, they sought to entangle Jesus in his teaching, Matt. 22.15-21

4. They conspired to trap Jesus, Mark 12.13.

F. Common traits of Jesus' contemporaries who opposed his public ministry

1. They all, in one way or another, related to Jesus because of how they viewed him vis-a-vis their agenda in light of Roman rule.

2. Viewed Jesus as a threat to the status quo; none of his opponents advocated him as the true Messiah

3. Felt that the overthrow and destruction of Jesus would benefit the Jewish nation in its relationship with Rome

4. Received Jesus' implicit and explicit rebuke and critique for not understanding the times (the root of his opposition was spiritual blindness), Luke 12.54-56

5. Elevated power, money, and position above a genuine desire to care for others, or recognize the obvious signs of Jesus' Messiahship

6. Jesus often warned against the unhealthy influence of their teaching, which was compared to "leaven."

a. Matt. 16.6

b. Matt. 16.11-12

c. Luke 12.1

7. With very little sanctified imagination, *we can easily find our own responses to Jesus within these groups.* (Take seriously what Jesus is saying because you are more like one of these groups than you probably know!)

8. Jesus forewarned that due to their opposition, plotting, and conspiracy he would be crucified, but also promised to rise again.

a. Matt. 20.17-19

b. Mark 8.31

c. Mark 10.32-34

Conclusion

» Jesus of Nazareth was born into a distinct social milieu which influenced every facet of his and his fellow Israelites life, government, and situation.

» The peculiar Roman historical context dramatically influenced the reactions of various groups within the Jewish nation, and affected the way in which they related to Jesus.

2

Please take as much time as you have available to answer these and other questions that the video brought out. Jesus was born and raised in a Roman historical context which impacted greatly the decisions and lifestyles of various competing Jewish contemporary groups of his period. Be clear and concise in your answers, and where possible, support with Scripture!

1. List two of the main elements of the historical context of the Roman empire at the time of Jesus? In your opinion, how did these elements impact the coming of the Lord at the time of his first advent?

2. Briefly describe the key features of the following groups which reacted to Jesus during his public ministry: the Sadducees, Pharisees, Essenes, Zealots, and Herodians.

3. In what way did the response of each of the above groups to the Roman occupation influence and affect their relationship and response to Jesus of Nazareth?

4. What group, in your opinion, was *furthest* away from the claims of Jesus of Nazareth as Messiah? Which group was closest to and most open to the claims of Jesus?

5. What do we detect in Jesus' response to these groups that shows that he was aware of their reaction to him? Was Jesus especially open to or critical of any one of the groups? Explain.

6. Do you think that the opposition that Jesus faced by one or more of the above groups was to be expected in light of the Roman occupation?

Segue 1

Student Questions and Response

page 257 📖 *6*

The Messiah Opposed

Segment 2: Opposition from Spiritual Forces

Rev. Dr. Don L. Davis

**Summary of
Segment 2**

page 257 📖 7

Even though the contemporary Jewish concept of the Kingdom of God at the time of Jesus emphasized the glory of Israel and defeat of the Gentiles, Jesus came announcing the Kingdom of God as present and visible in his person and works. In the person of Jesus of Nazareth, the long-awaited Kingdom of God had arrived, but not in a way that the Jews had predicted. Still, in his person and through his good deed works of miracles, Jesus proclaimed the Kingdom present, and demonstrated its reality in his healings and exorcisms.

Our objective for this segment, *Opposition from Spiritual Forces*, is to enable you to see that:

- The Jewish concept of the Kingdom of God at the time of Jesus was rooted in the power and glory of the nation of Israel, and the hope of Israel to defeat their oppressing Gentile powers.

- The Jewish concept further understood the Messiah as one who would come in mighty and awesome power, restoring the Kingdom of God in the material universe, and in a decisive moment of salvation would liberate humankind from the control of Satan.

- Jesus' view of the Kingdom conflicted with his contemporaries in that Jesus proclaimed the Kingdom to be present in his very person and works of power, demonstrated in his healings and exorcisms.

- As the true - albeit unexpected - Messiah, Jesus opposed those underlying spiritual powers which have held the world and humanity captive since the fall.

- Jesus of Nazareth fulfills the kingdom promise, and therefore as Messiah opposes the effects of the curse and the works of the kingdom of darkness.

2

I. Background of the Jewish Concept of the Kingdom of God

Video Segment 2
Outline

    A. "Kingdom" in the ancient world

        1. *"Kingdom"* at the time of Jesus in that milieu meant "lordship," "rule," "reign," or "sovereignty."

        2. *Sovereignty of God* or *Rule of God* = Kingdom of God

        3. In most Jewish sources, *"Kingdom of God"* and *"Kingdom of heaven"* both refer to God's reassertion of his rule over his creation (Dan 7.27).

    B. Old Testament references to the Kingdom of God (a representative sample)

        1. Exod. 15.18

        2. 1 Sam. 2.12

        3. 1 Chron. 29.11

        4. Ps. 22.29

        5. Pss. 93.1; 95.10; 97.1; 99.1

        6. Ps. 145.11-13

2

7. Isa. 9.6-7

8. Dan. 4.34

9. Dan. 7.14

10. Dan. 7.27

11. Much of the Jewish literature of the time of Jesus had numerous references to the idea of God's kingdom authority (e.g., Tobit 13.1; Wisdom of Solomon 6.4; 1 Enoch 41.1, etc.).

C. The Jewish worldview of the Kingdom at the time of Jesus

This overview is a summary of a few of the basic assumptions held by Jewish believers who were contemporaries of Jesus at his first coming. These ideas are assumed to serve as the backdrop of the events and teachings of the Hebrew Scriptures (i.e., our Old Testament).

1. God is the King of all heaven and earth (as Creator of the universe, he alone possesses the absolute right to rule over all the good things he has made).

2. God's sovereign right to rule has been contested in the universe.

    a. It has been contested by "*Satan*" (= "adversary"), a spiritual being which rebelled against God's right to rule.

b.   Through the deception of Satan, *humankind* fell into rebellion, losing their freedom under God, and passed under the control of Satan's rule and domination.

c.   Because of their rebellion against God, human beings have passed from the *Kingdom of God* (God's rule and influence) to the *kingdom of Satan* (the devil's rule and influence).

3.   The *kingdom of the devil* rules in the present world system.

a.   His influence and presence touches all phases of this present world order.

b.   The *kingdom of Satan* functions in both the material universe and the affairs of humankind.

4.   The *kingdom of the devil* and the *Kingdom of God* are in mortal conflict and combat with each other.

a.   God is reasserting his right to rule over his creation, and the *kingdom of the devil* resists this effort with all its fury and energy.

b.   At issue in this battle is this: *who will possess the absolute right to rule and reign over creation and humankind.*

D. Israel's special vision of the Kingdom related to its identity.

The idea of the Kingdom affected the Jewish view of spiritual opposition in regard to the forces of the material world, human affairs, and Israel's place as a nation.

1. Israel as a nation is wrapped up in this struggle between God and Satan for the control of the world.

   a. They are God's special people because of the Covenant, Gen. 12-17.

   b. Though called as God's special people, they live in a *milieu* (situation) that is dominated by the *kingdom of Satan*.

      (1) Political, governmental, and other social forces which were hostile to Israel are in fact under Satan's control.

      (2) God used these systems for his purposes (even though they were not aware of it).

2. The *Kingdom of God* would come in power through the Messiah and would bring an end to Satan's control and influence over the world and humankind.

   a. A dramatic invasion of God's power to once and for all end Satan's control over humankind

      (1) God's kingdom invasion would be immediate (it would happen suddenly).

      (2) God's kingdom invasion would be cataclysmic (it would involve all the world).

      (3) God's kingdom invasion would be decisive (it would bring an end to Satan's rule).

   b. A reversal of fortune for God's people (i.e., when the Kingdom came, Israel would become the greatest of all peoples on the earth)

3. The Kingdom of God would come through the line of the Hebrew kings.

    a. The kings of the Hebrews were rulers under the authority of God.

    b. God's Kingdom would come through the line of the Davidic kings (2 Samuel 7; Psalm 89).

    c. *Messiah* is spoken of often in Old Testament Scripture as a "*son of David*" (cf. Isa. 9.6-7; Jer. 23.5-6; Psalm 2).

    d. Appearance of the *Messiah* would be the evidence that the *Day of the Lord* had come, and that the Kingdom had arrived.

4. The *Kingdom of God*, when it finally arrived, would bring about dramatic change.

    a. It would produce *deliverance of the nation of Israel from political oppression and domination*.

    b. It would result in *the refreshing and renewing of all nature back to its Eden-like glory and splendor*.

    c. It would *establish peace and righteousness with justice* among all the nations, with Israel at its head.

    d. It would produce *global spiritual transformation*, with all nations changed to serve and worship the true God, YHWH.

e. It would be *apocalyptic* in its power: it would come suddenly, in the future, affecting all the world, both the material world and human affairs.

II. Jesus' Appearance Is the Presence of the Kingdom of God in the Here and Now: He Opposes and Overcomes the Effects of the Curse and the Kingdom of the Devil.

A. Jesus Christ in his person represents the *Kingdom of God in the here and now*.

1. Jesus announced himself to be the *promised Messiah* through whom all of the effects of the curse, sin, demonic oppression, and social injustice would be overcome.

    a. He announced with his coming the Kingdom as present, Mark 1.14-15.

    b. He declared himself to be Yahweh's Servant who would end all oppression in his person, Luke 4.18-19.

    c. He is *the Word made flesh*, the actual manifestation of God in human form come to earth, John 1.14-18.

2. Jesus is the *presence of the future*.

    a. The fulfillment of the promise of Abraham, Gal. 3.13-14

    b. The one appointed to rescind the effects of the curse, cf. Isaiah 11

c.   The Victor who would bring a final and full end to Satan's rule and authority, cf. Gen. 3.15 with 1 John 3.8

d.   The Messiah anointed by God to inaugurate the age to come in this present age

B.   General outline of Jesus' role as *Messiah* fulfills the kingdom promise of the one who would bring down the effects of the curse and the works of the devil

1.   The *mission* of Messiah Jesus was to destroy the works of the devil, 1 John 3.8.

2.   The *birth* of Messiah Jesus represents the invasion of God's reign into Satan's dominion, Luke 1.31-33.

3.   The *message* of Messiah Jesus was that the Kingdom of God was at hand, present for all to see in his person, Mark 1.14-15.

4.   The *teaching* of Messiah Jesus represents the ethics of the Kingdom, Matt. 5-7.

5.   The *miracles* of Messiah Jesus reveal to all his kingly authority and power to overcome the effects of the curse on God's material creation, e.g., in Mark 2.8-12 where he demonstrates his authority to forgive and heal.

6.   The *exorcisms* of Messiah Jesus represent the "binding of the strong man" as spoken in Luke 11.14-20.

7. The *matchless character* of Messiah reveal the Father's own divine splendor and glory, John 1.14-18.

8. The *death* of Messiah represents the payment for our sin debt and its penalty, along with the defeat of Satan, as Paul says in Colossians 2.15 made an open show and display of his victory on the cross, where our sin's indebtedness and unrighteousness was paid in full.

C. The Kingdom is Already, but Not Yet: two manifestations of the Kingdom of God.

1. In Jesus' presence, the Kingdom was displayed, and the reign of God inaugurated. Through his death and resurrection, the rebellious prince, Satan, the great deceiver and blasphemer was wounded, crippled, bound, but his destruction comes later, (cf. 1 John 3.8; Heb. 2.14-15; Col. 2.15).

2. At Christ's Second Coming (what scholars call the *Parousia* [Greek for "Second Arrival"]) Satan will be finally destroyed, his rule finally put down, and the full manifestation of God's kingly power will be revealed in the glorification of the saints, and in a restored heaven and earth, 1 Cor. 15.24-28.

III. Messiah Opposed by Spiritual Powers: Healings and Exorcisms in the Life of Jesus

A. The Kingdom has come in Jesus: healings and miracles

1. Jesus' healings were signs of his Messiahship and the Kingdom's presence in the world.

2. *Jesus opposed the effects of the curse*: he was endowed with authority over all the effects of the curse, including disease, corruption, even death.

   a. He opened blinded eyes, John 9.1-7.

   b. He fed over 5,000 with a few loaves and fish, Mark 6.30-44.

   c. He commanded the raging winds and storms, Matt. 8.23-27.

   d. He healed the lame, the paralyzed, and the crippled, Mark 2.1-12.

   e. He even raised the dead, John 11.

3. All of Jesus' miracles were signs of his kingly authority as Messiah to reassert God's kingdom rule on earth.

   a. Jesus' ministry is signs of his kingly right to demonstrate God's power in our world, Acts 10.36-38.

   b. Everywhere Jesus went, he demonstrated through his miracles and healings God's kingdom rule come to earth, Matt. 4.23-25.

B. The Kingdom come in Jesus: exorcisms and demonic oppression

1. Jesus' overthrow of the demons in exorcism and command are signs of his Messiahship.

a. He healed the demon-possessed boy, Mark 9.14-29.

    b. He cured the raving demoniac of the Gadarenes, Matt. 8.28-34.

    c. Demons wailed in terror at his presence, Mark 1.24-25.

2. *Jesus opposed the kingdom of the devil*: he was endowed with the authority to defeat and bind all the powers of the devil, and to destroy his works over God's creation and all humankind.

    a. Jesus' destruction and domination over the forces of the devil prove his kingly authority and the presence of the Kingdom in the earth, Luke 11.14-23.

    b. With Jesus' kingly presence, the Kingdom came in the midst of the people, Luke 17.20-21.

    c. Jesus' public ministry is a plundering of the house of the strong man, the devil, and the reassertion of God's right to rule over his own house, Matt. 12.24-29.

3. All of Jesus' encounters with the devil can be viewed as signs of his kingly authority as Messiah to reassert God's kingdom rule on earth.

    a. Heb. 2.14

    b. 1 John 3.8b

Conclusion

» Jesus is the fulfillment of the Messianic promise of the Old Testament in its hope for the Kingdom come.

» The coming of Messiah in Jesus differed from the contemporary Jewish view, and yet fulfilled the Messianic promises of the Kingdom.

» Jesus as Messiah received opposition from and overcame great spiritual forces during his public ministry on earth, including the effects of the curse and the renegade lordship of the devil.

The following questions were designed to help you review the material in the second video segment. In the person of Jesus of Nazareth the Kingdom of God has come, reasserting God's right to rule in the midst of a world plagued by the effects of the curse and the vicious oppression of the devil. Be clear and concise in your answers, and where possible, support with Scripture!

Segue 2

Student Questions and Response

1. In a short paragraph or statement, explain the various elements which made up the Jewish concept of the Kingdom of God at the time of Jesus. Why did the Jews of Jesus' day find it difficult to believe that he, a humble carpenter's son from Nazareth, might actually be the Messiah?

2. In regards to the element of time, how did the Jewish concept of the Kingdom differ from Jesus' own view of the Kingdom's coming?

3. In what sense does Jesus declare the prophecies of God's coming Kingdom to be fulfilled in his person at the time of his ministry? Be specific.

4. How do Christ's healings and exorcisms demonstrate that the promise of the Kingdom of God have actually come to pass in Jesus' own day?

5. Jesus' confrontation with the powers of the enemy reveal his authority in this world. How does his conflict help us to understand the ministry of Messiah in the world today?

6. If the Kingdom has come in Jesus, then why haven't all evil forces and influences been utterly destroyed? Is there a future dimension to Jesus' consummation of the Kingdom, and if so, what is it?

7. Jesus of Nazareth fulfills the kingdom promise, and therefore as Messiah opposes the effects of the curse and the works of the kingdom of darkness. How do we apply this kingdom authority in our own ministries and lives, here in the inner city?

CONNECTION

Summary of Key Concepts

This lesson focuses upon the opposition our Lord received, not only from his contemporaries in the nation of Israel, but those larger spiritual forces of the curse, the devil, and moral evil at work in the world. Jesus of Nazareth fulfills the kingdom promise of God, reasserting the rule of God in the earth, and demonstrating tangibly in his person and work God's victory over sin, Satan, and death.

- The historical context which surrounded Jesus at the time of his appearing in his public ministry was dominated by the occupation and influence of the Roman empire on the world in general, and Israel in particular.

- The Roman domination of the world utterly influenced the various worldviews of the groups of Jesus' contemporaries.

- This influence of Rome either negatively or positively on Jesus' contemporaries determined and shaped the reactions of these groups to the person and message of Jesus in his ministry to Israel.

- The critical groups which interacted with Jesus in his ministry were the Sadducees, Pharisees, Zealots, and Herodians, and various other groups connected with these.

- The Jewish concept of the Kingdom of God at the time of Jesus, influenced as it was by their oppression from political powers, included their belief that the Kingdom of God would come in power, restoring the material universe and saving humankind from the control of Satan.

- Jesus' view of the Kingdom conflicted with his contemporaries in that Jesus proclaimed the Kingdom to be present in his very person and works of power, demonstrated in his healings and exorcisms.

- As the true albeit unexpected Messiah, Jesus opposed those underlying spiritual powers which have held the world and humanity captive since the fall.

2

⌐ Jesus of Nazareth fulfills the kingdom promise, and therefore as Messiah opposes the effects of the curse and the works of the kingdom of darkness.

Now is the time for you to discuss with your fellow students your questions about the practical meaning of Jesus' opposition in his life and ministry as Messiah in Israel. A brief overview of the biblical teaching of Jesus' opposition reveals that the core principle of Jesus' work was to experience unrelenting conflict with those who opposed him in his kingdom advancing work. As you consider this critical element of Messiah's work, what kinds of questions do you have concerning your own life and ministry? How does opposition and conflict influence the various dimensions of your own service for the Lord today? Maybe some of the questions below might help you form your own, more specific and critical questions.

Student Application and Implications

*   What does the level and frequency of opposition, conflict, and persecution in the life of Jesus tell us about the nature of all kingdom advancing ministry today?

*   To what extent can the disciple of Jesus today expect the kind of rejection and opposition that accompanied Jesus' life? In what ways is Jesus' life a pattern for us, and in what ways is his life utterly unique to himself? Explain.

*   Jesus of Nazareth fulfills the kingdom promise in his person, so, in a very real sense, the Kingdom of God has come. What does this kind of teaching mean for inner city ministry and life? Are there signs of the Kingdom come in your neighborhood? Where?

*   How does the health-wealth version of the Gospel either agree with or conflict with Jesus' view of the Kingdom come in his own person?

*   In a sense, the Kingdom of God is already here, but not yet consummated (i.e., the Already/Not Yet Kingdom). What aspects of the Kingdom of God still await the full consummation and disclosure at Jesus' Second Coming?

*   In what ways do the ministries of the Church continue to display Jesus of Nazareth's fulfillment of the kingdom promise through his victory over the effects of the curse and the works of the kingdom of darkness?

Demonic Oppression, Possession, or Both?

page 259 📖 *8*

The fact that the Kingdom of God has come in the person of Jesus completely redefines the believer's and the Church's relationship to the devil. Because of Jesus' work on the cross, the believer is no longer subject to the domination and power of the devil; the victory of God is available to every believer who claims the work of Christ as his or her own (1 John 3.8; Heb. 2.13ff; James 4.7; 1 John 5.4; Eph. 6.10-18; 2 Cor. 10.3-5). What is the possibility of believers to be oppressed by demons, to be possessed by demons, or both, or neither? What must a believer do to experience continuously the victory won for him or her through the blood sacrifice of Jesus (Rev. 12.9ff.)?

Suffering: An Absolute Necessity?

According to Paul, it has been granted to believers not only to hold him in confidence, but also to suffer for the sake of the Lord Jesus (Phil. 1.29ff.). Some teach the Gospel as if the victory won by our Lord over sin and the devil means practically that we are no longer subject to suffering and persecution. This teaching would suggest that when a believer finds himself or herself sick, depressed, struggling, doubtful, or hurting, that the problem must be *self-caused*, due to a *lack of faith*. How would you describe the necessity or lack thereof of suffering in the life of the godly disciple of Jesus? Must every blood-washed believer also expect a baptism of fire of persecution from the enemy and God's enemies, or can they be avoided altogether by the proper walk with God?

A Shame to Christ?

A common teaching in many evangelical circles is that our Lord died expressly to eliminate the possibility for certain negative realities to be encountered and endured. By his stripes we are healed, they declare, and this means that we are to confess continuous, unbroken health and prosperity *on the very basis of Jesus' suffering on the cross*. The fact that Christ suffered for these things means that the believer ought not to attempt to shame Christ by either ignoring his victory or undercutting it by a weak or unbiblical faith. To what extent does the work of Jesus on the cross guarantee that certain effects of sin and the curse are to *no longer be experienced by believers in Jesus*?

We Killed Our Son

This is the title of book by a dear Christian couple who, confessing the healing of their diabetic son, saw him die due to a lack of insulin, and likewise saw themselves accused and found guilty of negligence in the death of their own son. How would you instruct new believers to pray the prayer of faith for healing, transformation, and blessing, while, at the same time, allowing God the right to withhold anything from his child for the sake of discipline, training, and growth?

The historical context which surrounded Jesus at the time of his appearing in his public ministry (i.e., Rome's domination of the world) influenced greatly the reaction of Jesus' contemporaries to his offer of the Kingdom. The critical groups included the Sadducees, Pharisees, Essenes, Zealots, and the Herodians. The Jewish concept of the Kingdom of God at the time of Jesus, influenced as it was by their oppression from political powers, included the belief that the Kingdom of God would come in power, restoring the material universe and saving humankind from the control of Satan. Jesus, on the other hand, proclaimed the Kingdom present in himself, and demonstrated its reality in his person and works of healings and exorcisms.

Restatement of the Lesson's Thesis

If you are interested in pursuing some of the ideas of *The Messiah Opposed*, you might want to give these books a try:

Ladd, George Eldon. *Crucial Questions About the Kingdom of God*. Grand Rapids: Eerdman's, 1952.

Willis, Wendell, ed. *The Kingdom of God in 20th-Century Interpretation*. Peabody, MA: Hendrickson Publishers, 1987.

Resources and Bibliographies

To understand the nature of the opposition that Messiah experienced is to begin to prepare for kingdom ministry today. After you have reflected much on the biblical evidence of Messiah's enduring of constant opposition to his person and work, you must apply this teaching to your own Christian life and service. If you are serving Jesus, you know already much of the truth of these simple texts. Now, in your life and ministry today, how would the Holy Spirit want you to be encouraged in your own struggle against sin, the devil, your flesh, and the world? What *internal*

Ministry Connections

struggles are you fighting with lust and passion, what external influences call for your distraction and disobedience in the world's temptation, and what *infernal* conflicts do you wage with the enemy's lies and doubts? Try to pinpoint those areas that the Lord would have you consider in your life and practical ministry, and prayerfully consider what steps he would have you take to re-engage in the fight as Christ's soldier and child.

Counseling and Prayer

page 259 📖 9

If anything is clear from the teaching of the Scriptures, many of the fights of the believer are done in a group; the enemy does not merely fight me, rather, he fights us. For your support, answerability, and growth, you need the prayers and counsel of others engaged in the same battle and struggle you face, even as they face the same (1 Pet. 5.8-10). Do not hesitate to ask believers whom you trust to pray specifically for you in the areas you need God's strengthening and aid. God will hear and answer the prayers of his believing children (James 5.16). Seek the face of the Lord together for his strength and power, and do not be discouraged; he knows we have need of him and his supply (Phil. 4.13).

ASSIGNMENTS

Scripture Memory

John 15.18-20

Reading Assignment

To prepare for class, please visit *www.tumi.org/books* to find next week's reading assignment, or ask your mentor.

Other Assignments

Please read carefully the assignments above, and as last week, write a brief summary for them and bring these summaries to class next week (please see the "Reading Completion Sheet" at the end of this lesson). Also, now is the time to begin to think about your ministry project, as well as decide your Scripture text for your exegetical project. These are weighty decisions, for these assignments possess great weight in the figuring of your final grade for this course. Therefore, do not delay in determining either your ministry or exegetical project. The sooner you select, the more time you will have to prepare!

In this lesson we carefully outlined those elements, both social and spiritual, which opposed the ministry of Jesus of Nazareth as the Messiah of God. Jesus came to earth reasserting God's right to rule in this world over the kingdom of the devil. Now, in our next lesson, we will see how the New Testament openly reveals the identity of Messiah Jesus in the glorious display of his majestic person and works, and ultimately and powerfully, in his suffering and death on behalf of the world.

Looking Forward to the Next Lesson

2

Name _____

Date _____

For each assigned reading, write a brief summary (one or two paragraphs) of the author's main point. (For additional readings, use the back of this sheet.)

Reading 1

Title and Author: _____ Pages _____

Reading 2

Title and Author: _____ Pages _____

LESSON

3

page 261 📖 *1*

The Messiah Revealed

Lesson Objectives

Welcome in the strong name of Jesus Christ! After your reading, study, discussion, and application of the materials in this lesson, you will be able to:

- Demonstrate your understanding of the richness of Jesus as Messiah in his personal revelation spoken of in the Gospel accounts.

- Show how from the New Testament Scriptures that Jesus' Messianic identity is powerfully revealed through his perfect life and character, his masterful leadership of the Apostles, and his submissive sonship to his Father.

- Describe how the Bible makes plain Jesus' Messianic identity in his prophetic teaching ministry, as well as in the mighty demonstrations of power, both in signs and wonders (miracles) and dramatic encounter with spiritual demons.

- Outline the episodes which make up the suffering and death of Jesus (i.e., his Passion), and show how his death provides a clear biblical revelation of his role as Messiah.

- Explain how Peter's confession of Jesus' true identity, accompanied by Jesus' prediction of his death, underwrites Jesus' Messiahship.

- List and briefly give commentary on the final events of Jesus' life on earth: his triumphal entry into Jerusalem, his Passover with his disciples, as well as the events surrounding his crucifixion and death, from his agony in prayer in the Garden to his burial after his death on the cross.

Devotion

page 263 📖 *2*

Blessed Is He Who Comes in the Name of the Lord

Read Matthew 21.1-16. In the Kingdom of God, nothing seems to be as it appears. At least this is what appears to be happening in the Triumphal Entry of our Lord into Jerusalem on the last week of his life on earth. In our day of fanfare and glorious pageantry, especially of the rich and powerful at their debuts and inaugurations, the Lord of the universe makes his entry into the capital of his compassion and love. The Lord of the heavens, the King of Israel, the long awaited Master of the people of

God enters into the great city–how does he do it? He borrows a donkey from a resident and comes into the cheering praises of the pilgrims entering the city for the annual Passover celebration. Where are the dignitaries, the glitz, the recognition, the hoopla? Where are the parades and tributes and monies and luxuries? The palms of trees, and coats of his disciples, the naysaying of his critics, and a donkey's testimony? Like everything else in our Lord's remarkable Messianic ministry, our Lord's public announcement of his Messiahship to the nation at the capital is unceremonious and lowly.

Who would think that the single greatest personage in the history of humankind would make his historic entry into the city as King on a donkey? The humility of our Lord is unfathomable and without equal; his willingness to serve the Father knows no bounds, and in his heart beats only one even pulse–the glory of his Father, the God of Israel. Do you, friend, have any idea what it means to have the same mind in you that was in Christ Jesus? Behold the grace, the humility, the lowliness, the meekness! Our Lord, the Most Famous of all, allowed himself to become a man, and as a man, humbled himself and became obedient to his Father, willing to enter into his city on a donkey, adorned with the good-will clothes of his rag-tag apostles, on a carpet of palm branches, with the pick-up band of the pilgrims. Nothing can describe the depths of love and lowliness of this gentle Carpenter, our Lord.

Even in the face of such lowliness, the crowds cry out, "Blessed is he who comes in the name of the Lord." Let's join their cry, and demonstrate in every area of our lives our allegiance to this great King who is also the Suffering Servant of Yahweh God.

After reciting and/or singing the Nicene Creed (located in the Appendix), pray the following prayer:

O God, to save us you gave your Son to a painful death on the cross and by his glorious resurrection delivered us from the power of the enemy. Grant us to die daily to sin that we may live closer to him, in the joy of the resurrection, through Christ our Lord.

~ Gregory the Great. **Praying with the Saints**. p. 43.

Nicene Creed and Prayer

Quiz

Put away your notes, gather up your thoughts and reflections, and take the quiz for Lesson 2, *The Messiah Opposed*.

Scripture Memorization Review

Review with a partner, write out and/or recite the text for last class session's assigned memory verse: John 15.18-20.

Assignments Due

Turn in your summary of the reading assignment for last week, that is, your brief response and explanation of the main points that the authors were seeking to make in the assigned reading (Reading Completion Sheet).

CONTACT

The Nature of True Greatness

In a society that measures success by size, number, and power, the Christian life offers a radical and revolutionary alternative. Jesus of Nazareth, although the greatest personage in the universe as heir of God and Son of the Father himself, demonstrates in his lowliness and humility a new vision of what constitutes "greatness," "success," "strength," and "power." Has the American experience of success caused the Church to reject the Christian view of true greatness and success? If so, how?

3

Why Would Messiah Have to Die?

One of the sticking points for many who find the Christian view compelling *as an ethical system* but reject its *theological understanding* is the rejection of the idea of vicarious sacrifice for sin. A vicarious sacrifice is a *substitutionary sacrifice*, one in which one thing is given in place of another. According to the Christian faith, the innocent and perfect Messiah of God was given as a sacrifice to die in the place of and on behalf of humankind, who transgressed and rejected the righteous law and will of God. This idea of blood sacrifice on behalf of the guilty, of one dying on behalf of the entire human race, is said to be hard to understand. How could the death of a single one be sufficient to satisfy the moral debt of billions of human beings? How can this be? In as few words as possible, provide your explanation for this critical doctrine of the Christian faith.

The Mystery of the Cross

Have you ever wondered what entered into the mind of our Lord as he hung on the Cross on behalf of the world. Rejected by his Father, abandoned by his friends and disciples, betrayed unjustly and punished cruelly, the Messiah of God received in his own body the blows and bruises deserved by us, guilty sinners. In a real sense, the Cross is a mystery–Almighty God the Son hangs on the tree to save us from the wrath of God the Father. No theology or creed, no poem or hymn, or sermon, or play, or cantata, or symphony, or work can capture the full mystery of what took place on the Cross, roughly from 9 a.m. to 3 p.m. on that remarkable Friday that Christians around the world have come to call Good Friday. Sanctify your imagination for a moment and ask yourself the question: *given what we know of Scripture and what we have seen of our Lord's ministry, what do you believe our Lord was pondering upon the Cross as he hung there, suffering for your sin, and mine?*

The Messiah Revealed

Segment 1: Revealed through His Person and Works

Rev. Dr. Don L. Davis

Jesus' identity as the Messiah is revealed through his perfect life and character, his masterful leadership of the Apostles, and his submissive sonship to his Father. His Messiahship is further vindicated and made plain through his prophetic teaching ministry, as well as in the mighty demonstrations of power, both in signs and wonders (miracles) and dramatic encounter with spiritual demons.

Our objective for this segment, *Revealed through His Person and Works* is to enable you to see that:

- Jesus' Messiahship is the express purpose and clear testimony of the Gospel accounts in the New Testament.

- The identity of Jesus of Nazareth as the Messiah of God is powerfully revealed through his perfect life and character, his masterful leadership of the Apostles, and his submissive sonship to his Father.

- The authentic identity of Jesus as Messiah is further seen through his prophetic teaching ministry, as well as in the mighty demonstrations of

Summary of Segment 1

page 264 📖 *3*

power, both in signs and wonders (miracles) and dramatic encounter with spiritual demons.

• The biblical evidence is both abundant and clear that Jesus of Nazareth is indeed the one, true promised Messiah of God.

Video Segment 1 Outline

I. The Messiahship of Jesus is Revealed through His Perfect Life.

A. The incarnation: the Word made flesh, John 1.14-18

1. The Word which was with God, and was God, was embodied.

2. He was the *agency* through which God created the worlds.

3. He was in his person and works a perfect revealer of the Father's own glory.

a. Heb. 1.1-3

b. 2 Cor. 4.4

c. Col. 1.15-16

4. From the beginning of his mission, *Jesus announces and reveals himself to be the Messiah promised of old, the fulfillment of the promise to Abraham, the Suffering Servant of the Lord, and King of the Kingdom of God.*

3

a. His opening announced his identity as the living presence of the Kingdom, Mark 1.14-15.

b. His inauguration announced his ministry as that of the Suffering Servant of YHWH, Isa. 61.1-4 (cf., Luke 4.18ff).

B. His character was matchless: all his character revealed the in-breaking of the Kingdom of God.

1. His birth and childhood revealed Jesus as the one chosen by God to bring God's *sovereign rule back to the world*, cf. Luke 1.31-33.

2. His baptism and temptation reveal the depths of his own righteous character.

a. The baptism reveals God's divine favor, Matt. 3.16-17.

b. The temptation reveals his resolve to obey the Father to the absolute exact degree that the Father desires and demands, Matt. 4.10.

3. His entire Galilean ministry (the first year of his public ministry) was not ease and comfort, but engagement and spiritual warfare, Matt. 4.23-25.

4. He glorified the Father in all that he said and did, John 17.3-5.

5. He did precisely what the Father commanded of him; he did nothing of his own accord or authority.

a. John 5.30

b. John 8.28

c. John 12.49

d. John 5.19-20

e. Phil. 2.6-8

6. He was a powerful and wonderfully attractive personality.

a. Although he was perfect and righteous, his demeanor and openness made him completely attractive to sinners and ungodly people.

(1) Matt. 9.10-11

(2) Matt. 11.19

b. He identified with the lowly and the poor, and included those who were socially ostracized within his own company, Luke 14.12-14, 21.

c. He went beyond the bounds of typical righteousness, and showed no partiality to anyone willing to embrace his call to the Kingdom, John 8.3-10.

d. He affirmed his mission to seek and save the lost, Luke 19.10.

7. His character was flawless; he was without sin, fault, or guilt (perfect holiness in all his thoughts, ways, and conduct).

    a. Isa. 53.9

    b. 2 Cor. 5.21

    c. Heb. 7.26

    d. 1 John 3.5

    e. Heb. 4.15

II. The Messiahship of Jesus Is Revealed through His Masterful Leadership and Sonship.

A. His selection of the Apostles

    1. He chose them in deep prayer to his Father, Mark 3.13-15.

    2. He chose them to minister alongside him and bear fruit in his name.

        a. Luke 6.13

        b. John 15.19

    c. John 15.16

3. He taught them regarding the kingdom promise, and his identity as the Messiah come, Matt. 13.

4. He loved them to the end.

    a. John 13.1

    b. John 17.16

    c. John 17.26

5. He modeled for them a kingdom lifestyle which they were to imitate and express, John 13.14-16.

B. He represented his Father with perfect faithfulness, Matt. 11.27.

1. He revealed the Father's glory.

    a. John 1.18

    b. John 17.6

    c. John 17.26

3

2. He communicated the Father's mind, John 15.15.

3. He delighted himself in the accomplishment of the Father's will.

    a. Ps. 40.8

    b. John 4.32, 34

4. He glorified the Father's name.

    a. John 13.31-32

    b. John 5.36

    c. John 14.31

    d. John 17.4

III. The Messiahship of Jesus Is Revealed through His Prophetic Teaching.

A. On his fulfillment of the salvation promises

1. Jesus taught that the *subject* of the Old Testament was his very own person.

a.   John 5.39-40

b.   Luke 24.27

c.   Luke 24.44

d.   Heb. 10.7

2.   Jesus shares the same attributes and qualities as YHWH.

a.   In him all things were created, John 1.3.

b.   He is the *Savior*, cf. Isa. 45.22 with John 4.42.

c.   He raises the dead, cf. 1 Sam. 2.6 with John 5.21.

d.   He is the *Judge* of all humankind, cf. Joel 3.12 with John 5.27.

e.   He is the *Light* of the world, cf. Isa. 60.19-20 with John 8.12.

f.   He is the *I Am*, cf. Exod. 3.14 with John 8.58.

g.   He is the *Shepherd*, Ps. 23.1 with John 10.11.

h.   He is the *First* and *Last*, Isa. 41.4 with Rev. 1.17.

i. He is the *Redeemer*, Hos. 13.14 with Rev. 5.9.

j. He is the *Bridegroom*, Isa. 62.5 with Matt. 25.1ff.

B. On the majesty of his kingdom ethics: Sermon on the Mount

1. Jesus' own person is the fulfillment of the righteousness required by God's law, Matt. 5.17-18.

2. He gave final interpretation to the meaning and significance of the Old Testament promise and commandment, e.g., Matt. 5.27-28.

3. Jesus' teaching represents the ethic of God's kingdom rule now proclaimed in his person and work.

   a. His work contrasts with Old Testament interpretation given by the rabbis, Matt. 7.28-29 (cf. Matt. 15.1-9; Mark 7.5ff.).

   b. His ethic super-extends the righteousness demanded by the tradition, Matt. 5.20.

   c. He spoke not as the scribes and rabbis: he spoke with absolute authority to interpret the Scriptures for *they testified of his person and work*, John 5.39-40.

4. Loving God and people: the commandments on which the entire Law hinges and swings, Matt. 22.36-40.

C. On the in-breaking of the Kingdom of God in his person: his parables

1. One-third of all his parables are on the Kingdom of God.

2. Through his parables he reveals a new picture of the Kingdom of God.

   a. It is not national blessing and Gentile destruction.

   b. It is spiritual, rooted in humility, grace, and love.

   c. It is both present and still future.

D. On his unique identification with the poor and the lost

1. His inauguration at Nazareth, Luke 4.18-19

2. His authentication of his Messiahship to John the Baptist, Luke 7.20-23

3. His verification of Zaccheus' salvation, Luke 19.8-10

4. His complete identification with the poor at the last judgment, Matt. 25.34-40

IV. The Messiahship of Jesus Is Revealed through the Mighty Power of His Works.

A. The miraculous signs and wonders which authenticated his Messiahship

   1. Jesus demonstrated his authority over all the effects of the curse (e.g., the raising of Jairus' daughter from death), Luke 8.40-56.

   2. Jesus manifested the blessing and abundance of the Kingdom of God present in his person, (e.g., the feeding of the five thousand), Luke 9.10-17.

B. The prevailing warfare and victory over the devil and his minions

   1. Jesus conceived his mission as one which was binding the devil in order to make the pillage of his house possible, Matt. 12.28-29.

   2. Jesus' person and work represented God reasserting his right to rule over his creation and in human affairs in the exact territory the devil had claimed for his own!, Luke 10.17-20.

C. The Transfiguration: window to the glory of the Son

   1. This incident reveals the glory which Jesus emptied himself of in his public ministry on earth.

      a. Matt. 17.1-3

b. Phil. 2.6-8

2. The significance of this is *prophetic and certain*: Jesus of Nazareth is confirmed to be the Messiah from the glory revealed in the Transfiguration, 2 Pet. 1.16-18.

Conclusion

» Jesus of Nazareth is the Messiah, revealed in the majesty of his person, specifically in his perfect life, his leadership, and his submissive sonship in relation to his Father.

» The Messianic identity of Jesus is further proven through the excellence of his prophetic teaching ministry, and through his mighty works of power which gave proof to the anointing of the Holy Spirit.

Segue 1

Student Questions and Response

page 265 📖 *4*

Please take as much time as you have available to answer these and other questions that the video brought out. Perhaps nothing reveals the majesty and greatness of Jesus' Messianic character more than the beauty of his person, his matchless virtue, and works of power and grace. Be clear and concise in your answers, and where possible, support with Scripture!

1. Why is it important to establish for us, as believers, the authentic evidence establishing Jesus' Messiahship from the Gospel accounts in the New Testament?

2. In what ways does Jesus' perfect life and character give testimony to his identity as Messiah? What about the way in which he called and led his disciples?

3. How does the teaching of Jesus offer support to the idea that he is the Messiah? What is so special about his teaching and understanding that it clearly gives witness to his claim to be God's anointed Servant?

4. How does the Gospel's testimony of Jesus' relationship to the Father support the claim that Jesus is the Messiah? What is special about their relationship that underscores the credibility of his claim to be the Messiah?

5. Why does Jesus appeal to his works as proof of his Messiahship? How do they help us defend our belief that Jesus indeed is the Messiah?

6. Describe the facts surrounding Jesus' transformation at the Transfiguration. How does this event help us understand Jesus' special relationship to the Old Testament prophets? To the Father? To his own past glory?

The Messiah Revealed

Segment 2: Revealed through His Passion and Resurrection

Rev. Dr. Don L. Davis

The suffering and death of Jesus (i.e., his Passion) provides us evidence of Jesus' identity as the promised Messiah. Peter's confession of Jesus' true identity as Messiah, accompanied by Jesus' prediction of his death, and his resolve to go toward Jerusalem support our claim that Jesus is Messiah. All of the events of Jesus' final week, from his triumphal entry into Jerusalem until his agony in prayer in the Garden, his suffering and crucifixion, and his burial give strong and undeniable testimony of his identity as God's Messiah.

Summary of Segment 2

page 265 📖 5

Our objective for this segment, *Revealed through His Passion and Resurrection*, is to enable you to see that:

- Jesus' suffering and death (i.e., his Passion) provide us with clear evidence of his claim to be the promised Messiah.

- Peter's confession of Jesus as the Messiah of the living God, accompanied by Jesus' prediction of his death and his resolve to go toward Jerusalem, reveal his intent to fulfill the biblical prophecy regarding Messiah.

- Jesus' last week includes his triumphal entry into Jerusalem, his encounters with the Jewish leaders, and sharing of the Passover meal with his disciples where he announces the new covenant in his blood.

- Messiah's final events during his Passion week include the various events surrounding his crucifixion and death, his agony in prayer in the Garden, his death on the cross, and his burial in the tomb. These events give strong and undeniable testimony of Jesus' identity as God's Messiah, the Son of God.

I. The Great Confession and Journey toward Jerusalem

A. The Confession of Peter, Matt. 16.15-18

　　1. Jesus is the Son of God, John 20.31.

　　2. Jesus is the Messiah of God, John 11.27.

　　3. Jesus is the Son of Man of Old Testament prophecy.

　　4. Jesus is the Suffering Servant of Old Testament prophecy.

　　5. The "Messianic Secret": (William Wrede, 1901)

　　　　a. Definition: Jesus' command to healed persons, disciples, and others not to report miraculous works of Jesus' identity to others

　　　　b. Possible explanation: John 6.15

B. The Passion predictions of Jesus

　　1. Of the suffering, death, and resurrection of Messiah

　　　　a. Mark 8.31

　　　　b. Mark 9.31

c. Mark 10.33-34

2. The nature of discipleship: sharing in the suffering and passion of Messiah (Mark 8.34ff.; 9.33; 10.3ff.)

a. Sharing in Messiah's stigma as a servant of all, Mark 9.34-35

b. Sharing in Messiah's suffering and death

(1) Mark 8.34-37

(2) John 12.23-26

C. The Transfiguration, Mark 9.2-4

1. A momentary display of his pre-existent glory, (cf. Phil. 2.6-8)

2. An authentication of Jesus' connection with the Old Testament revelation (notice Elijah and Moses)

3. A certain and sure word of prophecy: the Father's authentication of Jesus' identity, 2 Pet. 1.16-18

II. Jesus' Triumphal Entry into Jerusalem, Mark 11.7-10

A. The Triumphal Entry, Mark 11.1-11

1. Fulfillment of Old Testament Messianic prophecy, Zech. 9.9

2. Presents himself as Messiah and King of the Kingdom of God of a different sort

    a. It does not come with national preference to Israel.

    b. It does not result in cataclysmic glory and defeat of the Gentiles.

    c. It is presented in the lowliness of Jesus' person and the Kingdom of life he presents and proclaims.

B. Symbolic events picturing the end of Jesus' ministry

    1. Cursing of the fig tree, Mark 11.12-14 (The nation of Israel, God's pleasant fig tree, has failed to bear fruit in light of God's gracious revelation, cf. Hos. 9.10.)

    2. Second cleansing of the Temple, Matt. 21.12-13 (Jesus in the first cleansing, displayed himself as God's messenger and reformer; in this second cleansing, he boldly judges the Temple system and those who ran it.)

    3. Visit of the Greeks, John 12.20-50 (Jesus speaks of his death, and John provides commentary relating Jesus to the YHWH of Isa. 6.)

C. Encounters and controversy with Jewish leaders

    1. Desire for destruction and entrapment

a. Questions of Jesus' authority, Matt. 21.23-27

b. Three parables of warning, Mark 12.1-12

   (1) The two sons

   (2) The wicked tenants

   (3) The wedding feast

2. Jesus' judgment on the spirituality of the Pharisees, Matt. 23.1-39

D. The Olivet Discourse (Matt. 24-25): *Jesus claims to speak authoritatively about the end of time, and further claims that he himself would be at the center of these final events of human history.*

1. Jesus, as Messiah, predicts the destruction of the Temple and of Jerusalem.

2. Lessons: the fig tree, Noah's day, the thief in the night, the house-holder on a journey, the wise and evil stewards

3. Moral of the stories: watch and be ready, for you do not know precisely when the Son of Man will return (cf. Matt. 25.13).

E. Preparation for the betrayal: meeting of Judas and the leaders, Matt. 26.14-16

1. Jesus' rebuke of Judas for putting down the woman's anointing, Mark 14.3-9

2. "Payment up front": thirty pieces of silver as Judas' *price of betrayal* (see Exod. 21.32, Jesus was sold to his enemies for the same amount as a slave, gored by an ox!)

F. The Last Supper

1. The preparation of the Passover, Luke 22.7-13

   a. See Exodus 12.1-20 for what the preparation might have included.

   b. Powerful picture: *Jesus is the Lamb of God, preparing his own sacrifice to pay sin's debt and defeat the powers of the devil* (John 1.29; Heb. 2.14-15).

2. High drama of the New Testament: Jesus, the Paschal Lamb of God, shares the Passover with his disciples, Matt. 26.20.

3. Washing of the disciple's feet, *Jesus displays in dramatic power the true nature of his divine heart and servanthood*, John 13.1-20.

   a. A remarkable act of humility: typical task of a slave who washed the feet of guests who had come through the streets

   b. Done with a full sense of Jesus' own self-consciousness as to where he came from and where he was going

   c. The truest mark of sharing a life with Jesus as a disciple: washing one another's feet

4. Institution of the Lord's Supper, Matt. 26.26-29

    a. Jesus, the *Messianic mediator of the New Covenant*, institutes the Lord's Supper.

    b. Done as a prophetic act to remember the majesty of Jesus' sacrifice until he returns again, 1 Cor. 11.23-26

5. The Upper Room Discourse (John 13-16): *Jesus reveals clearly his understanding of the intimacy he has with God as his only begotten Son, and suggests that once glorified he will send the Holy Spirit upon the Apostles to aid them in their continuing mission.*

    a. Jesus predicts his departure, John 13.36-14.31.

    b. *Jesus is the source of all spiritual life and fruit*, John 15.1-27.

    c. Jesus reveals the future, including the sending of the Holy Spirit, John 16.1-33.

6. Jesus' great High Priestly prayer, John 17.1-26

    a. The Father's glory and the Son's prayer to be restored to that glory, John 17.1-5

    b. Jesus' petition for the Apostles, John 17.6-16

3

c. Jesus' prayer for the Word, John 17.17-19

    d. Jesus prayer for those who believe through the Apostles' words, and their relationship to God, one another, and the world, John 17.20-26

  7. Peter's denial predicted, Matt. 26.31-35

III. The Suffering of Jesus as the Lamb of God

A. The agony of Gethsemane, Mark 14.32-42

B. The Betrayal: Judas' betrayal and Peter's denial (Luke 22.47-54; John 18.2-12)

  1. The prophecy and its fulfillment of Peter's denial of Christ

  2. The prophecy and its fulfillment of Judas' remorse and suicide

  3. *Jesus reveals his Messiahship in his prophetic ministry, even in the midst of his Passion.*

C. The Jewish and Roman trials

  1. The Jewish trial: are you the Messiah or not?

a. Three instances of trial

   (1) Before Annas, *father-in-law to Caiaphas, the high priest that year*, John 18.13-14, 19-23

   (2) Before Caiaphas, Mark 14.53-65

   (3) Before the Final Council of the Sanhedrin, Luke 22.66-71

b. The blunt question to Jesus regarding his Messiahship, Mark 14.61-62

c. Jesus' equally blunt answer, cf. Dan. 7.13 and Ps. 110.1

2. The Roman trials: Pontius Pilate, Herod (only Luke is mentioned here)

   a. Three instances of trial

      (1) Before Pilate, Luke 23.1-5

      (2) Before King Herod, Luke 23.6-12

      (3) Before Pilate again, Luke 23.13-25

D. Peter's denial and Judas' suicide

   1. Peter's bitter cowardice and denial, John 18.15-18, 25-27

   2. Judas' remorse and suicide, Matt. 27.3-10

   3. Irony: *parcel of land bought in Judas's name, Acts 1.18-20; they could condemn the innocent Jesus illegally, but would not accept Judas' money since it was against the law!*

E. The Crucifixion of Messiah, Matt. 27.31-56; Mark 15.20-41; Luke 23.26-49; John 19.17-37

1. Crucifixion was a Roman method of execution that was *unbearably slow, publicly humiliating, and unbelievably painful.*

2. A form of execution reserved for slaves and criminals of the worst kind

3. The Seven Words of the Cross: Messiah's suffering and death

    a. Messiah reveals *mercy* for his executioners, Luke 23.34.

    b. Messiah promises *deliverance* for the penitent, Luke 23.43.

    c. Messiah, as beloved Son, makes *provision* for his mother, John 19.26-28.

    d. Messiah feels the *separation from the Lord*, Matt. 27.46.

    e. Messiah speaks in order to *fulfill the Scriptures*, John 19.28.

    f. Messiah exclaims the *completion of the biblical prophecy* and of our *redemption*, John 19.30.

    g. Messiah *commits his Spirit* into the hands of the Lord, Luke 23.46.

3

F. The burial of Messiah's body, Matt. 27.57-66

    1. Joseph of Arimathea, Matt. 27.57 (a devout member of the Sanhedrin) recovers the body of Jesus.

    2. Burial of Jesus' body the fulfillment of Isaiah 53.9

    3. Nicodemus and Joseph: Nicodemus provided the myrrh and aloes, and Joseph the wrappings and his new tomb

        a. Matt. 27.60

        b. John 19.39

    4. The tomb sealed with guards at the Jewish leader's request, John 19.38-42

Messiah Jesus is laid dead in the tomb. But the story does not end here . . .

Conclusion

» Jesus' last week provides compelling evidence of his claim to be the Messiah.

» In his suffering on Calvary's cross, Jesus gives clear and convincing evidence of his love for his Father, his commitment to humankind, and his identity as God's Passover Lamb.

» All the events that lead up to Jesus' death speak of him as the Innocent One whose death alone can end, once for all, our debt of sin to God, overcome the effects of the curse, and destroy the works of the devil.

Segue 2

Student Questions and Response

page 266 6

The following questions were designed to help you review the material in the second video segment. No greater mystery exists, no greater wonder has ever been told than the great humility and passion of our Lord Jesus who, in obedience to God, surrenders his will and gives up himself to die on behalf of those who would come to believe in him. Be clear and concise in your answers, and where possible, support with Scripture!

1. What is the significance of Peter's Confession of Jesus' Messiahship? How does Jesus describe the importance of this revelation of Peter? What does Jesus immediately begin to bear witness to after this significant recognition of his true identity?

2. In Jesus' words, what is the precise nature of discipleship, especially in light of the fact that the Messiah is going to be crucified? How does sharing in the sufferings of Messiah play into the true identity of all who profess to belong to him?

3. What is the biblical significance of Jesus' Triumphal Entry into Jerusalem on the last Sunday of his life? What do we learn here about the nature of true leadership and glory?

4. How does Jesus' encounters with the Jewish leaders help explain their inability to accept Jesus as their rightful Messiah?

5. In what way does Jesus reveal himself to be our Passover, even as he breaks the bread of the covenant with his disciples at the Last Supper? How does the New Covenant figure into this event?

6. What key truths did Jesus promise his disciples in his Upper Room discourse shortly before his betrayal and death? Also, what did Jesus ask on behalf of his own during his high priestly prayer before the disciples?

7. Describe Jesus' agony at Gethsemane. What was the precise nature of his request during this time of trial?

8. What was the essence of the reason for the three trials that Jesus had before the Sanhedrin, Herod, and Pilate? Were they just or not? Explain your answer.

9. What do we learn from the suffering and death of Jesus on the cross about his heart? About our Father's love? About Jesus' identity as Messiah?

3

10. How do the facts surrounding the burial of Jesus help support the notion that Jesus in fact died, and did not, as some claim, merely swoon upon the cross?

Summary of Key Concepts

This lesson highlights the events which lead up to the suffering, crucifixion, and death of Jesus the Messiah. In a real sense, Jesus' Passion proves that he is the Lamb of God, the one chosen by God to bear the sin and guilt of all the world. In this suffering, his identity as Messiah is fully revealed.

- The revelation of Jesus as Messiah is the express purpose and clear testimony of the Gospel accounts in the New Testament.

- Jesus of Nazareth is shown to be the Messiah of God through his perfect life and character, his masterful leadership of the Apostles, and his submissive sonship to his Father.

- Further proof is given regarding Jesus' Messianic calling in his prophetic teaching ministry, as well as in the mighty demonstrations of power, both in signs and wonders (miracles) and dramatic encounter with spiritual demons.

- The events leading up to Jesus' suffering and death (i.e., his Passion) provide us with additional compelling evidence of his claim to be the promised Messiah.

- The last events of Jesus' life, i.e., Peter's confession of Jesus as the Messiah of the living God, accompanied by Jesus' prediction of his death, show his resolve to fulfill the biblical prophecy regarding Messiah's sufferings on the cross.

- Jesus' last week includes his triumphal entry into Jerusalem, his encounters with the Jewish leaders, and sharing of the Passover meal with his disciples where he announces the New Covenant in his blood.

- The Gospels recount the final events during Jesus' Passion week. These events include his agony in prayer in the Garden, the trials before the Sanhedrin, Herod, and Pilate, his scourgings and condemnation, and finally his crucifixion and death on the cross, and his burial in the tomb. These events give strong and undeniable testimony of Jesus' identity as God's Messiah, the Son of God.

Student Application and Implications

Now is the time for you to discuss with your fellow students your questions about the revelation of Jesus and his true Messiahship shown in his suffering and crucifixion. In considering the weighty evidence of Jesus' Passion week, i.e., those events leading up to his death on the cross, what specific issues and concerns are raised in your study of this material? What particular questions arise now regarding your own understanding and appreciation of Jesus' suffering on our behalf? How does meditation on this material make you feel? How has God stirred your heart regarding the importance of the material you have just studied? Maybe some of the questions below might help you form your own, more specific and critical questions.

* Could Jesus truly be the Messiah without his suffering and death on the cross? Explain.

* Why is it absolutely necessary to be certain about the identity of the Messiah? Is there a difference between the *Christ of faith* and the *Jesus of history*, or must they always be understood to be *one and the same*?

* In what sense is Jesus' experience on the cross to be the *standard and pattern* of all authentic discipleship and spirituality? Explain your answer.

* What do you make of Jesus' awareness of the need to fulfill Scripture, even in the midst of his worst and most painful moments of torture and suffering? What does this suggest about the importance of Scripture in understanding the true identity of God's Messiah?

* How do the "Seven Words of the Cross" help us to understand the mind of Jesus in those final, nearly unbearable moments of his life?

* In what sense are we to understand our Lord Jesus as "our Passover" (1 Cor. 5.7)? How does the original Passover celebration and our Lord's celebration of the Passover help us to understand the nature of Jesus as *our Passover*?

* Jesus' body is buried in a borrowed tomb. Why do you believe that the burial of Jesus is so prominent, both in the Gospel message (e.g., 1 Cor. 15.3-4), and historically in documents as critical as the Nicene Creed (e.g., "was crucified, dead, and buried . . .")?

* Why must the Christian religion be understood only in the shadow of the agony and sufferings of Jesus on the cross? Why is it impossible to give a full and satisfying explanation of the nature of the Christian faith without highlighting and focusing on his suffering, crucifixion, death, and resurrection?

3

CASE STUDIES

You Are the Christ, the Son of the Living God

In discussing the importance of Peter's confession at Caesarea Philippi, one Sunday School student suggests, "Since we already knew that Jesus was the Messiah from the very beginning of the our reading of the Gospels, why does Jesus make Peter's realization and confession such a big deal? Many people today would say that Jesus is the Messiah, even a lot of people call him Jesus Christ (which means Messiah), but they don't act like it means anything to them at all. Can a person call Jesus the Christ, the Son of God, and it not mean what Peter took it to mean?" How would you answer this student's question?

page 267 📖 *7*

Not at First

In a growing church that focuses on being seeker sensitive, a looming argument is brewing among the Elders Council. Even though there has been great excitement about the church's growth (over 300% in the last two years), there is growing concern among the elders that their Gospel is becoming bloodless and crossless. Direct, blunt messages about the love of God shown on Calvary's Cross, the prospect of doom, and the need for saving grace, have been replaced with nice messages on the significance of family, the importance of integrity, and the need for care in our financial matters. These messages offend no one, but, as one elder suggests, neither do they awaken anyone to the their dire need for the Blood of the Cross. The strategy is to befriend these dear people first, share with them as friends and neighbors, and share the weighty matters of the Gospel after a relationship has been established. If you were called in to give the Council advice, what would your answer be to their challenge and situation?

An Anti-Semitic Hoax

A famous lecturer is causing a stir in the local neighborhood. At a free public lecture, one of the professors of one of the great Ivy-league divinity schools suggested recently that the Christian religion as it has been historically taught is completely false and untrue, as presented in the Gospels. The Jewish leaders of Jesus' day had a deep understanding of grace, longed for a Messiah who would deliver them, and have a keen understanding of salvation by God's mercy, not by one's works in obedience to the Law. The lecturer claims that, based on the most recent historical data available to us, the account of the Jewish leaders in the Gospels is simply "patently untrue." Some of your college students attended the lecture and are very upset about the implications of it. How would you answer the lecturers claims which throw the truthfulness of the Gospels into question?

Restatement of the Lesson's Thesis

The authenticity of Jesus as Messiah is established and grounded upon the Gospel accounts in our New Testament. Jesus' Messianic identity is powerfully revealed through his perfect life and character, his masterful leadership of the Apostles, and his submissive sonship to his Father. Further proof of Jesus' claim to be Messiah is found in the character of his prophetic teaching ministry, as well as in the mighty demonstrations of power, both in signs and wonders (miracles) and dramatic encounter with spiritual demons. The episodes and events that make up the suffering and death of Jesus (i.e., his Passion) underscore his identity as the Messiah. These events, from his triumphal entry into Jerusalem to his suffering and crucifixion, and his burial after his death all point to his identity as the promised Messiah of God.

Resources and Bibliographies

If you are interested in pursuing some of the ideas of *The Messiah Revealed*, you might want to give these books a try:

Aulen, Gustaf. *Christus Victor*. Trans. A. G. Hebert. New York: Collier Books, 1969.

Stott, John R. W. *The Cross of Christ*. Downers Grove: InterVarsity Press, 1986.

Ministry Connections

The power of Messiah's sufferings is so poignant and clear–in one way, there can be no understanding of ministry which doesn't comprehend the meaning of the suffering Savior for us. All preaching, teaching, ministry, and care are squarely anchored in the mind of the one who gave up everything for us, out of love and obedience to his Father. The great Apostle Paul could say that he himself was crucified with the Lord Jesus, yet he lived by the power of the indwelling Messiah within him, the very same one who loved him and gave himself for him (Gal. 2.20). Your ability to understand and embrace these truths and make them come alive in your own life and ministry through your church is precisely the reason for this curriculum. Ask yourself honestly: do I represent in my life the *meaning and power of the cross of Messiah*? Am I willing to enter into his sufferings on behalf of others so I too may be spent and poured out as an offering for the salvation of others? Has God

3

pricked some area of my heart, calling me to a greater love and faith in Jesus, and so, as his more cleansed vessel, better able to yield myself to him as his instrument? Listen carefully to the Holy Spirit, and explore the meaning of these truths for your life today, right where you are.

In a spirit of reverence and openness to God, commit the areas that God has revealed to you to him for his working and healing. Allow God the Holy Spirit to soften your heart, to break you in any area where you have denied his presence, to be cleansed from any besetting or hidden sin that you have toyed with or clung to. Let the Holy Spirit use your insights into the sufferings and death of Messiah to clarify the next steps you must take in your own ministry, as Christ's servant and minister, to change, to accept, to grow into. Share your insights with your prayer partner, pastor, spouse, or friend, seek their consistent intercession on your behalf. Trust God to continue to lead you step by step as you seek to apply the truths he has revealed in the midst of your meditation. Always know that your mentor is extremely open to walking with you on this, and your church leaders, especially your pastor, may be specially equipped to help you answer any difficult questions arising from your reflection on this study. Be open to God and allow him to lead you as he determines.

Counseling and Prayer

3

▶ **ASSIGNMENTS**

Luke 24.44-49

Scripture Memory

To prepare for class, please visit *www.tumi.org/books* to find next week's reading assignment, or ask your mentor.

Reading Assignment

As usual you ought to come with your reading assignment sheet containing your summary of the reading material for the week. Also, you must have selected the text for your exegetical project, and turn in your proposal for your ministry project.

Other Assignments

page 268 📖 *8*

Looking Forward to the Next Lesson

In this lesson we saw how the glory of Jesus as Messiah was revealed in his perfect life, his leadership and sonship, his prophetic teaching ministry, his works of miracles and his suffering and crucifixion. In our final lesson, we will look at the vindication of Jesus as Messiah, whose resurrection, ascension, and the gift of his Holy Spirit prove both his divine sonship and his certain exaltation to come.

3

Name _____

Date _____

For each assigned reading, write a brief summary (one or two paragraphs) of the author's main point. (For additional readings, use the back of this sheet.)

Reading 1

Title and Author: _____ Pages _____

Reading 2

Title and Author: _____ Pages _____

LESSON
4

The Messiah Vindicated

page 269 📖 1

Lesson Objectives

Welcome in the strong name of Jesus Christ! After your reading, study, discussion, and application of the materials in this lesson, you will be able to:

- Recite the basic facts related to the significance of the resurrection of Messiah Jesus, and how the entire credibility of our theology, faith, and ministry is based on the historical certainty of Jesus having been raised from the dead.

- Provide a listing of the various appearances of Jesus, beginning with his resurrection at the tomb up until his appearance to the Apostles at the Sea of Galilee.

- Cite biblical evidence to show the vindication of the Messianic identity of Jesus Christ through the apostolic testimony that he has been raised from the dead.

- State briefly how the Great Commission serves as a continuing vindication of Jesus' identity as Messiah, and the importance of this commission as it relates both to the fulfillment of prophecy as well as to global mission.

- Show how the Great Commission was repeated in Jesus' post-resurrection appearances, and how Jesus demonstrated his resurrection to the Apostles during a forty-day period of manifestation.

- Argue for the importance and relevance of the ascension of Christ as the final historical sign which gives evidence that Jesus of Nazareth is the Messiah of God.

4

Devotion

He Is Not Here. He Is Risen

page 269 📖 2

Read Mark 16.1-8. Can you imagine the level of brokenness and shattered spirits of the apostolic party following the crucifixion of Jesus? All their hopes and dreams, all their expectations for a new Kingdom, the restoration of Israel, the transformation of the earth, and the establishment of God's Kingdom–in a single weekend was brought down in a massive pile of unjust, murderous hatred poured out on Jesus. The one they were convinced would change it all, for good, forever, was tragically murdered, falsely accused, betrayed by one of their own. Can any of us imagine what must have been going on in their hearts? Can you taste the bitter herbs they had chewed upon, hour after hour, filled with a mix of emotions–fear, regret, sadness, despair, blame, and on and on and on. "What on earth is happening? What is God up to? We thought he was the Messiah–we had such hopes, such longings. Now all of that is gone. Dashed, crushed, ruined."

As it is, the sisters within our churches possess a special empathy and love. The Marys come early on the day after the Sabbath to anoint the body of the Lord. With hearts so heavy they must of seemed like stones, these dear sisters came to the tomb where the Lord lay with an intent to prepare his body with the love and care only known by those who cherished him from the first day of their meeting. In conversation on the way, they comment to one another about the problem of the stone. It was such a large stone, and they do not have the power to move it. Maybe they shared different possible solutions with each other on how to get the stone moved away. They were concerned about its weight and size. "We won't be able to anoint the Lord unless we get some help moving the stone . . ."

How strange, it must have seemed, to come upon the tomb's entrance, and to see that the very large stone had already been rolled back. What must have gripped their hearts at that moment? Horror? Excitement? Fear? The Scriptures declare that they immediately entered the tomb, and to their amazement saw a young man sitting on the right side of it, and he was dressed in a white robe. They were alarmed, but the young man said to them words which still ring out through time, as clear as a bell. He said to them, "Do not be alarmed. You seek Jesus of Nazareth, who was crucified. He has risen; he is not here. See the place where they laid him." After this, he told them to go and tell his disciples and Peter that Jesus would meet them in Galilee as he told them.

The biblical record says that they went out, fleeing from the tomb, being completely seized by trembling and astonishment, and said nothing to anyone because they were afraid.

The words of the young man were so concise, yet in his brief statement he summarized the most powerful and important truth in all Christian doctrine. Seeking the crucified Jesus of Nazareth in the tomb will always be a futile search. He is not in the tomb any longer; he is not there. The Lord of all is alive, he is risen. The place where they laid him proves it to be so. Let the power, wonder, and impact of that statement sink into your spirit, ignite your soul, and illumine your mind. The ancient promise of God for a Savior and Lord who will reign on David's throne has been fulfilled in this: the Messiah, Jesus of Nazareth, the same one crucified for our sins is alive. He is risen from the dead, and is alive forevermore. And soon, and very soon, he will return to finish what he started on the cross–setting up an everlasting Kingdom of peace and justice. *This* is our hope. *This* is our faith.

Nicene Creed and Prayer

After reciting and/or singing the Nicene Creed (located in the Appendix), pray the following prayer:

O God, whose blessed Son came into the world that he might destroy the works of the devil and make us children of God and heirs of eternal life: Grant that, having this hope, we may purify ourselves as he is pure; that, when he comes again with power and great glory, we may be made like him in his eternal and glorious Kingdom; where he lives and reigns with you and the Holy Spirit, one God, for ever and ever. Amen.

~ Episcopal Church. **The Book of Common Prayer and Administrations of the Sacraments and Other Rites and Ceremonies of the Church, Together with the Psalter or Psalms of David.**
New York: The Church Hymnal Corporation, 1979. p. 236

Quiz

Put away your notes, gather up your thoughts and reflections, and take the quiz for Lesson 3, *The Messiah Revealed.*

Scripture Memorization Review

Review with a partner, write out and/or recite the text for last class session's assigned memory verse: Luke 24.44-49.

Assignments Due

Turn in your summary of the reading assignment for last week, that is, your brief response and explanation of the main points that the authors were seeking to make in the assigned reading (Reading Completion Sheet).

4

The Need to Travel Light

Many today, especially those involved in Church growth, believe that the easiest and most credible way to see growth in numbers in the Church is to travel light, theologically speaking. Many churches no longer teach Christian doctrine proper, at least not directly. Convinced that such matters are too abstract and uninteresting for modern seekers, these churches concentrate their attention on matters which they believe will better strike the chords of people today. So, it is neither unusual nor odd to see the pulpits of these churches filled with messages about banking, romance, contemporary issues, or psychological insights regarding happiness and self-development. Messages about the resurrection, ascension, and Second Coming of Christ are seen to be both old-fashioned and ineffective, simply not relevant to an internet-savvy, modern 21st century crowd. What do you think about these trends in preaching and teaching–are they a sign of health or sickness in the Church today?

Resurrection Not a Scientific Possibility

Imagine being asked to join a panel of important figures from the scientific and religious communities to discuss the topic of the resurrection of the dead. How would you respond if one of the panelists denied the possibility of resurrection on the grounds that it cannot be proven scientifically? They are not suggesting that it may never happen, or did not happen in the past. Rather, they are suggesting that since we cannot verify it, show it to be a possibility through experimentation and scientific method, we simply cannot say that such a thing is possible. How would you answer this view on the resurrection? Should you even try to do so?

Materials Are Confusing, Scattered, and Inaccurate

On a long flight back home after a wonderful vacation, you encounter a passenger who is greatly interested in discussing religion, especially the Christian faith. He suggests that the most important doctrine of Christianity is its most difficult one. "In my own study of the Gospels and the different accounts of the resurrection, I just can't seem to harmonize what the different books say. As hard as I have tried, I find the various materials in the Gospels which speak of Jesus' resurrection to be confusing, scattered, and inaccurate. They just don't seem to fit together at all." What would be your argument to this seeker about the Gospels, and their testimonies regarding the resurrection of Jesus?

The Messiah Vindicated

Segment 1: The Resurrection and Appearances of Jesus

Rev. Dr. Don L. Davis

Summary of Segment 1

page 270 📖 *3*

For our faith and practice, for our understanding of the message of the New Testament, no doctrine or teaching is as significant to our conviction as the resurrection of Messiah Jesus. For believers, the entire credibility of our theology, faith, and ministry is based on the historical certainty of Jesus having been raised from the dead. The Gospel accounts provide several key citations of some of the various appearances of Jesus, beginning with his resurrection at the tomb up until his appearance to the Apostles at the Sea of Galilee. Of all the evidence given to testify as to Jesus of Nazareth's Messianic credential, nothing compares to the resurrection. It alone provides the clearest witness to the vindication of the Messianic identity of Jesus Christ.

Our objective for this segment, *The Resurrection and Appearances of Jesus*, is to enable you to see that:

- The doctrine of the resurrection and the resurrection of Christ is the most significant doctrine in Christian belief.

- The entire credibility of our theology, faith, and ministry is based on the historical certainty of Jesus having been raised from the dead.

- The New Testament provides a clear and compelling testimony about the appearances of Jesus after his resurrection, beginning with the fact of his resurrection at the tomb up until his appearance to the Apostles at the Sea of Galilee.

- No other fact or testimony provides a clearer witness to the vindication of the Messianic identity of Jesus Christ than this one unequivocal fact: Jesus Christ has been raised from the dead.

4

I.　The Centrality of the Resurrection to Christian Faith, 1 Cor. 15.12-20

Video Segment 1
Outline

A.　What Christianity is not

　　1.　We are not an *ethical system.*

　　2.　We are not a *community of religious practice.*

　　3.　We are not an *effort at escapism from the world's evils.*

B.　What Christianity is: *a lived faith anchored in the person and work of Jesus the Messiah whom we hold to have lived, died, and raised from the dead*

　　1.　*Christus Victum*: Messiah Jesus died and rose to pay the penalty for our sins, Rom. 5.8-10.

　　2.　*Christus Victor*: Messiah Jesus died and rose to defeat the powers of the enemy and transfer us from the kingdom of Satan to the Kingdom of God.

　　　　a.　Heb. 2.14

　　　　b.　1 John 3.8

　　　　c.　Col. 1.13

　　　　d.　Col. 2.15

3. No Christian faith exists without the resurrection!

C. The argument for the centrality of the resurrection, and the resurrection of Christ, 1 Cor. 15.12-20

   1. If no resurrection exists, then *Christ Jesus himself has not been raised*, v.13.

   2. And if Christ himself has not been raised:

      a. The Apostles' preaching is in vain (worthless), and our faith in that preaching is in vain (worthless), v.14.

      b. The Apostles misrepresented God (i.e., *they lied about God*) since they testified that God raised up Jesus from the dead, v.15.

   3. Again, if the dead are not raised, *not even Christ Jesus himself has been raised*, v. 16.

   4. And if Christ has not been raised:

      a. Our faith in Jesus is futile (completely meaningless), v.17.

      b. We are still in our sins, v. 17.

      c. Those who have fallen asleep in Messiah Jesus have perished, v. 18.

4

d.   If in this life alone we have hope, *we are the most pitiful people on the planet!* v.19.

5.   **The fact of the matter**: *Christ Jesus has been raised from the dead, the first fruits of those who have fallen asleep,* v. 20.

II.   The Resurrection and the Appearances

A.   The resurrection of Messiah Jesus and the first appearance at the tomb, Matt. 28.5-8; Mark 16.2-8; Luke 24.1-8; John 20.1

1.   Sunday, early morning, Spring A.D. 30?

2.   The violent earthquake and the stunned guards

3.   Mary Magdalene and the other Mary

4.   Angelic testimony: "He is not here; he has risen. Come see the place where he lay."

5.   Second appearance: Matt. 28.9-10

a.   Jesus meets the women, Matt. 28.9.

b.   Go tell my brothers to go to Galilee; there they will see me, Matt. 28.10.

6. Guards invited to lie regarding the angelic manifestations and events at the tomb, Matt. 28.11-15

B. Appearance on the road to Emmaus, Mark 16.12; Luke 24.13-33

   1. Sunday afternoon, Spring A.D. 30

   2. Third appearance, Cleopas and an unnamed man

   3. Walking and discussing: Jesus joins them

   4. Rebuke at their unbelief and ignorance of Scripture

   5. *Jesus reveals himself as the Messiah of Scripture, which was foretold to both die and rise again*, Luke 24.27.

C. Appearance to Peter and the Apostles, Mark 16.13-14; Luke 24.33-43; John 20.19-35

   1. Sunday evening, Spring A.D. 30

   2. Two disciples from Emmaus return to Jerusalem and report their encounter with Messiah to the Apostles.

      a. Spoke of their own encounter

4

b. Spoke of the Lord's appearance to Peter

  3. Fourth appearance: to Simon (cf. Luke 24.34 with 1 Cor. 15.5)

  4. While Emmaus disciples were speaking, Jesus appears to the entire group (with Thomas being absent, cf. John 20.24-25).

  5. Jesus' command: "Receive the Holy Spirit" (foreshadowing of the outpouring of the Holy Spirit at Pentecost?), cf. John 20.21-23

D. Appearance to disciples with Thomas present, John 20.26-31

  1. Sunday, one week after the resurrection, Spring, A.D. 30

  2. Difficulty from this time on to trace resurrection appearances

    a. A forty-day gap between verses 43 and 44 of Luke 24 (i.e., 43 takes place on the Resurrection day, 44 takes place on Ascension day.)

    b. Jesus' last forty days on earth demand critical tracing of what the Gospel accounts provide.

  3. Thomas' fundamental *scientific (?) attitude*: John 20.24-25

  4. Jesus' proof to Thomas and his reply: John 20.26-29

E. Appearance by the Sea of Galilee, John 21.1-25

   1. No date associated with the appearance (Spring A.D. 30)

   2. Jesus appears to seven disciples by the seashore in Galilee.

   3. Simon Peter's return to familiar territory, John 21.3-4

   4. Jesus' question about fish and a remarkable catch when they follow his instruction, John 21.5-7

   5. Critical historical reference in verse 14, John 21.14

   6. Jesus' three-fold question to Peter: "Do you love me?" "Tend my sheep." John 21.15-17

   7. Jesus' prophecy regarding Peter, and his rebuke against Peter's nosiness about John's future, John 21.18-23

F. The certainty of the apostolic testimony regarding the risen Messiah Jesus, John 21.24-25

   1. The Christian faith is anchored on *the resurrection of Messiah Jesus*.

   2. The testimony regarding the resurrection of Jesus is anchored on *the testimony of the Apostles, who tell us of Messiah Jesus' vindication through his risen life.*

Conclusion

page 272 📖 *4*

>> The resurrection of Messiah Jesus is the most significant doctrine of the Christian faith, and our entire faith and hope rests on the historical certainty of Jesus having been raised from the dead.

>> The New Testament provides clear testimony of Jesus' resurrection accounts, which all confirm his risen life and identity as Messiah.

"Christ is risen. He is risen, indeed!"

Please take as much time as you have available to answer these and other questions that the video brought out. No other teaching in the New Testament is more crucial for the identity of the Messiah than the resurrection of Jesus from the dead. Understanding the biblical testimony of Jesus' resurrection account is central to Christian leadership and ministry. Be clear and concise in your answers, and where possible, support with Scripture!

Segue 1

Student Questions and Response

page 273 📖 *5*

1. What is the difference between the Christian doctrines *Christus Victum* and *Christus Victor*?

2. Briefly define the statement: "Christianity is a lived faith in the person and work of Jesus the Messiah whom we hold to have lived, died, and raised from the dead."

3. Detail Paul's argument in 1 Corinthians 15.12-20 for the centrality of the resurrection of Christ for the Christian faith. Why does Paul say that a belief in the resurrection is absolutely critical for valid faith?

4. What are some of the critical facts surrounding the various appearances of Jesus after his resurrection, and the first appearance at the tomb?

5. How are we to understand Jesus' command to "Receive the Holy Spirit" to the apostolic company in his appearance after his Emmaus appearance?

6. What do you make of Thomas' critical doubt regarding the resurrection, and his unwillingness to believe without firsthand verification? In what sense does Thomas represent modern viewpoints regarding faith, proof, and history?

4

7. How does Jesus' three-fold question to Peter (i.e., "Do you love me?") help us understand the nature of Christian leadership in the world today?

The Messiah Vindicated

Segment 2:

The Great Commission, the Promise of the Spirit, and the Ascension to the Father

Rev. Dr. Don L. Davis

Summary of Segment 2

page 273 📖 6

The Great Commission is a token of Jesus' authority as the risen Lord and Messiah, relating both to the fulfillment of prophecy as well as to global mission. In the forty day period after his resurrection, Jesus demonstrates conclusively his risen life to the Apostles, repeats the commission to world evangelization, and promises to send them the Holy Spirit to fulfill it. The ascension of Christ is the final historical sign which vindicates Jesus of Nazareth as the Messiah of God.

Our objective for this segment, *The Great Commission, the Promise of the Holy Spirit, and the Ascension to the Father*, is to enable you to see that:

*   The Great Commission is an expression of the authority of the risen Lord Jesus, a token of his continuing vindication of his identity as Messiah, relating both to the fulfillment of prophecy as well as to global mission.

*   Jesus validated his resurrection objectively to the Apostles conclusively in the forty-day period after his resurrection.

*   During this period, Jesus repeats his commission to the Apostles to evangelize the world, and promises to send them the Holy Spirit to fulfill his commission to go and make disciples worldwide.

*   The ascension of Christ is the final historical sign which vindicates Jesus of Nazareth as the Messiah of God.

4

I. The Risen Messiah Gives the Apostles the Great Commission.

A. Background of the Great Commission

   1. Where given: Galilee

      a. Jesus had promised to meet the disciples in Galilee, so the disciples returned there to wait for him, Matt. 26.31-32.

      b. This is where, too, the women (informed by the angel and Jesus himself) had told them to go.

         (1) Matt. 28.6-7

         (2) Matt. 28.10

         (3) Matt. 28.16

   2. This was the fourth appearance that Jesus had made to the Apostles.

   3. The Great Commission text, Matt. 28.18-20

B. Five aspects of the Commission

   1. The *Lordship* of Jesus Christ, Matt. 28.18

      a. Matt. 16.28

      b. Acts 2.36

4

    c. Acts 10.36

    d. Rom. 14.9

    e. 1 Cor. 15.27

    f. Eph. 1.20-22

    g. Phil. 2.9-11

2. The *Mandate* to make disciples of Messiah among the nations, Matt. 28.19a

    a. Ps. 22.27-28

    b. Ps. 98.2-3

    c. Isa. 42.1-4

    d. Isa. 49.6

    e. Isa. 52.10

    f. Mark 16.15

4

3. The *Baptism* in the name of the triune God; Father, Son, and Holy Spirit, Matt. 28.19b

   a. Acts 2.38-39

   b. Acts 10.47-48

   c. 1 Pet. 3.21

4. *Teaching* disciples to practice everything Messiah commanded, Matt. 28.20a

   a. Matt. 7.24-27

   b. Acts 2.42

   c. Acts 20.20-21

   d. Acts 20.27

   e. Eph. 4.11-13

   f. Col. 1.28

   g. 1 John 3.22-24

5. The *Promise* of his presence until the end of the age, Matt. 28.20b

    a. Josh. 1.5

    b. Isa. 41.10

    c. Matt. 1.23

    d. Matt. 18.20

    e. John 14.18-20

    f. Acts 18.9-10

    g. 2 Tim. 4.17

C. Implications of the Great Commission

    1. The basis of all ministry in Messiah's name is the incontestable lordship of Jesus Christ.

    2. The mission of sharing this hope is now a global mission.

    3. Personal faith in Messiah is to be lived in the community and body that makes up his Church.

4

4. The heart of discipleship is instruction and obedience in the commands of Messiah, the greatest of which is love, John 13.34-35.

5. Christ's personal presence will accompany this work of proclamation until the very end of the age, when we are united, dead and living in Christ, forever, cf. 1 Thess. 4.13-18.

II. The Commission Repeated: Forty Days of Demonstration and Instruction, Acts 1.3-8, Luke 24.44-49

A. Luke's prologue in Acts, Acts 1.1-3

1. The book of Luke is for Luke a "Volume 1" in the story of Jesus, the Messiah.

2. After his resurrection, Jesus provided the Apostles instructions and commands through the Holy Spirit.

3. Forty-day period of post-resurrection contact with Jesus by the Apostles

a. "He [Jesus] presented himself alive after his suffering:" demonstrations of his actual resurrection person.

b. "By many proofs:" Jesus provided the Apostles with irrefutable evidence that he had been raised from the dead.

c. "Appearing to them during forty days and speaking about the Kingdom of God:" period of time was filled with appearances and teaching about the Kingdom of God, cf. Acts 1.4-7

  4. *Jesus as Messiah continues to make clear that the prophetic message regarding the global promise of salvation is now to be carried out by the Apostles*: the promise for Jerusalem and the nations, Isa. 52.9-10.

 B. The repeating of the Commission: variation of Messiah's mandate to mission

  1. Make disciples among all people groups, Matt. 28.19-20.

  2. Proclaim the Gospel to the whole creation, Mark 16.15.

  3. Repentance and forgiveness preached in Messiah's name to all nations, starting in Jerusalem, Luke 24.47

  4. Sent into the world as the Father sent Messiah, John 20.21

  5. Anointed by the Holy Spirit to be witnesses of Messiah from Jerusalem to the ends of the earth, Acts 1.8

page 275 📖 7
III. "But You Will Receive Power": the Promise of the Holy Spirit before the Ascension

 A. Outpourings of the Holy Spirit associated with the end of time: the Age to Come

1. The blessing on the offspring of God's people

   a. Isa. 44.3

   b. Isa. 59.21

2. As a sign of God's favor and acceptance, Ezek. 39.29

3. The outpouring of the Spirit is associated with the "*great and awesome day of the Lord*" (cf. v. 31 of Joel 2.28-32).

4. Associated with the regathering of repentant Israel to Messiah, Zech. 12.10

B. Promises given during Jesus' life about his baptism with the Holy Spirit

   1. John the Baptist's promise regarding Messiah

      a. Matt. 3.11

      b. Mark 1.8

      c. Luke 3.16

      d. John 1.33

2.   Jesus made mention of those who would ask the Father to send the Spirit.

   a.   Matt. 7.11

   b.   Luke 11.13

3.   Jesus promised to send the Spirit to his followers.

   a.   Luke 24.49

   b.   John 16.7

   c.   John 20.22

4.   Jesus would ask the Father to send the Spirit to his followers, John 14.16.

5.   Jesus spoke of the Spirit's outpouring in general terms.

   a.   John 7.37-39

   b.   Acts 1.5

   c.   Acts 1.8

4

C. The importance of the Holy Spirit in Messiah's vindication

    1. The Teacher and Interpreter of the Holy Scriptures

        a. 1 John 2.20

        b. 1 John 2.27

    2. The Spirit who bears witness of Messiah, John 15.26-27

    3. Assurance of Messiah's presence in the midst of his people, 1 John 4.13

    4. Revealer of the treasures of Messiah to his people, John 16.13-15

    5. Teacher of the truth, bringing the words of Messiah to the Apostles' remembrance, John 14.26

IV. The Ascension of Jesus Christ; Mark 16.19-20; Luke 24.50-53, Acts 1.9-12

page 276 📖 *8*

A. Its accuracy as to history

    1. At the end of his final charge to be his witnesses (cf. Acts 1.8), around the vicinity of Bethany

    2. Jesus pronounces his blessing upon them (cf. Luke 24.50-51a).

3. Jesus' "ascent": he was lifted up, carried up into heaven, sat down at the right hand of God.

4. The angels assurance, Acts 1.10 (the ascension as a sign of his return)

B. Its significance as to theology

    1. Ascension is the confirmation of his lordship: he has been exalted to a position of authority and honor, and as Head of the Church.

        a. Heb. 1.2-4

        b. 1 Pet. 1.21

        c. Eph. 1.20-23

    2. Ascension as sign of his high priestly ministry

        a. Heb. 4.14

        b. Heb. 8.1

        c. Heb. 10.12

        d. Heb. 12.2

4

3. Ascension as the installation of Messiah's kingship: he must reign until all his enemies are under his feet.

    a. Ps. 110.1-2

    b. 1 Cor. 15.25-27

    c. 1 Pet. 3.22

Conclusion

» The giving of the Great Commission vindicates Jesus' identity as Messiah, fulfilling Old Testament prophecy regarding God's offer of salvation to the nations.

» Jesus demonstrated his resurrection by many proofs to the Apostles, and ascended to heaven, from where he sent the Holy Spirit upon the Church.

» Our Lord Jesus must and will reign until the Father determines the time and season for him to return and consummate the Kingdom of God on the earth.

» As head of the Church and the Lord of all, Jesus' death, resurrection, and ascension gives ample evidence that he, Jesus of Nazareth, is the Messiah of God.

May God give us the strength and the wisdom to be his disciples,
and proclaim him alive throughout the earth,
as our Lord, our Savior, and our Messiah,
the anointed one of God.

Amen.

The following questions were designed to help you review the material in the second video segment. The Great Commission of our Lord fulfills the Old Testament prophecy regarding God's offer of salvation to the world, and serves as a strong evidence and ground for Jesus' authority as the risen Lord and Messiah. His proofs, the sending of the Spirit and ascension to the throne of God, serve as further signs which vindicate Jesus of Nazareth as the Messiah of God. Be clear and concise in your answers, and where possible, support with Scripture!

1. What are some of the various aspects of the Great Commission covered in our lesson today? How does the authority of Christ ground and serve as the basis for the Great Commission itself?

2. How does the Old Testament relate to the mandate of Jesus to go and make disciples among all nations? In what way does Jesus' commission fulfill Old Testament prophecy regarding God's kingdom offer of salvation to the nations?

3. Explain the sentence: "The heart of discipleship is instruction and obedience to the commands of the Messiah, the greatest of which is love."

4. What is the relationship between Jesus' commission to make disciples in Matthew 28.18-20, and the repeating of the command to go to the ends of the earth in Acts 1.8?

5. What is the significance of Jesus' forty-day period with his Apostles following his resurrection? How does Jesus make plain during this period that his kingdom offer is *global*, a promise not only for Jerusalem and Judea, but for the entire world?

6. How is the promise of the outpouring of the Holy Spirit a direct link to the end times, to the promises of the Age to Come? How did John the Baptist foresee Jesus' baptism of his own with the Holy Spirit?

7. What role does the sending of the Holy Spirit play in proving Jesus of Nazareth to be the Messiah of God?

8. What are the facts surrounding the ascension of Jesus to the throne? What is the importance of the ascension as to its meaning and importance for missions, the Church, and his current reign as Lord?

9. What is the connection between the ascension of Jesus and his coming in power, at the end of the age?

4

This lesson focuses upon the implications of the resurrection, Jesus' post-resurrection appearances, and his commission and ascension on his identity as Messiah.

Summary of Key Concepts

- The doctrine of the resurrection and the resurrection of Christ is the most significant doctrine in Christian belief.

- The entire credibility of our theology, faith, and ministry is based on the historical certainty of Jesus having been raised from the dead.

- The New Testament provides clear and compelling testimony about the appearances of Jesus after his resurrection, beginning with the fact of his resurrection at the tomb up until his appearance to the Apostles at the Sea of Galilee.

- No other fact or testimony provides a clearer witness to the vindication of the Messianic identity of Jesus Christ than this one unequivocal fact: Jesus Christ has been raised from the dead.

- The Great Commission is an expression of the authority of the risen Lord Jesus, a token of his continuing vindication of his identity as Messiah, relating both to the fulfillment of prophecy as well as to global mission.

- Jesus validated his resurrection objectively to the Apostles conclusively in the forty-day period after his resurrection, giving conclusive evidence of his life after his suffering, as well as teaching them regarding the Kingdom of God.

- During this period, Jesus repeats his commission to the Apostles to evangelize the world and promises to send them the Holy Spirit to fulfill his commission to go and make disciples worldwide.

- The ascension of Christ is that final historical sign which vindicates Jesus of Nazareth as the Messiah of God.

Student Application and Implications

Now is the time for you to discuss with your fellow students your questions about the implications of the resurrection on the vindication of Christ's identity as Messiah. No other doctrine or teaching carries such weight in the Christian theological framework as the resurrection of Jesus–it is the body and soul of Christian theology, and the heart of our conviction about who Jesus really was and is today. Your ability to relate this teaching to your life and teaching is critical to your ongoing spiritual health, and to Christian leadership and service. What particular questions do you have in light of the material you have just studied? Maybe some of the questions below might help you form your own, more specific and critical questions.

* Are you convinced that Jesus of Nazareth is alive, that he actually rose from the grave after his sufferings on the cross? How do you know for sure?

* How should we respond to those who say that the doctrine of the resurrection is untenable (not credible) because it simply doesn't agree with the laws of physics or the facts of science?

* Can you be a Christian and not believe in the resurrection of Jesus? Explain.

* How does the resurrection and ascension of Jesus prove beyond a shadow of a doubt that Jesus has been magnified to a position of authority and power by the Father?

* Why is it critical for us to believe *what the Apostles testify* about the resurrection of Jesus, more than any other source, logic, or argument? In what sense is the entire doctrine of the resurrection based on *what the Apostles claim to have seen, heard, and experienced*?

* How does the resurrection lay a foundation and provide a framework for understanding God's deliverance from the *power of sin* as well as the *penalty of sin*?

* Why is the Great Commission founded on the *authority of Christ as Lord*? What does this mean for us, in our sharing the good news of salvation with others?

* According to the New Testament, why can we be *absolutely certain* that our labor in the Lord is neither futile or pointless?

CASE STUDIES

His Body Is Preserved, As a Statement

For many years, the Jehovah's Witnesses taught their members that the body of Jesus did not rise from the dead. The foundation of their assertion was rooted in 1 Peter 3.18: "For Christ also suffered once for sins, the righteous for the unrighteous, that he might bring us to God, being put to death *in the flesh* but *made alive in the spirit*." On the basis of this text, they claimed that Jesus' body, his

page 277 ▢ 9

crucified body, was put to death as a fleshly body, but that he raised again in the spirit, not as a human being, but as a spirit (cf. 1 Cor. 15.45 - Thus it is written, "The first man Adam became a living being;" the last Adam became a life-giving spirit). Where is the body of Jesus today? It is preserved somewhere, as a statement to God's unmerited favor and love. . . . How would you answer this bold claim as to the "resurrection" of Jesus?

What We Have Seen and Heard

The doctrine of "apostolicity" (the idea that the Church is built on the testimony, experience, and teaching of the Apostles) lies at the center of all discussions about the authority of the Christian faith. In a Christian leadership training course, the instructor suggested to the class that our faith is not rooted on our own firsthand experience of the events of Jesus' death, resurrection, and ascension. Rather, our faith is anchored in what the Apostles saw, heard, and experienced. God gave to them the eye-witness experience and therefore their testimony carries the entirety of the Christian faith. All of what we believe is received from them. He even suggests that if we had been physically present at the foot of the cross we might not have understood at all what was taking place. Only through the help of the Apostles' eyewitness testimony and divine commentary can we even begin to make sense of the meaning of Jesus of Nazareth for our lives. These comments caused great debate among the students regarding *the ground and authority of our faith*. What do you think about the instructor's understanding of the doctrine of *apostolicity* applied to the resurrection of Jesus?

Apologetics Is the Way to Go

Excited about his recent purchase of the classic apologetic books on the Christian faith by Josh McDowell, *Evidence that Demands a Verdict*, a young pastor is convinced he has found the way to present the Gospel to modern skeptics. He is convinced that we must teach the doctrines of the faith carefully and critically, showing to unbelievers that there is plenty of evidence to show logically and plausibly that Jesus rose from the dead. He assumes that if we present the evidence logically and persuasively, that people will accept it, this being such a scientific age and culture (1 Pet. 3.15). On the other hand, others in the young pastor's church are not so convinced of the power of apologetics to make a difference in the mind of unbelievers. They claim that it is *not possible to argue anyone* into faith; even the most cogent and biblical presentation of the Gospel will not help anyone without the illumination of the Holy Spirit (1 Cor. 2.9-16). Only the conviction of the Spirit can possibly crack the code on the hardened hearts of those who do not believe. *What is the role of apologetics and argument in helping unbelievers understand and believe in the truth of God regarding the resurrection of Jesus?* Whose position is closer to the New Testament's view of apologetics? Are both correct, and if so, how?

Restatement of the Lesson's Thesis

The doctrine of the resurrection and the resurrection of Christ is the most significant doctrine in Christian belief. Our faith is based squarely on the historical validity of Jesus having arisen from the dead. The New Testament provides clear and compelling testimony about the appearances of Jesus after his resurrection, beginning with the fact of his resurrection at the tomb up until his appearance to the Apostles at the Sea of Galilee. The Great Commission is an expression of the authority of the risen Lord Jesus, a token of his continuing vindication of his identity as Messiah, relating both to the fulfillment of prophecy as well as to global mission. During the forty days after his crucifixion, Jesus validated his resurrection objectively to the Apostles, taught regarding the Kingdom of God, and commissioned the Apostles to evangelize the world. He promised to send them the Holy Spirit to empower them for this task. He ascended into heaven in the presence of his Apostles, which serves as that final historical sign which vindicates Jesus of Nazareth as the Messiah of God.

4

Resources and Bibliographies

If you are interested in pursuing some of the ideas of *The Messiah Vindicated,* you might want to give these books a try:

Baxter, J. Sidlow. *The Master Theme of the Bible*. 2nd ed. Grand Rapids: Kregel Publications, 1997.

Bonhoeffer, Dietrich. *Christ, the Center*. Trans. Edwin H. Robertson. San Francisco: Harper and Row Publishers, 1978.

Hunter, Archibald M. *The Work and Words of Jesus*. Philadelphia: Westminster Press, 1973.

Stott, John. *Life in Christ*. 2nd ed. Grand Rapids: Baker Books, 1996.

Ministry
Connections

Now you will have the opportunity to apply the insights from your study of these lessons in a practical sharing experience that you and your mentor agree to. To think through the vindication of the Messiah through his risen life lies at the core of your Christian identity and service. No other idea or doctrine of the Christian life carries such weight or significance as the truth of the resurrection of Jesus. Your ability to share this truth concisely, persuasively, and in a number of different contexts is critical for your ongoing ability to win people to Jesus, and make disciples of them. To think about your practicum, begin by thinking of all the ways that this teaching can influence your devotional life, your prayers, your response to your church, your attitude at work, and so on. The key to becoming a good communicator of the Gospel is to know it so well, to be so familiar with it that you are ready for any situation. This familiarity with the truths of the resurrection will mean that you will be able to apply this teaching in all phases of your life, work, and ministry.

The nature of this ministry project is to practice these skills in a tangible way, in a place and setting where you live, work, and minister. In the next days you will have the opportunity to share these insights in real-life, actual ministry environments. Pray that God will give you insight into his ways as you share your insights in your projects.

Counseling
and Prayer

Seek the Lord about the implications of these high truths on the resurrection. As you meditate upon these texts and truths, ponder your situation and ask the Lord to reveal to you any particular ways he wants you to respond to these insights. Are there any issues, persons, situations, or opportunities that need to be prayed for as a result of your studies in this lesson? What particular issues or people has God laid upon your heart that require focused supplication and prayer for in this lesson? Take the time to consider carefully what the Lord wants you to do or say, and receive the necessary support in counsel and prayer to respond immediately to what the Spirit has shown you.

ASSIGNMENTS

Scripture Memory

No assignment due.

Reading Assignment

No assignment due.

Other Assignments

page 277 📖 *10*

Your ministry project and your exegetical project should now be outlined, determined, and accepted by your instructor. Make sure that you plan ahead, so you will not be late in turning in your assignments.

Final Exam Notice

The final will be a take home exam, and will include questions taken from the first three quizzes, new questions on material drawn from this lesson, and essay questions which will ask for your short answer responses to key integrating questions. Also, you should plan on reciting or writing out the verses memorized for the course on the exam. When you have completed your exam, please notify your mentor and make certain that they get your copy.

Please note: Your module grade cannot be determined if you do not take the final exam and turn in all outstanding assignments to your mentor (ministry project, exegetical project, and final exam).

The Last Word about this Module

This module on the *New Testament Witness to Christ and His Kingdom* has been designed to give you, the student of Scripture, a cursory analysis of the historical witness in the Gospels to the person and work of Jesus Christ. No survey of a few lessons can possibly plumb the depths of truth that awaits your further study of this material. What should be plain, however, from this analysis of the Word of God on the subject of Christ is that Jesus' identity as the Messiah of God is the critical theme of all of the New Testament, and the subject proper of the Gospel accounts. From the birth of our Lord in the season of Roman occupation of Israel, through the announcement of his Messiahship at Nazareth, to his triumphal entry into Jerusalem during his final week before his death, our Lord demonstrated that he is the Messiah, the anointed one of God of whom Moses and the prophets spoke. Jesus of Nazareth through his life, death, resurrection, and ascension proves unequivocally that he is the Messiah, the Lord and Savior of the world.

Nothing is as crucial to your discipleship and leadership as the mastery of the teaching and truth regarding Jesus, and obedience to his commands contained in the

4

Gospels. As our Lord and King, nothing can be regarded as an acceptable sacrifice to him short of our complete allegiance and obedience to his will. Our prayer is that this study will prompt you to "Do your best to present yourself to God as one approved, a worker who has no need to be ashamed, rightly handling the word of truth" (2 Tim. 2.15). Only by mastering the word of the New Testament in its witness to Jesus as Messiah can you both become a disciple, and through that, be used of him to make disciples. Praise be to God! Jesus of Nazareth is the Messiah of God, and word of his coming and Second Coming is going out to all the world, even in the cities of America.

May God give us the grace to answer his call,
to tell the entire world that Jesus Christ is Lord of all,
and to proclaim him as living and coming again to all the peoples on the earth.

All glory be to the Father, and to his Son, Jesus of Nazareth,
our Lord, our Savior, who alone is our Messiah,
the anointed one of God.

Amen.

4

Appendices

APPENDIX 1

The Nicene Creed

Memory Verses ⇩

Rev. 4.11 (ESV) *Worthy are you, our Lord and God, to receive glory and honor and power, for you created all things, and by your will they existed and were created.*

John 1.1 (ESV) *In the beginning was the Word, and the Word was with God, and the Word was God.*

1 Cor.15.3-5 (ESV) *For what I received I passed on to you as of first importance: that Christ died for our sins according to the Scriptures, that he was buried, that he was raised on the third day according to the Scriptures, and that he appeared to Peter, and then to the Twelve.*

Rom. 8.11 (ESV) *If the Spirit of him who raised Jesus from the dead dwells in you, he who raised Christ Jesus from the dead will also give life to your mortal bodies through his Spirit who dwells in you.*

1 Pet. 2.9 (ESV) *But you are a chosen race, a royal priesthood, a holy nation, a people for his own possession, that you may proclaim the excellencies of him who called you out of darkness into his marvelous light.*

1 Thess. 4.16-17 (ESV) *For the Lord himself will descend from heaven with a cry of command, with the voice of an archangel, and with the sound of the trumpet of God. And the dead in Christ will rise first. Then we who are alive, who are left, will be caught up together with them in the clouds to meet the Lord in the air, and so we will always be with the Lord.*

We believe in one God,   *(Deut. 6.4-5; Mark 12.29; 1 Cor. 8.6)*
    the Father Almighty,   *(Gen. 17.1; Dan. 4.35; Matt. 6.9; Eph. 4.6; Rev. 1.8)*
    Maker of heaven and earth   *(Gen 1.1; Isa. 40.28; Rev. 10.6)*
    and of all things visible and invisible.   *(Ps. 148; Rom. 11.36; Rev. 4.11)*

We believe in one Lord Jesus Christ, the only Begotten Son of God,
    begotten of the Father before all ages,
    God from God, Light from Light, True God from True God,
    begotten not created,
    of the same essence as the Father,   *(John 1.1-2; 3.18; 8.58; 14.9-10; 20.28; Col. 1.15, 17; Heb. 1.3-6)*
    through whom all things were made.   *(John 1.3; Col. 1.16)*

Who for us men and for our salvation came down from heaven
    and was incarnate by the Holy Spirit and the virgin Mary
    and became human.   *(Matt. 1.20-23; John 1.14; 6.38; Luke 19.10)*
    Who for us too, was crucified under Pontius Pilate,
    suffered, and was buried.   *(Matt. 27.1-2; Mark 15.24-39, 43-47; Acts 13.29; Rom. 5.8; Heb. 2.10; 13.12)*
    The third day he rose again
    according to the Scriptures,   *(Mark 16.5-7; Luke 24.6-8; Acts 1.3; Rom. 6.9; 10.9; 2 Tim. 2.8)*
    ascended into heaven,
    and is seated at the right hand of the Father.   *(Mark 16.19; Eph. 1.19-20)*
    He will come again in glory
    to judge the living and the dead,
    and his Kingdom will have no end.
      (Isa. 9.7; Matt. 24.30; John 5.22; Acts 1.11; 17.31; Rom. 14.9; 2 Cor. 5.10; 2 Tim. 4.1)

We believe in the Holy Spirit, the Lord and life-giver,
      (Gen. 1.1-2; Job 33.4; Ps. 104.30; 139.7-8; Luke 4.18-19; John 3.5-6; Acts 1.1-2; 1 Cor. 2.11; Rev. 3.22)
    who proceeds from the Father and the Son,   *(John 14.16-18, 26; 15.26; 20.22)*
    who together with the Father and Son
    is worshiped and glorified,   *(Isa. 6.3; Matt. 28.19; 2 Cor. 13.14; Rev. 4.8)*
    who spoke by the prophets.   *(Num. 11.29; Mic. 3.8; Acts 2.17-18; 2 Pet. 1.21)*

We believe in one holy, catholic, and apostolic Church.
    (Matt. 16.18; Eph. 5.25-28; 1 Cor. 1.2; 10.17; 1 Tim. 3.15; Rev. 7.9)

We acknowledge one baptism for the forgiveness of sin,   *(Acts 22.16; 1 Pet. 3.21; Eph. 4.4-5)*
    And we look for the resurrection of the dead
    And the life of the age to come.   *(Isa. 11.6-10; Mic. 4.1-7; Luke 18.29-30; Rev. 21.1-5; 21.22-22.5)*

Amen.

APPENDIX 2

We Believe: Confession of the Nicene Creed (8.7.8.7. meter*)

Rev. Dr. Don L. Davis, 2007. All Rights Reserved.

* This song is adapted from the Nicene Creed, and set to 8.7.8.7. meter, meaning it can be sung to tunes of the same meter, such as:
Joyful, Joyful, We Adore Thee; I Will Sing of My Redeemer; What a Friend We Have in Jesus; Come, Thou Long Expected Jesus

Father God Almighty rules, the Maker of both earth and heav'n.

All things seen and those unseen, by him were made, by him were giv'n!

We believe in Jesus Christ, the Lord, God's one and only Son,

Begotten, not created, too, he and our Father God are one!

Begotten from the Father, same, in essence, as both God and Light;

Through him by God all things were made, in him all things were giv'n life.

Who for us all, for our salvation, did come down from heav'n to earth,

Incarnate by the Spirit's pow'r, and through the Virgin Mary's birth.

Who for us too, was crucified, by Pontius Pilate's rule and hand,

Suffered, and was buried, yet on the third day, he rose again.

According to the Sacred Scriptures all that happ'ned was meant to be.

Ascended high to God's right hand, in heav'n he sits in glory.

Christ will come again in glory to judge all those alive and dead.

His Kingdom rule shall never end, for he will rule and reign as Head.

We worship God, the Holy Spirit, Lord and the Life-giver known;

With Fath'r and Son is glorified, Who by the prophets ever spoke.

And we believe in one true Church, God's holy people for all time,

Cath'lic in its scope and broadness, built on the Apostles' line!

Acknowledging that one baptism, for forgiv'ness of our sin,

And we look for Resurrection, for the dead shall live again.

Looking for unending days, the life of the bright Age to come,

When Christ's Reign shall come to earth, the will of God shall then be done!

Praise to God, and to Christ Jesus, to the Spirit–triune Lord!

We confess the ancient teachings, clinging to God's holy Word!

APPENDIX 3

The Story of God: Our Sacred Roots

Rev. Dr. Don L. Davis

	The Alpha and the Omega	Christus Victor	Come, Holy Spirit	Your Word Is Truth	The Great Confession	His Life in Us	Living in the Way	Reborn to Serve
	The LORD God is the source, sustainer, and end of all things in the heavens and earth. All things were formed and exist by his will and for his eternal glory, the triune God, Father, Son, and Holy Spirit, Rom. 11.36.							
		THE TRIUNE GOD'S UNFOLDING DRAMA — God's Self-Revelation in Creation, Israel, and Christ			THE CHURCH'S PARTICIPATION IN GOD'S UNFOLDING DRAMA — Fidelity to the Apostolic Witness to Christ and His Kingdom			
		The Objective Foundation: The Sovereign Love of God — God's Narration of His Saving Work in Christ			The Subjective Practice: Salvation by Grace through Faith — The Redeemed's Joyous Response to God's Saving Work in Christ			
	The Author of the Story	*The Champion of the Story*	*The Interpreter of the Story*	*The Testimony of the Story*	*The People of the Story*	*Re-enactment of the Story*	*Embodiment of the Story*	*Continuation of the Story*
	The Father as Director	Jesus as Lead Actor	The Spirit as Narrator	Scripture as Script	As Saints, Confessors	As Worshipers, Ministers	As Followers, Sojourners	As Servants, Ambassadors
	Christian Worldview	Communal Identity	Spiritual Experience	Biblical Authority	Orthodox Theology	Priestly Worship	Congregational Discipleship	Kingdom Witness
	Theistic and Trinitarian Vision	Christ-centered Foundation	Spirit-Indwelt and -Filled Community	Canonical and Apostolic Witness	Ancient Creedal Affirmation of Faith	Weekly Gathering in Christian Assembly	Corporate, Ongoing Spiritual Formation	Active Agents of the Reign of God
	Sovereign Willing	Messianic Representing	Divine Comforting	Inspired Testifying	Truthful Retelling	Joyful Excelling	Faithful Indwelling	Hopeful Compelling
	Creator — True Maker of the Cosmos	Recapitulation — Typos and Fulfillment of the Covenant	Life-Giver — Regeneration and Adoption	Divine Inspiration — God-breathed Word	The Confession of Faith — Union with Christ	Song and Celebration — Historical Recitation	Pastoral Oversight — Shepherding the Flock	Explicit Unity — Love for the Saints
	Owner — Sovereign Disposer of Creation	Revealer — Incarnation of the Word	Teacher — Illuminator of the Truth	Sacred History — Historical Record	Baptism into Christ — Communion of Saints	Homilies and Teachings — Prophetic Proclamation	Shared Spirituality — Common Journey through the Spiritual Disciplines	Radical Hospitality — Evidence of God's Kingdom Reign
	Ruler — Blessed Controller of All Things	Redeemer — Reconciler of All Things	Helper — Endowment and the Power	Biblical Theology — Divine Commentary	The Rule of Faith — Apostles' Creed and Nicene Creed	The Lord's Supper — Dramatic Re-enactment	Embodiment — Anamnesis and Prolepsis through the Church Year	Extravagant Generosity — Good Works
	Covenant Keeper — Faithful Promisor	Restorer — Christ, the Victor over the powers of evil	Guide — Divine Presence and Shekinah	Spiritual Food — Sustenance for the Journey	The Vincentian Canon — Ubiquity, antiquity, universality	Eschatological Foreshadowing — The Already/Not Yet	Effective Discipling — Spiritual Formation in the Believing Assembly	Evangelical Witness — Making Disciples of All People Groups

APPENDIX 4

The Theology of Christus Victor

A Christ-Centered Biblical Motif for Integrating and Renewing the Urban Church

Rev. Dr. Don L. Davis

	The Promised Messiah	The Word Made Flesh	The Son of Man	The Suffering Servant	The Lamb of God	The Victorious Conqueror	The Reigning Lord in Heaven	The Bridegroom and Coming King
Biblical Framework	Israel's hope of Yahweh's anointed who would redeem his people	In the person of Jesus of Nazareth, the Lord has come to the world	As the promised king and divine Son of Man, Jesus reveals the Father's glory and salvation to the world	As Inaugurator of the Kingdom of God, Jesus demonstrates God's reign present through his words, wonders, and works	As both High Priest and Paschal Lamb, Jesus offers himself to God on our behalf as a sacrifice for sin	In his resurrection from the dead and ascension to God's right hand, Jesus is proclaimed as Victor over the power of sin and death	Now reigning at God's right hand till his enemies are made his footstool, Jesus pours out his benefits on his body	Soon the risen and ascended Lord will return to gather his Bride, the Church, and consummate his work
Scripture References	Isa. 9.6-7 Jer. 23.5-6 Isa. 11.1-10	John 1.14-18 Matt. 1.20-23 Phil. 2.6-8	Matt. 2.1-11 Num. 24.17 Luke 1.78-79	Mark 1.14-15 Matt. 12.25-30 Luke 17.20-21	2 Cor. 5.18-21 Isa. 52-53 John 1.29	Eph. 1.16-23 Phil. 2.5-11 Col. 1.15-20	1 Cor. 15.25 Eph. 4.15-16 Acts. 2.32-36	Rom. 14.7-9 Rev. 5.9-13 1 Thess. 4.13-18
Jesus' History	The pre-incarnate, only begotten Son of God in glory	His conception by the Spirit, and birth to Mary	His manifestation to the Magi and to the world	His teaching, exorcisms, miracles, and mighty works among the people	His suffering, crucifixion, death, and burial	His resurrection, with appearances to his witnesses, and his ascension to the Father	The sending of the Holy Spirit and his gifts, and Christ's session in heaven at the Father's right hand	His soon return from heaven to earth as Lord and Christ: the Second Coming
Description	The biblical promise for the seed of Abraham, the prophet like Moses, the son of David	In the Incarnation, God has come to us; Jesus reveals to humankind the Father's glory in fullness	In Jesus, God has shown his salvation to the entire world, including the Gentiles	In Jesus, the promised Kingdom of God has come visibly to earth, demonstrating his binding of Satan and rescinding the Curse	As God's perfect Lamb, Jesus offers himself up to God as a sin offering on behalf of the entire world	In his resurrection and ascension, Jesus destroyed death, disarmed Satan, and rescinded the Curse	Jesus is installed at the Father's right hand as Head of the Church, Firstborn from the dead, and supreme Lord in heaven	As we labor in his harvest field in the world, so we await Christ's return, the fulfillment of his promise
Church Year	Advent	Christmas	Season after Epiphany Baptism and Transfiguration	Lent	Holy Week Passion	Eastertide Easter, Ascension Day, Pentecost	Season after Pentecost Trinity Sunday	Season after Pentecost All Saints Day, Reign of Christ the King
Spiritual Formation	*The Coming of Christ* As we await his Coming, let us proclaim and affirm the hope of Christ	*The Birth of Christ* O Word made flesh, let us every heart prepare him room to dwell	*The Manifestation of Christ* Divine Son of Man, show the nations your salvation and glory	*The Ministry of Christ* In the person of Christ, the power of the reign of God has come to earth and to the Church	*The Suffering and Death of Christ* May those who share the Lord's death be resurrected with him	*The Resurrection and Ascension of Christ* Let us participate by faith in the victory of Christ over the power of sin, Satan, and death	*The Heavenly Session of Christ* Come, indwell us, Holy Spirit, and empower us to advance Christ's Kingdom in the world	*The Reign of Christ* We live and work in expectation of his soon return, seeking to please him in all things

APPENDIX 5

Christus Victor

An Integrated Vision for the Christian Life

Rev. Dr. Don L. Davis

For the Church

- The Church is the primary extension of Jesus in the world
- Ransomed treasure of the victorious, risen Christ
- *Laos:* The people of God
- God's new creation: presence of the future
- Locus and agent of the Already/Not Yet Kingdom

For Gifts

- God's gracious endowments and benefits from *Christus Victor*
- Pastoral offices to the Church
- The Holy Spirit's sovereign dispensing of the gifts
- Stewardship: divine, diverse gifts for the common good

For Theology and Doctrine

- The authoritative Word of Christ's victory: the Apostolic Tradition: the Holy Scriptures
- Theology as commentary on the grand narrative of God
- *Christus Victor* as core theological framework for meaning in the world
- The Nicene Creed: the Story of God's triumphant grace

Christus Victor

**Destroyer of Evil and Death
Restorer of Creation
Victor o'er Hades and Sin
Crusher of Satan**

For Spirituality

- The Holy Spirit's presence and power in the midst of God's people
- Sharing in the disciplines of the Spirit
- Gatherings, lectionary, liturgy, and our observances in the Church Year
- Living the life of the risen Christ in the rhythm of our ordinary lives

For Worship

- People of the Resurrection: unending celebration of the people of God
- Remembering, participating in the Christ event in our worship
- Listen and respond to the Word
- Transformed at the Table, the Lord's Supper
- The presence of the Father through the Son in the Spirit

For Evangelism and Mission

- Evangelism as unashamed declaration and demonstration of *Christus Victor* to the world
- The Gospel as Good News of kingdom pledge
- We proclaim God's Kingdom come in the person of Jesus of Nazareth
- The Great Commission: go to all people groups making disciples of Christ and his Kingdom
- Proclaiming Christ as Lord and Messiah

For Justice and Compassion

- The gracious and generous expressions of Jesus through the Church
- The Church displays the very life of the Kingdom
- The Church demonstrates the very life of the Kingdom of heaven right here and now
- Having freely received, we freely give (no sense of merit or pride)
- Justice as tangible evidence of the Kingdom come

APPENDIX 6

Old Testament Witness to Christ and His Kingdom

Rev. Dr. Don L. Davis

Christ Is Seen in the OT's:	Covenant Promise and Fulfillment	Moral Law	Christophanies	Typology	Tabernacle, Festival, and Levitical Priesthood	Messianic Prophecy	Salvation Promises
Passage	Gen. 12.1-3	Matt. 5.17-18	John 1.18	1 Cor. 15.45	Heb. 8.1-6	Mic. 5.2	Isa. 9.6-7
Example	The Promised Seed of the Abrahamic covenant	The Law given on Mount Sinai	Commander of the Lord's army	Jonah and the great fish	Melchizedek, as both High Priest and King	The Lord's Suffering Servant	Righteous Branch of David
Christ As	Seed of the woman	The Prophet of God	God's present Revelation	Antitype of God's drama	Our eternal High Priest	The coming Son of Man	Israel's Redeemer and King
Where Illustrated	Galatians	Matthew	John	Matthew	Hebrews	Luke and Acts	John and Revelation
Exegetical Goal	To see Christ as heart of God's sacred drama	To see Christ as fulfillment of the Law	To see Christ as God's revealer	To see Christ as antitype of divine typos	To see Christ in the Temple *cultus*	To see Christ as true Messiah	To see Christ as coming King
How Seen in the NT	As fulfillment of God's sacred oath	As telos of the Law	As full, final, and superior revelation	As substance behind the historical shadows	As reality behind the rules and roles	As the Kingdom made present	As the One who will rule on David's throne
Our Response in Worship	God's veracity and faithfulness	God's perfect righteousness	God's presence among us	God's inspired Scripture	God's ontology: his realm as primary and determinative	God's anointed servant and mediator	God's resolve to restore his kingdom authority
How God Is Vindicated	God does not lie: he's true to his word	Jesus fulfills all righteousness	God's fulness is revealed to us in Jesus of Nazareth	The Spirit spoke by the prophets	The Lord has provided a mediator for humankind	Every jot and tittle written of him will occur	Evil will be put down, creation restored, under his reign

APPENDIX 7

Summary Outline of the Scriptures

Rev. Dr. Don L. Davis

1. GENESIS - Beginnings
   a. Adam
   b. Noah
   c. Abraham
   d. Isaac
   e. Jacob
   f. Joseph

2. EXODUS - Redemption, (out of)
   a. Slavery
   b. Deliverance
   c. Law
   d. Tabernacle

3. LEVITICUS - Worship and Fellowship
   a. Offerings, sacrifices
   b. Priests
   c. Feasts, festivals

4. NUMBERS - Service and Walk
   a. Organized
   b. Wanderings

5. DEUTERONOMY - Obedience
   a. Moses reviews history and law
   b. Civil and social laws
   c. Palestinian Covenant
   d. Moses' blessing and death

6. JOSHUA - Redemption (into)
   a. Conquer the land
   b. Divide up the land
   c. Joshua's farewell

7. JUDGES - God's Deliverance
   a. Disobedience and judgment
   b. Israel's twelve judges
   c. Lawless conditions

8. RUTH - Love
   a. Ruth chooses
   b. Ruth works
   c. Ruth waits
   d. Ruth rewarded

9. 1 SAMUEL - Kings, Priestly Perspective
   a. Eli
   b. Samuel
   c. Saul
   d. David

10. 2 SAMUEL - David
    a. King of Judah
       (9 years - Hebron)
    b. King of all Israel
       (33 years - Jerusalem)

11. 1 KINGS - Solomon's Glory, Kingdom's Decline
    a. Solomon's glory
    b. Kingdom's decline
    c. Elijah the prophet

12. 2 KINGS- Divided Kingdom
    a. Elisha
    b. Israel (N. Kingdom falls)
    c. Judah (S. Kingdom falls)

13. 1 CHRONICLES - David's Temple Arrangements
    a. Genealogies
    b. End of Saul's reign
    c. Reign of David
    d. Temple preparations

14. 2 CHRONICLES - Temple and Worship Abandoned
    a. Solomon
    b. Kings of Judah

15. EZRA - The Minority (Remnant)
    a. First return from exile - Zerubbabel
    b. Second return from exile - Ezra (priest)

16. NEHEMIAH - Rebuilding by Faith
    a. Rebuild walls
    b. Revival
    c. Religious reform

17. ESTHER - Female Savior
    a. Esther
    b. Haman
    c. Mordecai
    d. Deliverance: Feast of Purim

18. JOB - Why the Righteous Suffer
    a. Godly Job
    b. Satan's attack
    c. Four philosophical friends
    d. God lives

19. PSALMS - Prayer and Praise
    a. Prayers of David
    b. Godly suffer; deliverance
    c. God deals with Israel
    d. Suffering of God's people - end with the Lord's reign
    e. The Word of God (Messiah's suffering and glorious return)

20. PROVERBS - Wisdom
    a. Wisdom versus folly
    b. Solomon
    c. Solomon - Hezekiah
    d. Agur
    e. Lemuel

21. ECCLESIASTES - Vanity
    a. Experimentation
    b. Observation
    c. Consideration

22. SONG OF SOLOMON - Love Story

23. ISAIAH - The Justice (Judgment) and Grace (Comfort) of God
    a. Prophecies of punishment
    b. History
    c. Prophecies of blessing

24. JEREMIAH - Judah's Sin Leads to Babylonian Captivity
    a. Jeremiah's call; empowered
    b. Judah condemned; predicted Babylonian captivity
    c. Restoration promised
    d. Prophesied judgment inflicted
    e. Prophesies against Gentiles
    f. Summary of Judah's captivity

25. LAMENTATIONS - Lament over Jerusalem
    a. Affliction of Jerusalem
    b. Destroyed because of sin
    c. The prophet's suffering
    d. Present desolation versus past splendor
    e. Appeal to God for mercy

26. EZEKIEL - Israel's Captivity and Restoration
    a. Judgment on Judah and Jerusalem
    b. Judgment on Gentile nations
    c. Israel restored; Jerusalem's future glory

27. DANIEL - The Time of the Gentiles
    a. History; Nebuchadnezzar, Belshazzar, Daniel
    b. Prophecy

28. HOSEA - Unfaithfulness
    a. Unfaithfulness
    b. Punishment
    c. Restoration

29. JOEL - The Day of the Lord
    a. Locust plague
    b. Events of the future day of the Lord
    c. Order of the future day of the Lord

30. AMOS - God Judges Sin
    a. Neighbors judged
    b. Israel judged
    c. Visions of future judgment
    d. Israel's past judgment blessings

31. OBADIAH - Edom's Destruction
    a. Destruction prophesied
    b. Reasons for destruction
    c. Israel's future blessing

32. JONAH - Gentile Salvation
    a. Jonah disobeys
    b. Other suffer
    c. Jonah punished
    d. Jonah obeys; thousands saved
    e. Jonah displeased, no love for souls

33. MICAH - Israel's Sins, Judgment, and Restoration
    a. Sin and judgment
    b. Grace and future restoration
    c. Appeal and petition

34. NAHUM - Nineveh Condemned
    a. God hates sin
    b. Nineveh's doom prophesied
    c. Reasons for doom

35. HABAKKUK - The Just Shall Live by Faith
    a. Complaint of Judah's unjudged sin
    b. Chaldeans will punish
    c. Complaint of Chaldeans' wickedness
    d. Punishment promised
    e. Prayer for revival; faith in God

36. ZEPHANIAH - Babylonian Invasion Prefigures the Day of the Lord
    a. Judgment on Judah foreshadows the Great Day of the Lord
    b. Judgment on Jerusalem and neighbors foreshadows final judgment of all nations
    c. Israel restored after judgments

37. HAGGAI - Rebuild the Temple
    a. Negligence
    b. Courage
    c. Separation
    d. Judgment

38. ZECHARIAH - Two Comings of Christ
    a. Zechariah's vision
    b. Bethel's question; Jehovah's answer
    c. Nation's downfall and salvation

39. MALACHI - Neglect
    a. The priest's sins
    b. The people's sins
    c. The faithful few

Summary Outline of the Scriptures (continued)

1. MATTHEW - Jesus the King
   a. The Person of the King
   b. The Preparation of the King
   c. The Propaganda of the King
   d. The Program of the King
   e. The Passion of the King
   f. The Power of the King

2. MARK - Jesus the Servant
   a. John introduces the Servant
   b. God the Father identifies the Servant
   c. The temptation initiates the Servant
   d. Work and word of the Servant
   e. Death, burial, resurrection

3. LUKE - Jesus Christ the Perfect Man
   a. Birth and family of the Perfect Man
   b. Testing of the Perfect Man; hometown
   c. Ministry of the Perfect Man
   d. Betrayal, trial, and death of the Perfect Man
   e. Resurrection of the Perfect Man

4. JOHN - Jesus Christ is God
   a. Prologue - the Incarnation
   b. Introduction
   c. Witness of Jesus to his Apostles
   d. Passion - witness to the world
   e. Epilogue

5. ACTS - The Holy Spirit Working in the Church
   a. The Lord Jesus at work by the Holy Spirit through the Apostles at Jerusalem
   b. In Judea and Samaria
   c. To the uttermost parts of the Earth

6. ROMANS - The Righteousness of God
   a. Salutation
   b. Sin and salvation
   c. Sanctification
   d. Struggle
   e. Spirit-filled living
   f. Security of salvation
   g. Segregation
   h. Sacrifice and service
   i. Separation and salutation

7. 1 CORINTHIANS - The Lordship of Christ
   a. Salutation and thanksgiving
   b. Conditions in the Corinthian body
   c. Concerning the Gospel
   d. Concerning collections

8. 2 CORINTHIANS - The Ministry in the Church
   a. The comfort of God
   b. Collection for the poor
   c. Calling of the Apostle Paul

9. GALATIANS - Justification by Faith
   a. Introduction
   b. Personal - Authority of the Apostle and glory of the Gospel
   c. Doctrinal - Justification by faith
   d. Practical - Sanctification by the Holy Spirit
   e. Autographed conclusion and exhortation

10. EPHESIANS - The Church of Jesus Christ
    a. Doctrinal - the heavenly calling of the Church
       A Body
       A Temple
       A Mystery
    b. Practical - The earthly conduct of the Church
       A New Man
       A Bride
       An Army

11. PHILIPPIANS - Joy in the Christian Life
    a. Philosophy for Christian living
    b. Pattern for Christian living
    c. Prize for Christian living
    d. Power for Christian living

12. COLOSSIANS - Christ the Fullness of God
    a. Doctrinal - In Christ believers are made full
    b. Practical - Christ's life poured out in believers, and through them

13. 1 THESSALONIANS - The Second Coming of Christ:
    a. Is an inspiring hope
    b. Is a working hope
    c. Is a purifying hope
    d. Is a comforting hope
    e. Is a rousing, stimulating hope

14. 2 THESSALONIANS - The Second Coming of Christ
    a. Persecution of believers now; judgment of unbelievers hereafter (at coming of Christ)
    b. Program of the world in connection with the coming of Christ
    c. Practical issues associated with the coming of Christ

15. 1 TIMOTHY - Government and Order in the Local Church
    a. The faith of the Church
    b. Public prayer and women's place in the Church
    c. Officers in the Church
    d. Apostasy in the Church
    e. Duties of the officer of the Church

16. 2 TIMOTHY - Loyalty in the Days of Apostasy
    a. Afflictions of the Gospel
    b. Active in service
    c. Apostasy coming; authority of the Scriptures
    d. Allegiance to the Lord

17. TITUS - The Ideal New Testament Church
    a. The Church is an organization
    b. The Church is to teach and preach the Word of God
    c. The Church is to perform good works

18. PHILEMON - Reveal Christ's Love and Teach Brotherly Love
    a. Genial greeting to Philemon and family
    b. Good reputation of Philemon
    c. Gracious plea for Onesimus
    d. Guiltless illustration of Imputation
    e. General and personal requests

19. HEBREWS - The Superiority of Christ
    a. Doctrinal - Christ is better than the Old Testament economy
    b. Practical - Christ brings better benefits and duties

20. JAMES - Ethics of Christianity
    a. Faith tested
    b. Difficulty of controlling the tongue
    c. Warning against worldliness
    d. Admonitions in view of the Lord's coming

21. 1 PETER - Christian Hope in the Time of Persecution and Trial
    a. Suffering and security of believers
    b. Suffering and the Scriptures
    c. Suffering and the sufferings of Christ
    d. Suffering and the Second Coming of Christ

22. 2 PETER - Warning Against False Teachers
    a. Addition of Christian graces gives assurance
    b. Authority of the Scriptures
    c. Apostasy brought in by false testimony
    d. Attitude toward Return of Christ: test for apostasy
    e. Agenda of God in the world
    f. Admonition to believers

23. 1 JOHN - The Family of God
    a. God is Light
    b. God is Love
    c. God is Life

24. 2 JOHN - Warning against Receiving Deceivers
    a. Walk in truth
    b. Love one another
    c. Receive not deceivers
    d. Find joy in fellowship

25. 3 JOHN - Admonition to Receive True Believers
    a. Gaius, brother in the Church
    b. Diotrephes
    c. Demetrius

26. JUDE - Contending for the Faith
    a. Occasion of the epistle
    b. Occurrences of apostasy
    c. Occupation of believers in the days of apostasy

27. REVELATION - The Unveiling of Christ Glorified
    a. The person of Christ in glory
    b. The possession of Jesus Christ - the Church in the World
    c. The program of Jesus Christ - the scene in Heaven
    d. The seven seals
    e. The seven trumpets
    f. Important persons in the last days
    g. The seven vials
    h. The fall of Babylon
    i. The eternal state

APPENDIX 8

From Before to Beyond Time:

The Plan of God and Human History

Adapted from: Suzanne de Dietrich. **God's Unfolding Purpose.** *Philadelphia: Westminster Press, 1976.*

I. Before Time (Eternity Past) 1 Cor. 2.7
  A. The Eternal Triune God
  B. God's Eternal Purpose
  C. The Mystery of Iniquity
  D. The Principalities and Powers

II. Beginning of Time (Creation and Fall) Gen. 1.1
  A. Creative Word
  B. Humanity
  C. Fall
  D. Reign of Death and First Signs of Grace

III. Unfolding of Time (God's Plan Revealed Through Israel) Gal. 3.8
  A. Promise (Patriarchs)
  B. Exodus and Covenant at Sinai
  C. Promised Land
  D. The City, the Temple, and the Throne (Prophet, Priest, and King)
  E. Exile
  F. Remnant

IV. Fullness of Time (Incarnation of the Messiah) Gal. 4.4-5
  A. The King Comes to His Kingdom
  B. The Present Reality of His Reign
  C. The Secret of the Kingdom: the Already and the Not Yet
  D. The Crucified King
  E. The Risen Lord

V. The Last Times (The Descent of the Holy Spirit) Acts 2.16-18
  A. Between the Times: the Church as Foretaste of the Kingdom
  B. The Church as Agent of the Kingdom
  C. The Conflict Between the Kingdoms of Darkness and Light

VI. The Fulfillment of Time (The Second Coming) Matt. 13.40-43
  A. The Return of Christ
  B. Judgment
  C. The Consummation of His Kingdom

VII. Beyond Time (Eternity Future) 1 Cor. 15.24-28
  A. Kingdom Handed Over to God the Father
  B. God as All in All

From Before to Beyond Time
Scriptures for Major Outline Points

I. Before Time (Eternity Past)

1 Cor. 2.7 (ESV) - But we impart a secret and hidden wisdom of God, *which God decreed before the ages* for our glory (cf. Titus 1.2).

II. Beginning of Time (Creation and Fall)

Gen. 1.1 (ESV) - *In the beginning*, God created the heavens and the earth.

III. Unfolding of Time (God's Plan Revealed Through Israel)

Gal. 3.8 (ESV) - And the Scripture, foreseeing that God would justify the Gentiles by faith, *preached the Gospel beforehand to Abraham*, saying, "In you shall all the nations be blessed" (cf. Rom. 9.4-5).

IV. Fullness of Time (The Incarnation of the Messiah)

Gal. 4.4-5 (ESV) - *But when the fullness of time had come*, God sent forth his Son, born of woman, born under the law, to redeem those who were under the law, so that we might receive adoption as sons.

V. The Last Times (The Descent of the Holy Spirit)

Acts 2.16-18 (ESV) - But this is what was uttered through the prophet Joel: "'*And in the last days it shall be*,' God declares, 'that I will pour out my Spirit on all flesh, and your sons and your daughters shall prophesy, and your young men shall see visions, and your old men shall dream dreams; even on my male servants and female servants in those days I will pour out my Spirit, and they shall prophesy.'"

VI. The Fulfillment of Time (The Second Coming)

Matt. 13.40-43 (ESV) - Just as the weeds are gathered and burned with fire, *so will it be at the close of the age*. The Son of Man will send his angels, and they will gather out of his kingdom all causes of sin and all lawbreakers, and throw them into the fiery furnace. In that place there will be weeping and gnashing of teeth. Then the righteous will shine like the sun in the Kingdom of their Father. He who has ears, let him hear.

VII. Beyond Time (Eternity Future)

1 Cor. 15.24-28 (ESV) - Then comes the end, when he delivers the Kingdom to God the Father after destroying every rule and every authority and power. For he must reign until he has put all his enemies under his feet. The last enemy to be destroyed is death. For "God has put all things in subjection under his feet." But when it says, "all things are put in subjection," it is plain that he is excepted who put all things in subjection under him. When all things are subjected to him, then the Son himself will also be subjected to him who put all things in subjection under him, that God may be all in all.

APPENDIX 9

"There Is a River"

Identifying the Streams of a Revitalized Authentic Christian Community in the City[1]

Rev. Dr. Don L. Davis • Psalm 46.4 (ESV) - There is a river whose streams make glad the city of God, the holy habitation of the Most High.

Tributaries of Authentic Historic Biblical Faith			
Recognized Biblical Identity	Revived Urban Spirituality	Reaffirmed Historical Connectivity	Refocused Kingdom Authority
The Church Is **One**	The Church Is **Holy**	The Church Is **Catholic**	The Church Is **Apostolic**
A Call to Biblical Fidelity *Recognizing the Scriptures as the anchor and foundation of the Christian faith and practice*	A Call to the Freedom, Power, and Fullness of the Holy Spirit *Walking in the holiness, power, gifting, and liberty of the Holy Spirit in the body of Christ*	A Call to Historic Roots and Continuity *Confessing the common historical identity and continuity of authentic Christian faith*	A Call to the Apostolic Faith *Affirming the apostolic tradition as the authoritative ground of the Christian hope*
A Call to Messianic Kingdom Identity *Rediscovering the story of the promised Messiah and his Kingdom in Jesus of Nazareth*	A Call to Live as Sojourners and Aliens as the People of God *Defining authentic Christian discipleship as faithful membership among God's people*	A Call to Affirm and Express the Global Communion of Saints *Expressing cooperation and collaboration with all other believers, both local and global*	A Call to Representative Authority *Submitting joyfully to God's gifted servants in the Church as undershepherds of true faith*
A Call to Creedal Affinity *Embracing the Nicene Creed as the shared rule of faith of historic orthodoxy*	A Call to Liturgical, Sacramental, and Catechetical Vitality *Experiencing God's presence in the context of the Word, sacrament, and instruction*	A Call to Radical Hospitality and Good Works *Expressing kingdom love to all, and especially to those of the household of faith*	A Call to Prophetic and Holistic Witness *Proclaiming Christ and his Kingdom in word and deed to our neighbors and all peoples*

[1] *This schema is an adaptation and is based on the insights of the **Chicago Call** statement of May 1977, where various leading evangelical scholars and practitioners met to discuss the relationship of modern evangelicalism to the historic Christian faith.*

APPENDIX 10

A Schematic for a Theology of the Kingdom and the Church

The Urban Ministry Institute

The Reign of the One, True, Sovereign, and Triune God, the LORD God, Yahweh, God the Father, Son, and Holy Spirit

The Father	The Son	The Spirit
Love - 1 John 4.8 Maker of heaven and earth and of all things visible and invisible	Faith - Heb. 12.2 Prophet, Priest, and King	Hope - Rom. 15.13 Lord of the Church

Creation
All that exists through the creative action of God.

Kingdom
The Reign of God expressed in the rule of his Son Jesus the Messiah.

Church
The one, holy, apostolic community which functions as a witness to (Acts 28.31) and a foretaste of (Col. 1.12; James 1.18; 1 Pet. 2.9; Rev. 1.6) the Kingdom of God.

Rom. 8.18-21 →

The eternal God, sovereign in power, infinite in wisdom, perfect in holiness, and steadfast in love, is the source and goal of all things.

Freedom
(Slavery)

Jesus answered them, "Truly, truly, I say to you, everyone who commits sin is a slave to sin. The slave does not remain in the house forever; the son remains forever. So if the Son sets you free, you will be free indeed." - John 8.34-36 (ESV)

The Church is an Apostolic Community Where the Word is Rightly Preached, Therefore it is a Community of:

Calling - For freedom Christ has set us free; stand firm therefore, and do not submit again to a yoke of slavery. - Gal. 5.1 (ESV) (cf. Rom. 8.28-30; 1 Cor. 1.26-31; Eph. 1.18; 2 Thess. 2.13-14; Jude 1.1)

Faith - ". . . for unless you believe that I am he you will die in your sins". . . . So Jesus said to the Jews who had believed in him, "If you abide in my word, you are truly my disciples, and you will know the truth, and the truth will set you free." - John 8.24b, 31-32 (ESV) (cf. Ps. 119.45; Rom. 1.17; 5.1-2; Eph. 2.8-9; 2 Tim. 1.13-14; Heb. 2.14-15; James 1.25)

Witness - The Spirit of the Lord is upon me, because he has anointed me to proclaim good news to the poor. He has sent me to proclaim liberty to the captives and recovering of sight to the blind, to set at liberty those who are oppressed, to proclaim the year of the Lord's favor. - Luke 4.18-19 (ESV) (cf. Lev. 25.10; Prov. 31.8; Matt. 4.17; 28.18-20; Mark 13.10; Acts 1.8; 8.4, 12; 13.1-3; 25.20; 28.30-31)

Rev. 21.1-5 →

O, the depth of the riches and wisdom and knowledge of God! How unsearchable are his judgments, and how inscrutable his ways! For who has known the mind of the Lord, or who has been his counselor? Or who has ever given a gift to him, that he might be repaid?" For from him and through him and to him are all things. To him be glory forever! Amen! - Rom. 11.33-36 (ESV) (cf. 1 Cor. 15.23-28; Rev.)

Wholeness
(Sickness)

But he was wounded for our transgressions; he was crushed for our iniquities; upon him was the chastisement that brought us peace, and with his stripes we are healed. - Isa. 53.5 (ESV)

The Church is One Community Where the Sacraments are Rightly Administered, Therefore it is a Community of:

Worship - You shall serve the Lord your God, and he will bless your bread and your water, and I will take sickness away from among you. - Exod. 23.25 (ESV) (cf. Ps. 147.1-3; Heb. 12.28; Col. 3.16; Rev. 15.3-4; 19.5)

Covenant - And the Holy Spirit also bears witness to us; for after the saying, "This is the covenant that I will make with them after those days, declares the Lord: I will put my laws on their hearts, and write them on their minds," then he adds, "I will remember their sins and their lawless deeds no more." - Heb. 10.15-17 (ESV) (cf. Isa. 54.10-17; Ezek. 34.25-31; 37.26-27; Mal. 2.4-5; Luke 22.20; 2 Cor. 3.6; Col. 3.15; Heb. 8.7-13; 12.22-24; 13.20-21)

Presence - In him you also are being built together into a dwelling place for God by his Spirit. - Eph. 2.22 (ESV) (cf. Exod. 40.34-38; Ezek. 48.35; Matt. 18.18-20)

Isa. 11.6-9 →

Justice
(Selfishness)

Behold, my servant whom I have chosen, my beloved with whom my soul is well pleased. I will put my Spirit upon him, and he will proclaim justice to the Gentiles. He will not quarrel or cry aloud, nor will anyone hear his voice in the streets; a bruised reed he will not break, and a smoldering wick he will not quench, until he brings justice to victory. - Matt. 12.18-20 (ESV)

The Church is a Holy Community Where Discipline is Rightly Ordered, Therefore it is a Community of:

Reconciliation - For he himself is our peace, who has made us both one and has broken down in his flesh the dividing wall of hostility by abolishing the law of commandments and ordinances, that he might create in himself one new man in place of the two, so making peace, and might reconcile us both to God in one body through the cross, thereby killing the hostility. And he came and preached peace to you who were far off and peace to those who were near. For through him we both have access in one Spirit to the Father. - Eph. 2.14-18 (ESV) (cf. Exod. 23.4-9; Lev. 19.34; Deut. 10.18-19; Ezek. 22.29; Mic. 6.8; 2 Cor. 5.16-21)

Suffering - Since therefore Christ suffered in the flesh, arm yourselves with the same way of thinking, for whoever has suffered in the flesh has ceased from sin, so as to live for the rest of the time in the flesh no longer for human passions but for the will of God. - 1 Pet. 4.1-2 (ESV) (cf. Luke 6.22; 10.3; Rom. 8.17; 2 Tim. 2.3; 3.12; 1 Pet. 2.20-24; Heb. 5.8; 13.11-14)

Service - But Jesus called them to him and said, "You know that the rulers of the Gentiles lord it over them, and their great ones exercise authority over them. It shall not be so among you. But whoever would be great among you must be your servant, and whoever would be first among you must be your slave even as the Son of Man came not to be served but to serve, and to give his life as a ransom for many." - Matt. 20.25-28 (ESV) (cf. 1 John 4.16-18; Gal. 2.10)

APPENDIX 11

Living in the Already and the Not Yet Kingdom

Rev. Dr. Don L. Davis

The Spirit: The pledge of the inheritance **(arrabon)**
The Church: The foretaste **(aparche)** of the Kingdom
"In Christ": The rich life **(en Christos)** we share as citizens of the Kingdom

Internal enemy: The flesh (*sarx*) and the sin nature
External enemy: The world (*kosmos*) the systems of greed, lust, and pride
Infernal enemy: The devil (*kakos*) the animating spirit of falsehood and fear

Jewish View of Time

This Present Age   The Age to Come

The Coming of Messiah
The restoration of Israel
The end of Gentile oppression
The return of the earth to Edenic glory
Universal knowledge of the Lord

APPENDIX 12

Jesus of Nazareth: The Presence of the Future

Rev. Dr. Don L. Davis

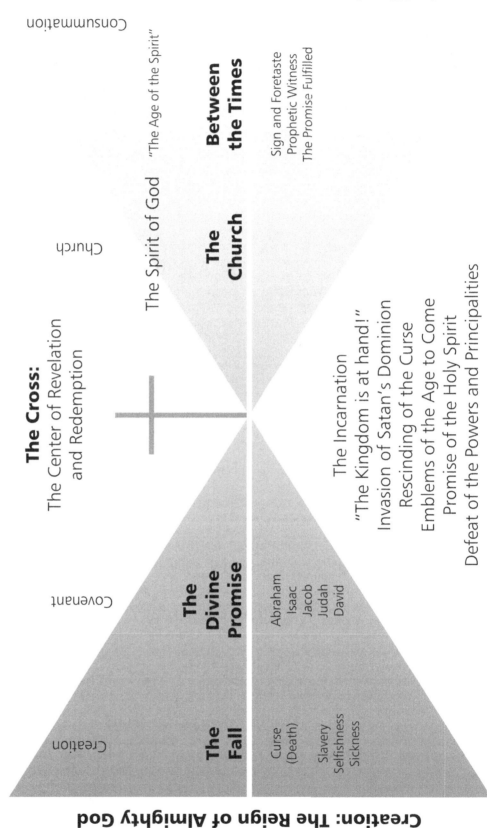

Glorification: New Heavens and New Earth

Consummation

"The Age of the Spirit"

Between the Times

Sign and Foretaste
Prophetic Witness
The Promise Fulfilled

The Spirit of God

Church

The Church

The Cross:
The Center of Revelation and Redemption

The Incarnation
"The Kingdom is at hand!"
Invasion of Satan's Dominion
Rescinding of the Curse
Emblems of the Age to Come
Promise of the Holy Spirit
Defeat of the Powers and Principalities

Covenant

The Divine Promise

Abraham
Isaac
Jacob
Judah
David

The Fall

Creation

Curse (Death)

Slavery
Selfishness
Sickness

Creation: The Reign of Almighty God

APPENDIX 13

Traditions

(Paradosis)

Dr. Don L. Davis and Rev. Terry G. Cornett

Strong's Definition

Paradosis. Transmission, i.e. (concretely) a precept; specifically, the Jewish traditionary law

Vine's Explanation

denotes "a tradition," and hence, by metonymy, (a) "the teachings of the rabbis," . . . (b) "apostolic teaching," . . . of instructions concerning the gatherings of believers, of Christian doctrine in general . . . of instructions concerning everyday conduct.

1. **The concept of tradition in Scripture is essentially positive.**

Jer. 6.16 (ESV) - Thus says the Lord: "Stand by the roads, and look, and ask for the ancient paths, where the good way is; and walk in it, and find rest for your souls. But they said, 'We will not walk in it'" (cf. Exod. 3.15; Judg. 2.17; 1 Kings 8.57-58; Ps. 78.1-6).

2 Chron. 35.25 (ESV) - Jeremiah also uttered a lament for Josiah; and all the singing men and singing women have spoken of Josiah in their laments to this day. They made these a rule in Israel; behold, they are written in the Laments (cf. Gen. 32.32; Judg. 11.38-40).

Jer. 35.14-19 (ESV) - The command that Jonadab the son of Rechab gave to his sons, to drink no wine, has been kept, and they drink none to this day, for they have obeyed their father's command. I have spoken to you persistently, but you have not listened to me. I have sent to you all my servants the prophets, sending them persistently, saying, 'Turn now every one of you from his evil way, and amend your deeds, and do not go after other gods to serve them, and then you shall dwell in the land that I gave to you and your fathers.' But you did not incline your ear or listen to me. The sons of Jonadab the son of Rechab have kept the command that their father gave them, but this people has not obeyed me. Therefore, thus says the

Traditions (continued)

Lord, the God of hosts, the God of Israel: Behold, I am bringing upon Judah and all the inhabitants of Jerusalem all the disaster that I have pronounced against them, because I have spoken to them and they have not listened, I have called to them and they have not answered." But to the house of the Rechabites Jeremiah said, "Thus says the Lord of hosts, the God of Israel: Because you have obeyed the command of Jonadab your father and kept all his precepts and done all that he commanded you, therefore thus says the Lord of hosts, the God of Israel: Jonadab the son of Rechab shall never lack a man to stand before me."

2. **Godly tradition is a wonderful thing, but not all tradition is godly.**

Any individual tradition must be judged by its faithfulness to the Word of God and its usefulness in helping people maintain obedience to Christ's example and teaching.[1] In the Gospels, Jesus frequently rebukes the Pharisees for establishing traditions that nullify rather than uphold God's commands.

Mark 7.8 (ESV) - You leave the commandment of God and hold to the tradition of men" (cf. Matt. 15.2-6; Mark 7.13).

Col. 2.8 (ESV) - See to it that no one takes you captive by philosophy and empty deceit, according to human tradition, according to the elemental spirits of the world, and not according to Christ.

3. **Without the fullness of the Holy Spirit, and the constant edification provided to us by the Word of God, tradition will inevitably lead to dead formalism.**

Those who are spiritual are filled with the Holy Spirit, whose power and leading alone provides individuals and congregations a sense of freedom and vitality in all they practice and believe. However, when the practices and teachings of any given tradition are no longer infused by the power of the Holy Spirit and the Word of God, tradition loses its effectiveness, and may actually become counterproductive to our discipleship in Jesus Christ.

Eph. 5.18 (ESV) - And do not get drunk with wine, for that is debauchery, but be filled with the Spirit.

[1] *"All Protestants insist that these traditions must ever be tested against Scripture and can never possess an independent apostolic authority over or alongside of Scripture." (J. Van Engen, "Tradition,"* **Evangelical Dictionary of Theology,** *Walter Elwell, Gen. ed.) We would add that Scripture is itself the "authoritative tradition" by which all other traditions are judged. See "Appendix A, The Founders of Tradition: Three Levels of Christian Authority," p. 4.*

Gal. 5.22-25 (ESV) - But the fruit of the Spirit is love, joy, peace, patience, kindness, goodness, faithfulness, gentleness, self-control; against such things there is no law. And those who belong to Christ Jesus have crucified the flesh with its passions and desires. If we live by the Spirit, let us also walk by the Spirit.

2 Cor. 3.5-6 (ESV) - Not that we are sufficient in ourselves to claim anything as coming from us, but our sufficiency is from God, who has made us competent to be ministers of a new covenant, not of the letter but of the Spirit. For the letter kills, but the Spirit gives life.

4. **Fidelity to the Apostolic Tradition (teaching and modeling) is the essence of Christian maturity.**

2 Tim. 2.2 (ESV) - and what you have heard from me in the presence of many witnesses entrust to faithful men who will be able to teach others also.

1 Cor. 11.1-2 (ESV) - Be imitators of me, as I am of Christ. Now I commend you because you remember me in everything and maintain the traditions even as I delivered them to you (cf.1 Cor. 4.16-17, 2 Tim. 1.13-14, 2 Thess. 3.7-9, Phil. 4.9).

1 Cor. 15.3-8 (ESV) - For I delivered to you as of first importance what I also received: that Christ died for our sins in accordance with the Scriptures, that he was buried, that he was raised on the third day in accordance with the Scriptures, and that he appeared to Cephas, then to the twelve. Then he appeared to more than five hundred brothers at one time, most of whom are still alive, though some have fallen asleep. Then he appeared to James, then to all the apostles. Last of all, as to one untimely born, he appeared also to me.

5. **The Apostle Paul often includes an appeal to the tradition for support in doctrinal practices.**

1 Cor. 11.16 (ESV) - If anyone is inclined to be contentious, we have no such practice, nor do the churches of God (cf. 1 Cor. 1.2, 7.17, 15.3).

Traditions (continued)

1 Cor. 14.33-34 (ESV) - For God is not a God of confusion but of peace. As in all the churches of the saints, the women should keep silent in the churches. For they are not permitted to speak, but should be in submission, as the Law also says.

6. When a congregation uses received tradition to remain faithful to the "Word of God," they are commended by the apostles.

1 Cor. 11.2 (ESV) - Now I commend you because you remember me in everything and maintain the traditions even as I delivered them to you.

2 Thess. 2.15 (ESV) - So then, brothers, stand firm and hold to the traditions that you were taught by us, either by our spoken word or by our letter.

2 Thess. 3.6 (ESV) - Now we command you, brothers, in the name of our Lord Jesus Christ, that you keep away from any brother who is walking in idleness and not in accord with the tradition that you received from us.

Appendix A

The Founders of Tradition: Three Levels of Christian Authority

Exod. 3.15 (ESV) - God also said to Moses, "Say this to the people of Israel, 'The Lord, the God of your fathers, the God of Abraham, the God of Isaac, and the God of Jacob, has sent me to you.' This is my name forever, and thus I am to be remembered throughout all generations."

1. The Authoritative Tradition: the Apostles and the Prophets (The Holy Scriptures)

Eph. 2.19-21 (ESV) - So then you are no longer strangers and aliens, but you are fellow citizens with the saints and members of the household of God, built on the foundation of the apostles and prophets, Christ Jesus himself being the cornerstone, in whom the whole structure, being joined together, grows into a holy temple in the Lord.

~ The Apostle Paul

Traditions (continued)

Those who gave eyewitness testimony to the revelation and saving acts of Yahweh, first in Israel, and ultimately in Jesus Christ the Messiah. This testimony is binding for all people, at all times, and in all places. It is the authoritative tradition by which all subsequent tradition is judged.

2. The Great Tradition: the Ecumenical Councils and their Creeds[2]

See Appendix B, "Defining the Great Tradition."

What has been believed everywhere, always, and by all.

~ Vincent of Lerins

The Great Tradition is the core dogma (doctrine) of the Church. It represents the teaching of the Church as it has understood the Authoritative Tradition (the Holy Scriptures), and summarizes those essential truths that Christians of all ages have confessed and believed. To these doctrinal statements the whole Church, (Catholic, Orthodox, and Protestant)[3] gives its assent. The worship and theology of the Church reflects this core dogma, which finds its summation and fulfillment in the person and work of Jesus Christ. From earliest times, Christians have expressed their devotion to God in its Church calendar, a yearly pattern of worship which summarizes and reenacts the events of Christ's life.

[3] *Even the more radical wing of the Protestant reformation (Anabaptists) who were the most reluctant to embrace the creeds as dogmatic instruments of faith, did not disagree with the essential content found in them. "They assumed the Apostolic Creed–they called it 'The Faith,' Der Glaube, as did most people." See John Howard Yoder,* **Preface to Theology: Christology and Theological Method.** *Grand Rapids: Brazos Press, 2002. pp. 222-223.*

3. Specific Church Traditions: the Founders of Denominations and Orders

The Presbyterian Church (U.S.A.) has approximately 2.5 million members, 11,200 congregations and 21,000 ordained ministers. Presbyterians trace their history to the 16th century and the Protestant Reformation. Our heritage, and much of what we believe, began with the French lawyer John Calvin (1509-1564), whose writings crystallized much of the Reformed thinking that came before him.

~ The Presbyterian Church, U.S.A.

Christians have expressed their faith in Jesus Christ in various ways through specific movements and traditions which embrace and express the Authoritative Tradition and the Great Tradition in unique ways. For instance,

Traditions (continued)

Catholic movements have arisen around people like Benedict, Francis, or Dominic, and among Protestants people like Martin Luther, John Calvin, Ulrich Zwingli, and John Wesley. Women have founded vital movements of Christian faith (e.g., Aimee Semple McPherson of the Foursquare Church), as well as minorities (e.g., Richard Allen of the African Methodist Episcopal Church or Charles H. Mason of the Church of God in Christ, who also helped to spawn the Assemblies of God), all which attempted to express the Authoritative Tradition and the Great Tradition in a specific way consistent with their time and expression.

The emergence of vital, dynamic movements of the faith at different times and among different peoples reveal the fresh working of the Holy Spirit throughout history. Thus, inside Catholicism, new communities have arisen such as the Benedictines, Franciscans, and Dominicans; and outside Catholicism, new denominations have emerged (Lutherans, Presbyterians, Methodists, Church of God in Christ, etc.). Each of these specific traditions have "founders," key leaders whose energy and vision helped to establish a unique expression of Christian faith and practice. Of course, to be legitimate, these movements must adhere to and faithfully express both the Authoritative Tradition and the Great Tradition. Members of these specific traditions embrace their own unique practices and patterns of spirituality, but these unique features are not necessarily binding on the Church at large. They represent the unique expressions of that community's understanding of and faithfulness to the Authoritative and Great Traditions.

Specific traditions seek to express and live out this faithfulness to the Authoritative and Great Traditions through their worship, teaching, and service. They seek to make the Gospel clear within new cultures or sub-cultures, speaking and modeling the hope of Christ into new situations shaped by their own set of questions posed in light of their own unique circumstances. These movements, therefore, seek to contextualize the Authoritative tradition in a way that faithfully and effectively leads new groups of people to faith in Jesus Christ, and incorporates those who believe into the community of faith that obeys his teachings and gives witness of him to others.

Appendix B

Defining the "Great Tradition"

The Great Tradition (sometimes called the "classical Christian tradition") is defined by Robert E. Webber as follows:

[It is] the broad outline of Christian belief and practice developed from the Scriptures between the time of Christ and the middle of the fifth century

~ Webber. **The Majestic Tapestry**.
Nashville: Thomas Nelson Publishers, 1986. p. 10.

This tradition is widely affirmed by Protestant theologians both ancient and modern.

Thus those ancient Councils of Nicea, Constantinople, the first of Ephesus, Chalcedon, and the like, which were held for refuting errors, we willingly embrace, and reverence as sacred, in so far as relates to doctrines of faith, for they contain nothing but the pure and genuine interpretation of Scripture, which the holy Fathers with spiritual prudence adopted to crush the enemies of religion who had then arisen.

~ John Calvin. **Institutes**. IV, ix. 8.

. . . most of what is enduringly valuable in contemporary biblical exegesis was discovered by the fifth century.

~ Thomas C. Oden. **The Word of Life**.
San Francisco: HarperSanFrancisco, 1989. p. xi

The first four Councils are by far the most important, as they settled the orthodox faith on the Trinity and the Incarnation.

~ Philip Schaff. **The Creeds of Christendom**. Vol. 1.
Grand Rapids: Baker Book House, 1996. p. 44.

Our reference to the Ecumenical Councils and Creeds is, therefore, focused on those Councils which retain a widespread agreement in the Church among Catholics, Orthodox, and Protestants. While Catholic and Orthodox share common agreement on the first seven councils, Protestants tend to affirm and use primarily the first four. Therefore, those councils which continue to be shared by the whole Church are completed with the Council of Chalcedon in 451.

Traditions (continued)

It is worth noting that each of these four Ecumenical Councils took place in a pre-European cultural context and that none of them were held in Europe. They were councils of the whole Church and they reflected a time in which Christianity was primarily an eastern religion in it's geographic core. By modern reckoning, their participants were African, Asian, and European. The councils reflected a church that ". . . has roots in cultures far distant from Europe and preceded the development of modern European identity, and [of which] some of its greatest minds have been African" (Oden, *The Living God*, San Francisco: HarperSanFrancisco, 1987, p. 9).

Perhaps the most important achievement of the Councils was the creation of what is now commonly called the Nicene Creed. It serves as a summary statement of the Christian faith that can be agreed on by Catholic, Orthodox, and Protestant Christians.

The first four Ecumenical Councils are summarized in the following chart:

Name/Date/Location	Purpose
First Ecumenical Council 325 A.D. Nicea, Asia Minor	Defending against: *Arianism* Question answered: *Was Jesus God?* Action: *Developed the initial form of the Nicene Creed to serve as a summary of the Christian faith*
Second Ecumenical Council 381 A.D. Constantinople, Asia Minor	Defending against: *Macedonianism* Question answered: *Is the Holy Spirit a personal and equal part of the Godhead?* Action: *Completed the Nicene Creed by expanding the article dealing with the Holy Spirit*
Third Ecumenical Council 431 A.D. Ephesus, Asia Minor	Defending against: *Nestorianism* Question answered: *Is Jesus Christ both God and man in one person?* Action: *Defined Christ as the Incarnate Word of God and affirmed his mother Mary as **theotokos** (God-bearer)*
Fourth Ecumenical Council 451 A.D. Chalcedon, Asia Minor	Defending against: *Monophysitism* Question answered: *How can Jesus be both God and man?* Action: *Explained the relationship between Jesus' two natures (human and Divine)*

APPENDIX 14

Readings on Christ

Rev. Dr. Don L. Davis

What Is Christianity without Christ?

Christianity without Christ is a chest without its treasure, a frame without a portrait, a corpse without breath.

> ~ John Stott. **Focus on Christ.**
> Cleveland: William Collins Publishers, Inc., 1979.

What Is the Bible all About?

What is the Bible all about? How can I understand its meaning? Why are there sixty-six books in the Bible? How do I know it is the Word of God?

All of these questions can be answered in one word - Christ.

Jesus Christ is the key to both the inspiration and the interpretation of the Bible. Further, it is Christ who confirmed the collection of books as both complete and authoritative.

> ~ Norman Geisler. **A Popular Survey of the Old Testament.**
> Grand Rapids: Baker Book House, 1977. p. 11.

The End of the Line

[Matthew] is being deliberately schematic [i.e., providing us with a big picture], with a theological intention. He is pointing out that Old Testament history falls into three approximately equal spans of time between the critical events:

- from the foundational covenant with Abraham to the establishing of the monarchy under David;

- from David to the destruction and loss of the monarchy in the Babylonian exile;

- and from the exile to the coming of the Messiah himself who alone could occupy the throne of David.

Jesus is thus 'the end of the line,' as far as the Old Testament story goes. It has run its completed course in preparation for him, and now its goal and climax has been reached.

> ~ Christopher J. H. Wright. **Knowing Jesus through the Old Testament.**
> Downers Grove: InterVarsity Press, 1992. pp. 6-7.

Readings on Christ (continued)

The Cosmic and All-Sufficient Center

Jesus of Nazareth continues to enjoy an extraordinary boom. People are fascinated by him, even in spite of themselves. Many who never reach the point of confessing him as God and Savior yet regard him with profound admiration. True, there are others who resent and reject him. But the one thing people seem unable to do is to ignore him and leave him alone.

Even in other religions and ideologies Jesus is held in high honor. . . . As T.R. Glover wrote in *The Jesus of History*: "Jesus remains the very heart and soul of the Christian movement, still controlling men, still capturing men. . . . In fine, there is no figure in human history that signifies more. Men may love him or hate him, but they do it intensely."

. . . Jesus Christ is the center of Christianity, and therefore both the Christian faith and the Christian life, if they are to be authentic, must be focused on Christ. In his work *Christian Faith and Other Faiths*, the late Bishop Stephen Neill wrote: "The old saying 'Christianity is Christ' is almost exactly true. The historical figure of Jesus of Nazareth is the criterion by which every Christian affirmation has to be judged, and in the light of which it stands or falls."

~ John Stott. **Life in Christ**.
Grand Rapids: Baker Books, 1991. p. 7.

The Magnetism of Jesus' Teaching: Where Did it Come From?

Why was Jesus such a fascinating teacher? What caused these large crowds to follow him? In reply one might say that it was what Jesus said that drew the crowds. With Jesus the voice of prophecy had once again returned to Israel after 400 years. In the ministry of Jesus, the Spirit of God was once again active in Israel (cf. Matt. 12.28; Luke 4.16-21). God was once again visiting his people and proclaiming his will. One reason people came to hear Jesus was that many were convinced that God was speaking through Jesus of Nazareth and that what he was saying was indeed the Word of God (Luke 5.1; 11.28; Mark 4.14-20). . . .

No doubt an additional factor that enters the picture involves the personality of Jesus, for the personality of Jesus gave life and vitality to his message. It was the Word made flesh (John 1.14) which was the medium through which and by which the Word of God came. People loved to listen to Jesus because of the kind of person he was. Publicans, sinners, children, the crowds–all found in Jesus one whom they enjoyed being near. It was therefore not only *what* he taught but also *who* he was that attracted people to hear him. . . . The *what* of his message and the *who*, i.e., the "personality" and "authority" of the messenger, all played a part in making Jesus an exciting teacher.

> ~ Robert H. Stein. **The Method and Message of Jesus' Teachings**.
> Philadelphia: The Westminster Press, 1978. pp.7-8.

The Challenge of the Biblical Stories

John Dominic Crossan

John Dominic Crossan is an original member and former co-chair of the Jesus Seminar as well as chairman of the Historical Jesus Section of the Society of Biblical Literature. He earned a doctorate in divinity from Maynooth College, Ireland. His postdoctoral studies have been in biblical research at the Pontifical Biblical Institute, Rome, and in archeological research at the Ecole Biblique, Jerusalem. Crossan has taught at several seminaries in the Chicago area and was professor of religious studies at DePaul University for twenty-six years. He has written over a dozen books on the historical Jesus.

The Gospels are normative, I think for us as Christians not just in their production, in what they have created, but in the way they are written. A Gospel goes back, as it were, to the twenties. It writes Jesus from the 20s into the 70s, the 80s, the 90s. A Gospel always takes the historical Jesus and laminates him together with the Christ we believe in–the two of them together. John rewrites the 20s as Mark had done before him. The historical Jesus remains crucial for Christianity because we must in each generation of the Church redo our historical work and redo our theological work. We can't skip it. . . .

When I look a Buddhist friend in the face, I cannot say with integrity: "Our story about Jesus' virginal birth is true and factual. Your story that when the Buddha came out of his mother's womb, he was walking, talking, teaching, and preaching (which I must admit is even better than our story)–that's a myth. We have the truth; you have a lie."

I don't think that can be said any longer, for our insistence that our faith is fact and that others' faith is a lie is, I think, a cancer that eats at the heart of Christianity.

> ~ William F. Buckley, Jr. **Will the Real Jesus Please Stand Up?** Paul Copan, ed.
> Grand Rapids: Baker Books, 1998. p. 39.

Readings on Christ (continued)

Christus Victor: The Warrior Who Is Messiah

> Ps. 68.10 - You ascended on high, leading a host of captives in your train and receiving gifts among men, even among the rebellious, that the Lord God may dwell there.

> Ps. 110.1-2 - The Lord says to my Lord: "Sit at my right hand, until I make your enemies your footstool." The Lord sends forth from Zion your mighty scepter. Rule in the midst of your enemies!

[*Christus Victor's*] central theme is the idea of the Atonement as a Divine conflict and victory; Christ–*Christus Victor*–fights against and triumphs over the evil powers of the world, the 'tyrant' under which mankind is in bondage and suffering, and in him God reconciles the world to himself . . . . The background of the idea is dualistic; God is pictured as in Christ carrying through a victorious conflict against powers of evil which are hostile to his will. This constitutes Atonement, because the drama is a cosmic drama, and the victory over the powers bring to pass a new relation, a relation of reconciliation, between God and the world; and, still more, because in a measure the hostile powers are regarded as in the service of the will of God the Judge of all, and the executants of his judgment. Seen from this side, the triumph over the opposing powers is regarded as a reconciling of God himself; he is reconciled by the very act in which he reconciles the world to himself.

> ~ Gustaf Aulen, **Christus Victor**.
> New York: MacMillan Publishers, 1969. pp. 20-21.

The Risen Messiah Himself Is Our Life

> Col. 3.1-4 - If then you have been raised with Christ, seek the things that are above, where Christ is, seated at the right hand of God. Set your minds on things that are above, not on things that are on earth. For you have died, and your life is hidden with Christ in God. When Christ who is your life appears, then you also will appear with him in glory.

Let us keep in mind that instead of giving us one object after another, God gives his Son to us. Because of this, we can always lift up our hearts and look to the Lord, saying, "Lord, You are my way; Lord, You are my truth; Lord, You are my life. It is you, Lord, who is related to me, not your things." May we ask God to give us grace that we may see Christ in all spiritual things. Day by day we are convinced that aside from Christ there is no way, nor truth, nor life. How easily we make things as way, truth, and life. Or, we call hot atmosphere as life, we label clear thought as life. We consider strong emotion or outward conduct as life. In reality, though, these are not life. We ought to realize that only the Lord is life, Christ is our life. And it is the Lord who lives out this life in us. Let us ask him to deliver us from the many external and fragmentary affairs that we may touch only him. May we see the Lord in all things –way, truth, and life are all found in knowing him. May we really meet the Son of God and let him live in us. Amen.

~ Watchman Nee. **Christ, the Sum of All Spiritual Things.**
New York: Christian Fellowship Publishers, 1973. p. 20.

APPENDIX 15

Re-presenting Messiah

Don L. Davis

"Gentilization" of modern Christian faith expressions

Contextualization: freedom in Christ to enculturate the gospel

Common modern portrayal of Messianic hope as Gentile faith

Tendency of tradition/culture to usurp biblical authority

Present day eclipse of biblical framework by "captivities"

Strange fires on the altar: examples of socio-cultural captivities

Nationalism

Capitalism

Scientific rationalism

Denominationalism

Personal existentialism

Asceticism/moralism

Ethnocentrism

Nuclear family life

Jesus' critique of socio-cultural captivity

Bondage to religious tradition, Matt. 15.3-9

Ignorance of Scripture and God's power, Matt. 22.29

Zealous effort without knowledge, Romans 10.1-3

Hermeneutic habits that lead toward a syncretistic faith

Selective choice of texts

Tradition viewed as canon

Cultural readings of texts

Preaching and teaching based on eisegesis and audience

Uncritical approaches to one's own doctrine and practice

Apologetics for socio-cultural identity

"Paradigm paralysis" & biblical faith

Blind to one's own historical conditionedness

Limited vantage point and perspective

Privilege and power: political manipulation

Inability to receive criticism

Persecution of opposite viewpoints and new interpretations of faith

---

Rediscover the Hebraic roots of the biblical Messianic hope (return)

Recognize the socio-cultural captivity of Christian profession (exile)

Re-present Messiah Yeshua with passion and clarity

with fidelity to Scripture in sync with historic orthodoxy without cultural distortion without theological bias

---

Rediscovery of the Jewish origins of biblical faith, John 4.22

YHWH as God of lovingkindness in covenant faithfulness

Messianic fulfillment in OT: prophecy, type, story, ceremony, and symbol

Hebraic roots of the Promise: YHWH as a Warrior God

People of Israel as community of Messianic hope

Psalms and Prophets emphasize divine rulership of Messiah

Tracing the Seed

Seed of the Woman, Gen. 3.15

Seed of Shem, Gen. 9.26-27

Seed of Abraham, Gen. 12.3

Seed of Isaac and Jacob, Gen. 26.2-5; 28.10-15

Seed of Judah, Gen. 49.10

Seed of David, 2 Sam. 7

Suffering Servant of YHWH: humiliation and lowliness of God's Davidic king

Glimmers of Gentile salvation and global transformation

Live the adventure of NT apocalyptic myth (possession)

Apocalyptic as the "mother tongue and native language" of the apostles and early Church as eschatological community

Yeshua Messiah as the Cosmic Warrior: YHWH as God who wins ultimate victory over his enemies

Messiah Yeshua as Anointed One and Binder of the Strong Man: the Messianic Age to come inaugurated in Jesus of Nazareth

"Already/Not Yet" Kingdom orientation: The Reign of God as both manifest but not consummated

The Evidence and Guarantee of the Age to Come: The Spirit as down payment, first fruits, and seal of God

Messianic Prophecies Cited in the New Testament

Rev. Dr. Don L. Davis

	NT Citation	OT Reference	Indication of the Fulfillment of the Messianic Prophecy
1	Matt. 1.23	Isa. 7.14	The virgin birth of Jesus of Nazareth
2	Matt. 2.6	Mic. 5.2	The birth of Messiah in Bethlehem
3	Matt. 2.15	Hos. 11.1	That Yahweh would call Messiah out of Egypt, the second Israel
4	Matt. 2.18	Jer. 31.15	Rachel weeping over infants slain by Herod seeking to destroy Messianic seed
5	Matt. 3.3	Isa. 40.3	John the Baptist's preaching fulfills the Messianic forerunner of Isaiah
6	Matt. 4.15-16	Isa. 9.1-2	Galilean ministry of Jesus fulfills Isaiah's prophecy of Messiah's light to the Gentiles
7	Matt. 8.17	Isa. 53.4	Healing ministry of Jesus fulfills Isaiah prophecy regarding Messiah's power to exorcize and heal
8	Matt. 11.14-15	Isa. 35.5-6; 61.1	Jesus' healing ministry confirms his identity as Yahweh's anointed Messiah
9	Matt. 11.10	Mal. 3.1	Jesus confirms John the Baptist's identity as the messenger of Yahweh in Malachi
10	Matt. 12.18-21	Isa. 42.1-4	Jesus' healing ministry fulfills Isaiah's prophecy of Messiah's compassion for the weak
11	Matt. 12.40	Jon. 1.17	As Jonah was three days and nights in the belly of the sea monster, so Jesus would be in the earth
12	Matt. 13.14-15	Isa. 6.9-10	The spiritual dullness of Jesus' audience
13	Matt. 13.35	Ps. 78.2	Messiah would teach in parables to the people
14	Matt. 15.8-9	Isa. 29.13	Hypocritical nature of the audience of Jesus
15	Matt. 21.5	Zech. 9.9	Triumphal entry of Messiah the King into Jerusalem upon the foal of a donkey
16	Matt. 21.9	Ps. 118.26-27	Hosannas to the King of Jerusalem
17	Matt. 21.16	Ps. 8.2	Out of the mouth of babes Yahweh declares salvation
18	Matt. 21.42	Ps. 118.22	The Stone which the builders rejected has become the Capstone
19	Matt. 23.39	Ps. 110.1	The enthronement of Yahweh's Lord

Messianic Prophecies Cited in the New Testament (continued)

	NT Citation	OT Reference	Indication of the Fulfillment of the Messianic Prophecy
20	Matt. 24.30	Dan. 7.13	The Son of Man to come, of Daniel's prophecy, is none other than Jesus of Nazareth
21	Matt. 26.31	Zech. 13.7	The Shepherd smitten by Yahweh and the sheep scattered
22	Matt. 26.64	Ps. 110.1	Jesus of Nazareth is the fulfillment of Daniel's Messianic Son of Man
23	Matt. 26.64	Dan. 7.3	Jesus will come in the clouds of heaven as Daniel's exalted ruler
24	Matt. 27.9-10	Zech. 11.12-13	Messiah is betrayed for thirty pieces of silver
25	Matt. 27.34-35	Ps. 69.21	God's anointed is given wine mingled with gall
26	Matt. 27.43	Ps. 22.18	The soldiers cast lots for the garments of the Messiah
27	Matt. 27.43	Ps. 22.8	Messiah receives mockery and derision upon the cross
28	Matt. 27.46	Ps. 22.1	Messiah forsaken by God for the sake of others
29	Mark 1.2	Mal. 3.1	John the Baptist is the fulfillment of the prophecy regarding the Lord's messenger
30	Mark 1.3	Isa. 40.3	John the Baptist is the voice calling in the wilderness to prepare the Lord's way
31	Mark 4.12	Isa. 6.9	The spiritual dullness of the audience in regards to Messiah's message
32	Mark 7.6	Isa. 29.13	Hypocrisy of the audience in their response to Messiah
33	Mark 11.9	Ps. 118.25	Hosanna's given to Messiah's entry as King into Jerusalem
34	Mark 12.10-11	Ps. 118.25	The stone which the builders rejected has become the chief cornerstone
35	Mark 12.36	Ps. 110.1	The Lord enthrones the Lord of David upon his throne in Zion
36	Mark 13.26	Dan. 7.13	Jesus is the prophesied Son of Man who will return in glory in the clouds
37	Mark 14.27	Zech 13.7	Jesus will be forsaken by his own, for the shepherd will be smitten and the sheep scattered
38	Mark 14.62	Dan. 7.13	Jesus is the Messiah, the Son of Man of Daniel's vision
39	Mark 14.62	Ps. 110.1	The Son of Man, who is Jesus, will come from the right hand of Yahweh
40	Mark 15.24	Ps. 22.18	Lots are cast for the garments of Messiah during his passion
41	Mark 15.34	Ps. 22.1	Messiah is forsaken by God for the redemption of the world

Messianic Prophecies Cited in the New Testament (continued)

	NT Citation	OT Reference	Indication of the Fulfillment of the Messianic Prophecy
42	Luke 1.17	Mal. 4.6	John the Baptist will come in the power and the spirit of Elijah
43	Luke 1.76	Mal. 3.1	John goes before the Lord to prepare the way
44	Luke 1.79	Isa. 9.1-2	Messiah will give light to those who dwell in darkness
45	Luke 2.32	Isa. 42.6; 49.6	Messiah will be a light to the Gentiles
46	Luke 3.4-5	Isa. 40.3	John is Isaiah's voice that cries in the wilderness to prepare the Lord's way
47	Luke 4.18-19	Isa. 61.1-2	Jesus is Yahweh's servant, anointed by his Spirit to bring the good news of the Kingdom
48	Luke 7.27	Mal. 3.1	Jesus confirms John's identity as the preparer of the Lord's way
49	Luke 8.10	Isa. 6.9	The dullness of the audience to Messiah Jesus
50	Luke 19.38	Ps. 118.26	Jesus fulfills in his entry into Jerusalem the Messianic prophecy of the King of Israel
51	Luke 20.17	Ps. 118.26	Jesus is Yahweh's stone which the builders rejected, which has become the Capstone
52	Luke 20.42-43	Ps. 110.1	David calls his lord the Messiah and Lord, who is enthroned in Zion by Yahweh
53	Luke 22.37	Isa. 53.12	Messiah is classed among criminals
54	Luke 22.69	Ps. 110.1	Jesus will return from the right hand of God, from where he has been enthroned
55	Luke 23.34	Ps. 22.18	Lots are cast for the garments of Messiah
56	John 1.23	Isa. 40.3	John's preaching is the fulfillment of Isaiah's prophecy about the forerunner of the Messiah
57	John 2.17	Ps. 69.17	Zeal for the house of the Lord will consume the Messiah
58	John 6.45	Isa. 54.13	All those whom God teaches will come to Messiah
59	John 7.42	Ps. 89.4; Mic. 5.2	Messiah, the seed of David, will be from Bethlehem
60	John 12.13	Ps. 118.25-26	Hosannas are given to Israel's triumphant Messiah King
61	John 12.15	Zech. 9.9	The King of Israel enters Jerusalem upon the foal of a donkey
62	John 12.38	Isa. 53.1	As Isaiah prophesied, few believed the report of Yahweh about his anointed one
63	John 12.40	Isa. 6.10	Isaiah saw the glory of Messiah and spoke of the dullness of his audience to him

Messianic Prophecies Cited in the New Testament (continued)

	NT Citation	OT Reference	Indication of the Fulfillment of the Messianic Prophecy
64	John 13.18; cf. 17.12	Ps. 41.9	Betrayal of Messiah by one of his intimate followers
65	John 15.25	Pss. 35.19; 69.4	Messiah will be hated without cause
66	John 19.24	Ps. 22.18	The garments of Messiah will be divided
67	John 19.28	Ps. 69.21	Messiah will be offered wine upon the cross
68	John 19.36	Exod. 12.46; Num. 9.12; Ps. 34.20	Not one bone of the Messiah will be broken
69	John 19.37	Zech. 12.10	The repentant nation of Israel will look upon him whom they have pierced
70	Acts 1.20	Pss. 69.25; 109.8	Judas is to be replaced with another
71	Acts 2.16-21	Joel 2.28-32	The Spirit is to be poured out in the last days upon all flesh
72	Acts 2.25-28	Ps. 16.8-11	Messiah could not undergo decay or corruption in Sheol
73	Acts 2.34-35	Ps. 110.1	Messiah is enthroned at Yahweh's right hand until his enemies are defeated
74	Acts 3.22-23	Deut. 18.15, 19	God would raise up for the people a prophet like Moses
75	Acts 3.25	Gen. 22.18	All nations of the earth would be blessed in the seed of Abraham
76	Acts 4.11	Ps. 118.22	Messiah Jesus is the rejected stone whom God has made the cornerstone
77	Acts 4.25	Ps. 2.1	Yahweh will laugh at the opposition given by the nations to him and his anointed
78	Acts 7.37	Deut. 18.15	Yahweh will give to Israel a prophet like Moses
79	Acts 8.32-33	Isa. 53.7-9	Messiah Jesus is the Suffering Servant of Yahweh
80	Acts 13.33	Ps. 2.7	God has fulfilled the promise to Israel in Jesus by raising him from the dead
81	Acts 13.34	Isa. 53.3	Messiah Jesus is the fulfillment of the sure mercies of David
82	Acts 13.35	Ps. 16.10	Messiah would not undergo corruption in the grave
83	Acts 13.47	Isa. 49.6	Through Paul, the message of Messiah becomes a light to the nations
84	Acts 15.16-18	Amos 9.11-12	The dynasty of David is restored in Jesus, and Gentiles are welcomed into the Kingdom
85	Rom. 9.25-26	Hos. 2.23; 1.10	Gentiles are to become the people of God

Messianic Prophecies Cited in the New Testament (continued)

	NT Citation	OT Reference	Indication of the Fulfillment of the Messianic Prophecy
86	Rom. 9.33; 10.11	Isa. 28.16	Messiah becomes a stone of stumbling to those who reject God's salvation
87	Rom. 10.13	Joel 2.32	Anyone calling on the name of the Lord will be saved
88	Rom. 11.8	Isa. 29.10	Israel through unbelief has been hardened to Messiah
89	Rom. 11.9-10	Ps. 69.22-23	Judgment has hardened upon Israel
90	Rom. 11.26	Isa. 59.20-21	A deliverer will come from Zion
91	Rom. 11.27	Isa. 27.9	Forgiveness of sins will be given through a new covenant
92	Rom. 14.11	Isa. 45.23	All will be finally judged by Yahweh
93	Rom. 15.9	Ps. 18.49	Gentiles praise God through faith in Messiah
94	Rom. 15.10	Deut. 32.43	God receives praise from the nations
95	Rom. 15.11	Ps. 117.1	The peoples of the earth give God glory
96	Rom. 15.12	Isa. 11.10	Gentiles will hope in the root of Jesse
97	Rom. 15.21	Isa. 52.15	The Good News will be preached to those without understanding
98	1 Cor. 15.27	Ps. 8.7	All things are under the feet of God's representative head
99	1 Cor. 15.54	Isa. 25.8	Death will be swallowed up in victory
100	1 Cor. 15.55	Hos. 13.14	Death will one day lose its sting altogether
101	2 Cor. 6.2	Isa. 49.8	Now is the day of salvation through faith in Messiah Jesus
102	2 Cor. 6.16	Ezek. 37.27	God will dwell with his people
103	2 Cor. 6.18	Hos. 1.10; Isa 43.6	Believers in Messiah Jesus are the sons and daughters of God
104	Gal. 3.8, 16	Gen. 12.3; 13.15; 17.8	The Scriptures, foreseeing Gentile justification by faith, preached the Gospel beforehand through the promise to Abraham, that all nations would be blessed in his seed
105	Gal. 4.27	Isa. 54.1	Jerusalem is the mother of us all
106	Eph. 2.17	Isa. 57.19	Peace of Messiah Jesus is preached both to the Jew and the Gentile
107	Eph. 4.8	Ps. 68.18	Messiah in his ascension has conquered and given gifts to us all by his grace
108	Eph. 5.14	Isa. 26.19; 51.17; 52.1; 60.1	The regeneration of the Lord has occurred; his light has shined on us

Messianic Prophecies Cited in the New Testament (continued)

	NT Citation	OT Reference	Indication of the Fulfillment of the Messianic Prophecy
109	Heb. 1.5	Ps. 2.7	Messiah is God's Son
110	Heb. 1.5	2 Sam. 7.14	Messiah Jesus is the anointed Son of God
111	Heb. 1.6	Deut. 32.43	Angels worshiped Messiah when he entered the world
112	Heb. 1.8-9	Ps. 45.6-7	Messiah Jesus is referred to as God by Yahweh in direct address
113	Heb. 1.10-12	Ps. 102.25-27	The Son is the agent of God's creation and is eternal
114	Heb. 1.13	Ps. 110.1	Messiah Jesus is enthroned at the Father's right hand
115	Heb. 2.6-8	Ps. 8.4-6	All things have been made subject to the Son's authority
116	Heb. 2.12	Ps. 22.22	Messiah Jesus is a brother to all of the redeemed
117	Heb. 2.13	Isa. 8.17-18	Messiah puts his trust in Yahweh God
118	Heb. 5.5	Ps. 2.7	Messiah is God's Son
119	Heb. 5.6	Ps. 110.4	Messiah is an eternal priest after the order of Melchizedek
120	Heb. 7.17, 21	Ps. 110.4	Messiah Jesus is an eternal High Priest
121	Heb. 8.8-12	Jer. 31.31-34	A new covenant has been made in the blood of Jesus
122	Heb. 10.5-9	Ps. 40.6	The death of Messiah Jesus replaces the atoning system of Temple sacrifice
123	Heb. 10.13	Ps. 110.1	Yahweh has enthroned Messiah Jesus as Lord
124	Heb. 10.16-17	Jer. 31.33-34	The Holy Spirit bears witness of the sufficiency of the New Covenant
125	Heb. 10.37-38	Hab. 2.3-4	He who will come will do so, in a little while
126	Heb. 12.26	Hag. 2.6	All heaven and earth will be shaken
127	1 Pet. 2.6	Isa. 28.16	God lays a cornerstone in Zion
128	1 Pet. 2.7	Ps. 118.22	The stone which the builders rejected, God has made the Capstone
129	1 Pet. 2.8	Isa. 8.14	Messiah is a stone of stumbling to those who do not believe
130	1 Pet. 2.10	Hos. 1.10; 2.23	Gentiles through Messiah are now invited to become the people of God
131	1 Pet. 2.22	Isa. 53.9	The sinless Messiah Jesus was sacrificed for us

The Prophetic Vision as Source of Biblical Faith Commitment

Rev. Dr. Don L. Davis

Faith is an essential part of human life. Humans are confessing, believing and trusting creatures. *And where we place our faith determines the world view which we will adopt. Put another way, our ultimate faith commitment sets the contours of our world view.* It shapes our vision for a way of life. People who doubt their world view are restless and feel they have no ground to stand on. They are often in the throes of a psychological crisis. *But the emotional crisis is fundamentally religious because our world view rests on a faith commitment.*

What is a faith commitment? It is the way we answer four basic questions facing everyone:

1) *Who am I?* Or, what is the nature, task, and purpose of human beings?

2) *Where am I?* Or, what is the nature of the world and universe I live in?

3) *What's wrong?* Or, what is the basic problem or obstacle that keeps me from attaining fulfillment? In other words, how do I understand evil?

4) *What is the remedy?* Or, how is it possible to overcome this hindrance to my fulfillment? In other words, how do I find salvation?

When we've answered these questions, that is, when our faith is settled, then we begin to see reality in some sensible pattern. *Out of our faith proceeds a world view, without which human life simply cannot go on.*

~ Brian J. Walsh and J. Richard Middleton. **The Transforming Vision**.
Downers Grove: InterVarsity Press, 1984. p. 35.

APPENDIX 18

Preaching and Teaching Jesus of Nazareth as Messiah and Lord Is the Heart of All Biblical Ministry

Don L. Davis

Phil. 3.8 (ESV) - Indeed, I count everything as loss because of the surpassing worth of *knowing Christ [Messiah] Jesus my Lord*. For his sake I have suffered the loss of all things and count them as rubbish, in order *that I may gain Christ [Messiah]*.

Acts 5.42 (ESV) - And every day, in the temple and from house to house, they *did not cease teaching and preaching Jesus as the Christ [Messiah]*.

1 Cor. 1.23 (ESV) - but we preach *Christ [Messiah] crucified*, a stumbling block to Jews and folly to Gentiles.

2 Cor. 4.5 (ESV) - For what we proclaim is not ourselves, but *Jesus Christ [Messiah] as Lord*, with ourselves as your servants for Jesus' sake.

1 Cor. 2.2 (ESV) - For I decided to know nothing among you except *Jesus Christ [Messiah] and him crucified*.

Eph. 3.8 (ESV) - To me, though I am the very least of all the saints, this grace was given, *to preach to the Gentiles the unsearchable riches of Christ [Messiah]*.

Phil. 1.18 (ESV) - What then? Only that in every way, whether in pretense or in truth, *Christ [Messiah] is proclaimed*, and in that I rejoice. Yes, and I will rejoice.

Col. 1.27-29 (ESV) - To them God chose to make known how great among the Gentiles are the riches of the glory of this mystery, which is *Christ [Messiah] in you, the hope of glory*. [28] Him we proclaim, warning everyone and teaching everyone with all wisdom, that we may *present everyone mature in Christ [Messiah]*. [29] *For this I toil, struggling with all his energy* that he powerfully works within me.

APPENDIX 19

Summary of Messianic Interpretations in the Old Testament

Rev. Dr. Don L. Davis, adapted from James Smith, The Promised Messiah

Legend

EJ - Early Jewish Interpretation   NTA - New Testament Allusion

NTE - New Testament Exegesis   CF - Church Fathers

	Bible Reference	Summary of the Messianic Prophecy	EJ	NTA	NTE	CF
1	Gen. 3.15	One from the ranks of the seed of the woman will crush the head of the serpent	X	X		X
2	Gen. 9.25-27	God will come and dwell in the tents of Shem	X	X		X
3	Gen. 12.3; 18.18; 22.18; 26.4; 28.14	All nations of the earth will be blessed through the seed of Abraham, Isaac, and Jacob	X	X	X	X
4	Gen. 49.10-11	The scepter won't depart from Judah until Shiloh comes, and all the nations will be obedient to him	X	X		X
5	Num. 24.16-24	A powerful ruler from Israel will come and crush the enemies of God's people	X	X		X
6	Deut. 18.15-18	A prophet like Moses will come and all the righteous will listen to him		X	X	X
7	Deut. 32.43	The angels of God commanded to rejoice as the Firstborn of God comes into the world		X		
8	1 Sam. 2.10	God will judge the ends of the earth but will give strength to his anointed	X			X
9	1 Sam. 2.35-36	A faithful Priest will come and dispense blessing upon the people				
10	2 Sam. 7.12-16	The Seed of David will sit upon an eternal throne and will build the house of God		X		X
11	Ps. 89	God's covenant to send Messiah through David cannot be revoked	X			
12	Ps. 132	God has chosen David and Zion		X		
13	Ps. 8	The Son of Man is made a little lower than the angels, and is exalted as ruler over all creation		X	X	X
14	Ps. 40	Messiah volunteers to enter the world, to suffer, and is delivered			X	X

Summary of Messianic Interpretations in the Old Testament (continued)

	Bible Reference	Summary of the Messianic Prophecy	EJ	NTA	NTE	CF
15	Ps. 118	Messiah survives the power of death to become the chief Cornerstone, the Capstone of God's building			X	X
16	Ps. 78.1-2	Messiah will speak to the people in parables			X	
17	Ps. 69	Messiah's zeal for the house of God will bring hatred and abuse, but his enemies will receive their just dues			X	X
18	Ps. 109	The one who betrays Messiah will suffer a terrible fate			X	X
19	Ps. 22	After unparalleled suffering, Messiah conquers death and rejoices with his brethren			X	X
20	Ps. 2	Messiah is enthroned in Zion, defeats his opposition, and rules over creation	X		X	X
21	Ps. 16	Yahweh will not allow Messiah to see corruption in Sheol			X	X
22	Ps. 102	Messiah the Creator is eternal, though suffering severe persecution				X
23	Ps. 45	Messiah is God, and has been anointed by God to sit upon an eternal throne; his people are his lovely bride	X			X
24	Ps. 110	Messiah is a priest-king after the order of Melchizedek, and he sits at the right hand of God, ruling over all humankind	X		X	X
25	Ps. 72	Messiah reigns over a universal and righteous kingdom of blessing	X			X
26	Ps. 68	Messiah wins a great victory, then ascends back on high	X		X	X
27	Job 9.33; 16.19-21; 17.3; 33.23-28	A Mediator, Interpreter, Advocate, and Witness will walk in the latter days upon the earth				
28	Job 19.23-27	A Redeemer will stand upon the earth in the latter days and the righteous will see him				X
29	Joel 2.23	A Wonderful Teacher will arise and usher in an age of great abundance	X			X
30	Hos. 1.10-2.1	A Second Moses will lead God's people out of bondage into a glorious new era			X	
31	Hos. 3.5	After the exile, God's people will serve Yahweh their God, and David their king	X			
32	Hos. 11.1	God calls his Son, the Second Israel, out of Egypt			X	

Summary of Messianic Interpretations in the Old Testament (continued)

	Bible Reference	Summary of the Messianic Prophecy	EJ	NTA	NTE	CF
33	Isa. 4.2-6	The beautiful and glorious Shoot of Yahweh will be the pride of the remnant of Israel	X			
34	Isa. 7.14-15	A virgin will conceive and bear a son whose name will be called Immanuel			X	X
35	Isa. 8.17-18	Messiah waits for the time of his coming, and he and his children are signs and wonders in Israel		X	X	
36	Isa. 9.1-7	Messiah will bring light to Galilee and one will sit on the throne of David to usher in the reign of God in righteousness and justice	X	X		X
37	Isa. 11.1-16	A Shoot from the stem of Jesse will be filled with the Spirit of Yahweh, and will usher into the earth a Kingdom of righteousness and peace	X	X	X	X
38	Isa. 16.5	Downtrodden peoples will look to the house of David for justice and lovingkindness				
39	Isa. 28.16	God is going to lay in Zion a tried and tested Stone, a precious Cornerstone	X	X	X	X
40	Isa. 30.19-26	The people of God will see their divine Teacher and will enjoy his abundant blessing as a result of listening to him	X			
41	Isa. 32.1-2	A Leader of the future will be a shelter from the storm, like water in a dry place				
42	Isa. 33.17	The eyes of the people of God will see the King in his beauty				
43	Isa. 42.17	Yahweh's Servant will bring forth justice to the nations, and will be a Covenant to the people, a Light to the nations	X		X	X
44	Isa. 49.1-13	Yahweh's Servant is divinely appointed to teach, to raise up the tribes of Jacob, and to be a Light to the Gentiles	X			CX
45	Isa. 50.4-11	Yahweh's Servant is an obedient disciple who endures suffering and indignity				X
46	Isa. 52.13-53.12	God's Servant is rejected, suffers horribly for the sins of others, dies, but then sees his seed and is satisfied	X	X	X	X
47	Isa. 55.3-5	A son of David will be made a Witness, Leader, and Commander for the peoples				X
48	Isa. 59.20-21	A Redeemer will come to penitent Zion	X		X	

Summary of Messianic Interpretations in the Old Testament (continued)

	Bible Reference	Summary of the Messianic Prophecy	EJ	NTA	NTE	CF
49	Isa. 61.1-11	Messiah has been anointed by the Spirit of Yahweh to proclaim the Good News to the poor, and liberty and deliverance to the captives	X		X	X
50	Mic. 2.12-13	The divine Breaker will lead the people of God out of bondage	X			
51	Mic. 5.1-5	A glorious Ruler will arise from Bethlehem to shepherd the people of God and give them victory over their enemies	X	X	X	X
52	Hab. 3.12-15	Yahweh comes forth from the salvation of his Anointed, and will strike through the head of the house of evil				
53	Jer. 23.5-6	God will raise up a Righteous Branch who will act wisely and execute justice and righteousness in the land	X			
54	Jer. 30.9, 21	Upon return from exile, God's people will serve David their King who will serve as Mediator and draw near to God for them	X			
55	Jer. 31.21-22	God will create a new thing in the land	X			X
56	Jer. 33.14-26	Yahweh will raise up his righteous Servant in the land, and will not fail to fulfill his promise to David and to Levi	X			
57	Ezek. 17.22-24	A tender Twig from the house of David will become a stately Cedar with birds of every kind nesting under it	X			X
58	Ezek. 21.25-27	The crown is removed from the last king of Judah until he comes whose right it is				
59	Ezek. 34.23-31	God will set over those who return from Babylon one Shepherd, his servant, David		X		
60	Ezek. 37.21-28	God's people will be united and will have one King, "My Servant David"		X		
61	Ezek. 44.48	A Prince in the future age will be accorded honor, and through him sacrifices will be offered to God	X			
62	Dan. 7.13-14	One like a Son of Man will come before the Ancient of Days to receive an everlasting Kingdom and Dominion	X	X	X	X
63	Dan. 9.24-27	After 69 "weeks" of years, Messiah will appear, he will be cut off, and will cause sacrifice and oblation to cease	X			X
64	Hag. 2.6-9	After the shaking of the nations, the Desire of all Nations will come and fill the Temple of God with glory	X		X	

Summary of Messianic Interpretations in the Old Testament (continued)

	Bible Reference	Summary of the Messianic Prophecy	EJ	NTA	NTE	CF
65	Hag. 2.21-23	Zerubbabel will be made God's signet Ring in the day when the thrones of kingdoms and the Gentiles are overthrown by Yahweh				
66	Zech. 3.8-10	The Servant of Yahweh, his Shoot, is symbolized by Joshua the High Priest and by an engraved stone	X			X
67	Zech. 6.12-13	A man whose name is Shoot shall build the Temple of the Lord, and he will be a Priest and a King	X			X
68	Zech. 9.9-11	The King of Zion comes riding upon the foal of a donkey	X		X	X
69	Zech. 10.3-4	God will send one who is the Cornerstone, the Tent Peg, the Battle Bow, the one who possesses all sovereignty	X			
70	Zech. 11.4-14	Thirty pieces of silver thrown to the potter in the house of God			X	X
71	Zech. 13.7	The sword of divine justice smites the Shepherd and the sheep are scattered			X	X
72	Mal. 3.1	The Lord's messenger will clear the way before him, and the Lord will suddenly come to his Temple	X	X	X	X
73	Mal. 4.2	The Sun of Righteousness will arise with healing in his wings	X	X		

APPENDIX 20
Messiah Yeshua in Every Book of the Bible
Adapted from Norman L. Geisler, A Popular Survey of the Old Testament

Christ in the Books of the Old Testament

1. The Seed of the Woman (Gen. 3.15)

2. The Passover Lamb (Exod. 12.3-4)

3. The Atoning Sacrifice (Lev. 17.11)

4. The Smitten Rock (Num. 20.8, 11)

5. The Faithful Prophet (Deut. 18.18)

6. The Captain of the Lord's Host (Josh. 5.15)

7. The Divine Deliverer (Judg. 2.18)

8. The Kinsman Redeemer (Ruth 3.12)

9. The Anointed One (1 Sam. 2.10)

10. The Son of David (2 Sam. 7.14)

11. The Coming King (1 Kings)

12. The Coming King (2 Kings)

13. The Builder of the Temple (1 Chron. 28.20)

14. The Builder of the Temple (2 Chron.)

15. The Restorer of the Temple (Ezra 6.14, 15)

16. The Restorer of the Nation (Neh. 6.15)

17. The Preserver of the Nation (Esther 4.14)

18. The Living Redeemer (Job 19.25)

19. The Praise of Israel (Ps. 150.6)

20. The Wisdom of God (Prov. 8.22, 23)

21. The Great Teacher (Eccles. 12.11)

22. The Fairest of Ten Thousand (Song of Sol. 5.10)

23. The Suffering Servant (Isa. 53.11)

24. The Maker of the New Covenant (Jer. 31.31)

25. The Man of Sorrows (Lam. 3.28-30)

26. The Glory of God (Ezek. 43.2)

27. The Coming Messiah (Dan. 9.25)

28. The Lover of the Unfaithful (Hos. 3.1)

29. The Hope of Israel (Joel 3.16)

30. The Husbandman (Amos 9.13)

31. The Savior (Obad. 21)

32. The Resurrected One (Jon. 2.10)

33. The Ruler in Israel (Mic. 5.2)

34. The Avenger (Nah. 2.1)

35. The Holy God (Hab. 1.13)

36. The King of Israel (Zeph. 3.15)

37. The Desire of Nations (Hag. 2.7)

38. The Righteous Branch (Zech. 3.8)

39. The Sun of Righteousness (Mal. 4.2)

Christ in the Books of the New Testament

1. The King of the Jews (Matt. 2.2)

2. The Servant of the Lord (Mark 10.45)

3. The Son of Man (Luke 19.10)

4. The Son of God (John 1.1)

5. The Ascended Lord (Acts 1.10)

6. The Believer's Righteousness (Rom. 1.17)

7. Our Sanctification (1 Cor. 1.30)

8. Our Sufficiency (2 Cor. 12.9)

9. Our Liberty (Gal. 2.4)

10. The Exalted Head of the Church (Eph. 1.22)

11. The Christian's Joy (Phil. 1.26)

12. The Fullness of Deity (Col. 2.9)

13. The Believer's Comfort (1 Thess. 4.16, 17)

14. The Believer's Glory (2 Thess. 1.12)

15. The Christian's Preserver (1 Tim. 4.10)

16. The Christian's Rewarder (2 Tim. 4.8)

17. The Blessed Hope (Titus 2.13)

18. Our Substitute (Philem. 17)

19. The Great High Priest (Heb. 4.15)

20. The Giver of Wisdom (James 1.5)

21. The Rock (1 Pet. 2.6)

22. The Precious Promise (2 Pet. 1.4)

23. The Life (1 John)

24. The Truth (2 John)

25. The Way (3 John)

26. The Advocate (Jude)

27. The King of kings and Lord of lords (Rev. 19.16)

APPENDIX 21

Old Testament Names, Titles, and Epithets for the Messiah

Adapted from Norman L. Geisler, A Popular Survey of the Old Testament

1. Advocate, Job 16.19

2. Angel (messenger), Job 33.23

3. Anointed, 1 Sam. 2.19; Ps. 2.2

4. Battle-bow, Zech. 10.4

5. Bethlehem's Ruler, Mic. 5.2

6. Breaker, Mic. 2.13

7. Commander, Isa. 55.4

8. Cornerstone (Capstone), Ps. 118.22; Isa. 28.16

9. Covenant of the People, Isa. 42.6

10. Crusher, Gen. 3.15

11. David, Hos. 3.5; Jer. 30.9

12. Desire of all Nations, Hag. 2.7

13. Eternal One, Ps. 102.25-27

14. Eternal Priest, Ps. 110.4

15. Everlasting Father, Isa. 9.6

16. Faithful Priest, 1 Sam. 2.35

17. Firstborn, Ps. 89.27

18. Forsaken Sufferer, Ps. 22

19. Foundation, Isa. 28.16; Zech. 10.4

20. God, Ps. 45.6-7

21. Head, Hos. 1.11; Mic. 2.13

22. Healer, Isa. 42.7

23. He who Comes, Ps. 118.26

24. Horn of David, Ps. 132.17

25. Immanuel, Isa. 7.14

26. Interpreter, Job 33.23

27. Israel, Hos. 11.1; Isa. 49.3

28. King, Ps. 2.5; Hos. 3.5

29. Lamp for David, Ps. 132.17

30. Last, Job 19.25

31. Launderer, Mal. 3.2

32. Leader, Isa. 55.4

33. Liberator, Isa. 42.7

34. Light, Isa. 9.2

35. Light of the Gentiles, Isa. 42.6; 49.6

36. Lord, Mal. 3.1

37. Man, Zech. 6.12; 13.7

38. Man of Sorrows, Isa. 53.3

39. Mediator, Job 33.23

40. Messenger of the Covenant, Mal. 3.1

41. Messiah-Prince, Dan. 9.25

42. Mighty God, Isa. 9.6

43. Mighty Hero, Ps. 45.3

44. My Equal, Zech. 13.7

45. Nail (peg), Zech. 10.4

46. Our Peace, Mic. 5.5

47. Parable Teller, Ps. 78.1-2

48. Pierced One, Zech. 12.10

Old Testament Names, Titles, and Epithets for the Messiah (continued)

49. Poor and Afflicted, Ps. 69.29

50. Priestly Ruler, Jer. 30.21; Zech. 6.13

51. Prince, Ezek. 37.25; 44-48

52. Prince of Peace, Isa. 9.6

53. Proclaimer of Good Tidings to the Poor, Isa. 61.2

54. Prophet like Moses, Deut. 18.15,18

55. Redeemer, Job 19.25; Isa. 59.20

56. Refiner, Mal. 3.2

57. Refuge, Isa. 32.1

58. Rejected Shepherd, Zech. 11

59. Rejected Stone, Ps. 118.22

60. Righteous Shoot, Jer. 23.5; 33.15

61. Root out of Dry Ground, Isa. 53.2

62. Ruler of all Nature, Ps. 8.5-8

63. Ruler of the Earth, Isa. 16.5

64. Scepter, Num. 24.17

65. Second Moses, Hos. 11.1

66. Seed of Abraham, Gen. 12.3; 18.18

67. Seed of David, 2 Sam. 2.12

68. Seed of the Woman, Gen. 3.15

69. Servant, Isa. 42.1; 49.3, 6

70. Shade, Isa. 32.2

71. Shelter, Isa. 32.1

72. Shepherd, Ezek. 34.23; 37.24

73. Shiloh, Gen. 49.10

74. Shoot, Zech. 3.8; 6.12

75. Shoot from the Stump of Jesse, Isa. 11.1

76. Shoot of Yahweh, Isa. 4.2

77. Sign and Wonder, Isa. 8.18

78. Signet Ring, Hag. 2.23

79. Son of God, 2 Sam. 7.14; Ps. 2.7

80. Son of Man, Ps. 8.4; Dan. 7.13

81. Star, Num. 24.17

82. Stone, Zech. 3.9

83. Substitutionary Sufferer, Isa. 53

84. Sun of Righteousness, Mal. 4.5

85. Teacher, Isa. 30.20

86. Teacher for Righteousness, Joel 2.23

87. Tender Shoot, Isa. 53.2

88. Tender Twig, Ezek. 17.22

89. Temple Builder, Zech. 6.12

90. Tent Dweller, Gen. 9.26-27

91. Tested Stone, Isa. 28.16

92. Trailblazer, Ps. 16.11

93. Victor, Ps. 68.18

94. Volunteer, Ps. 40.7

95. Water of Life, Isa. 32.2

96. Witness, Job 16.19

97. Witness to the Peoples, Isa. 55.4

98. Wonderful Counselor, Isa. 9.6

99. Yahweh, Our Righteousness, Jer. 23.6

100. Zerubbabel, Hag. 2.23

APPENDIX 22

Promise vs. Prediction

The Apostolic Hermeneutic of the Old Testament

Adapted from Christopher J. H. Wright

And So It Was Fulfilled: Five Scenes of Jesus' Early Life				
Incident in Jesus' Life	Matthew Citation	The Old Testament Reference	Commentary on the Actual Historical Context of the Old Testament Text	Hermeneutic Significance
Assurance to Joseph concerning the child conceived in Mary	Matt. 1.18-25	Isa. 7.14, the Immanuel sign given to King Ahaz by Isaiah	Immanuel prophecy was given as a sign to King Ahaz in his own historical context, and does not immediately provide any sense of a long range prediction of Messianic relevance	The Holy Spirit provided the Apostles with divine wisdom in making connections with not only the plain Messianic predictions, but also those aspects of the history of Israel which represent in a direct way some aspect of the life and ministry of Jesus.

The ability to correlate particular events of Israel to the life and ministry of Messiah Jesus is precisely the nature of the apostolic Spirit-illumined hermeneutic which coincides with divine and Spirit-inspired Scripture.

We are invited to exegete the Scriptures and make correlations in the same way as the Lord and the Apostles, although our connections should never be considered normative in the same way as theirs. |
Jesus' birth in Bethlehem, the city of David	Matt. 2.1-12	Mic. 5.2, prophecy of the Governor and Ruler of Israel to come from Bethlehem	A direct Messianic prediction about the birthplace of the future Governor of Israel and the nations	
The escape to Egypt, and the return from there	Matt. 2.13-15	Hos. 11.1, God's deliverance of his people Israel, his "son," out of Egypt at the Exodus	No prediction present; Hosea reference is a prophetic allusion to the Exodus of the people of God from Egypt	
Herod's murder of the boys in Bethlehem	Matt. 2.16-18	Jer. 31.15, Jeremiah's lament for the Israelite nation who were going into exile, into Babylonian captivity	The OT text is a figurative picture of the mourning of Rachel (Israel) at the time of the Exile in 587 BC after the fall of Jerusalem to the Babylonians. No explicit Messianic prediction is contained in the text.	
Jesus' family settlement in Nazareth of Galilee	Matt. 2.19-23	Several possible allusions in the OT, Judg. 13.5; 1 Sam. 1.11; Amos 2.10-11	Texts have relevance within their setting, but not in an explicit way to fulfill Messianic predictions	

APPENDIX 23

Messiah Jesus: Fulfillment of the Old Testament Types

*Adapted from Norman Geisler, **To Understand the Bible, Look for Jesus**, pp. 38-41.*

Messiah Jesus Fulfills the Tabernacle Types

Tabernacle Types	Jesus of Nazareth as the Antitype
The One Door	I am the Door John 10.9
The Brazen Altar	Gives his life as a ransom for many Mark 10.45
The Laver	If I do not wash you, you have no part with me John 13.8, 10; 1 John 1.7
The Lampstand	I am the Light of the Word John 8.12
The Shewbread	I am the Bread of Life John 6.48
The Altar of Incense	I am praying for them John 17.9
The Veil	This is my body Matt. 26.26
The Mercy Seat	I lay down my life for the sheep John 10.15

Messiah Jesus: Fulfillment of the Old Testament Types (continued)

Contrast Between Aaron's and Melchizedek's Priesthood

Nature of the Order	The Order of Aaron's Levitical Priesthood	The Order of Messiah Jesus' Priesthood (Melchizedek's Priesthood)
Consecration	Temporal and fading	Eternal priesthood Heb. 7.21-23
Priest	Fallible, vulnerable to sin	Sinless and perfect Heb. 7.26
Priesthood	Changeable	Unchangeable priesthood Heb. 7.24
Ministry	Continual offering of sacrifice	Secured an eternal redemption once for all Heb. 9.12, 26
Mediation	Imperfect representation	Perfect representation between God and humankind Heb. 2.14-18
Sacrifice	Unable and insufficient to take the sin of the offenders away	Offered a single sacrifice for sin for all time Heb. 10.11-12
Intercession	Was interrupted by weakness and death	Always lives to make intercession for us Heb. 7.25

Messiah Jesus Fulfills the Levitical Sacrifices and Offerings

The Levitical Offering	How Offering is Fulfilled in Jesus of Nazareth
The Burnt Offering	The perfection of his life Heb. 9.14
The Meal Offering	The dedication and presentation of his life Heb. 5.7; John 4.34
The Peace Offering	He is the peace of our relationships and souls Heb. 4.1-2; Eph. 2.14
The Sin Offering	He bore the penalty for our offense Heb. 10.12; 1 John 2.2
The Trespass Offering	Provision for the offender Heb. 10.20-21; 1 John 1.7

Messiah Jesus: Fulfillment of the Old Testament Types (continued)

Messiah Jesus Fulfills the Levitical Feasts and Festivals

Levitical Feast (Lev. 23)	The Fulfillment in Jesus of Nazareth
The Passover (April)	The death of Jesus Christ 2 Cor. 5.17
Unleavened Bread (April)	Holy and humble walk for Jesus 1 Cor. 5.8
First Fruits (April)	The resurrection of Messiah Jesus 1 Cor. 15.23
The Feast of Pentecost (June)	Outpouring of the Spirit by the Father and the Son Acts 1.5; 2.4
Trumpets (September)	Messiah Jesus' regathering of the Nation Israel Matt. 24.31
The Day of Atonement (September)	Propitiation and cleansing through Jesus Rom. 11.26
Tabernacles (September)	Rest and reunion with Messiah Jesus Zech. 14.16-18

APPENDIX 24

Picking Up on Different Wavelengths
Integrated vs. Fragmented Mindsets and Lifestyles
Dr. Don L. Davis

A Fragmented Mindset and Lifestyle	An Integrated Lifestyle and Mindset
Sees things primarily in relation to one's own needs	Sees all things as one and whole
Sees something other than God as a substitute point of reference and coordination for meaning and truth	Sees God in Christ as the ultimate point of reference and coordination for all meaning and truth
Seeks God's blessing upon one's own personal enhancement	Aligns personal goals with God's ultimate plan and purposes
Understands the purpose of life to experience the greatest level of personal fulfillment and enhancement possible	Understands the purpose of life to make the maximum contribution possible to God's purpose in the world
Only relates to others in connection to their effect upon and place within one's individual personal space	Deeply identifies with all people and things as an integral part of God's great plan for his own glory
Defines theology as seeking to express someone's perspective on some religious idea or concept	Defines theology as seeking to comprehend God's ultimate designs and plans for himself in Jesus Christ
Applications are rooted in seeking right responses to particular issues and situations	Applications are byproducts of understanding what God is doing for himself in the world
Focuses on the style of analysis (to discern the processes and make-up of things)	Focuses on the style of synthesis (to discern the connection and unity of all things)
Seeks to understand biblical revelation primarily from the standpoint of one's private life ("God's plan for my life")	Seeks to understand biblical revelation primarily from the standpoint of God's plan for whole ("God's plan for the ages")
Governed by pressing concerns to ensure one's own security and significance in one's chosen endeavors ("My personal life plan")	Decision making is governed by commitment to participate as co-workers with God in the overall vision ("God's working in the world")
Coordinates itself around personal need as a working paradigm and project	Connects and correlates itself around God's vision and plan as a working paradigm
Sees mission and ministry as the expression of one's personal giftedness and burden, bringing personal satisfaction and security	Sees mission and ministry as the present, practical expression of one's identity vis-a-vis the panoramic vision of God
Relates knowledge, opportunity, and activity to the goals of personal enhancement and fulfillment	Relates knowledge, opportunity, and activity to a single, integrated vision and purpose
All of life is perceived to revolve around the personal identity and needs of the individual	All of life is perceived to revolve around a single theme: the revelation of God in Jesus of Nazareth

Picking Up on Different Wavelengths (continued)

Scriptures on the Validity of Seeing All Things as Unified and Whole

Ps. 27.4 (ESV) - One thing have I asked of the Lord, that will I seek after: that I may dwell in the house of the Lord all the days of my life, to gaze upon the beauty of the Lord and to inquire in his temple.

Luke 10.39-42 (ESV) - And she had a sister called Mary, who sat at the Lord's feet and listened to his teaching. [40] But Martha was distracted with much serving. And she went up to him and said, "Lord, do you not care that my sister has left me to serve alone? Tell her then to help me." [41] But the Lord answered her, "Martha, Martha, you are anxious and troubled about many things, [42] but one thing is necessary. Mary has chosen the good portion, which will not be taken away from her."

Phil. 3.13-14 (ESV) - Brothers, I do not consider that I have made it my own. But one thing I do: forgetting what lies behind and straining forward to what lies ahead [14] I press on toward the goal for the prize of the upward call of God in Christ Jesus.

Ps. 73.25 (ESV) - Whom have I in heaven but you? And there is nothing on earth that I desire besides you.

Mark 8.36 (ESV) - For what does it profit a man to gain the whole world and forfeit his life?

Luke 18.22 (ESV) - When Jesus heard this, he said to him, "One thing you still lack. Sell all that you have and distribute to the poor, and you will have treasure in heaven; and come, follow me."

John 17.3 (ESV) - And this is eternal life, that they know you the only true God, and Jesus Christ whom you have sent.

1 Cor. 13.3 (ESV) - If I give away all I have, and if I deliver up my body to be burned, but have not love, I gain nothing.

Gal. 5.6 (ESV) - For in Christ Jesus neither circumcision nor uncircumcision counts for anything, but only faith working through love.

Col. 2.8-10 (ESV) - See to it that no one takes you captive by philosophy and empty deceit, according to human tradition, according to the elemental spirits of the world, and not according to Christ. [9] For in him the whole fullness of deity dwells bodily, [10] and you have been filled in him, who is the head of all rule and authority.

1 John 5.11-12 (ESV) - And this is the testimony, that God gave us eternal life, and this life is in his Son. [12] Whoever has the Son has life; whoever does not have the Son of God does not have life.

Ps. 16.5 (ESV) - The Lord is my chosen portion and my cup; you hold my lot.

Ps. 16.11 (ESV) - You make known to me the path of life; in your presence there is fullness of joy; at your right hand are pleasures forevermore.

Ps. 17.15 (ESV) - As for me, I shall behold your face in righteousness; when I awake, I shall be satisfied with your likeness.

Eph. 1.9-10 (ESV) - making known to us the mystery of his will, according to his purpose, which he set forth in Christ [10] as a plan for the fullness of time, to unite all things in him, things in heaven and things on earth.

John 15.5 (ESV) - I am the vine; you are the branches. Whoever abides in me and I in him, he it is that bears much fruit, for apart from me you can do nothing.

Ps. 42.1 (ESV) - As a deer pants for flowing streams, so pants my soul for you, O God.

Hab. 3.17-18 (ESV) - Though the fig tree should not blossom, nor fruit be on the vines, the produce of the olive fail and the fields yield no food, the flock be cut off from the fold and there be no herd in the stalls, [18] yet I will rejoice in the Lord; I will take joy in the God of my salvation.

Matt. 10.37 (ESV) - Whoever loves father or mother more than me is not worthy of me, and whoever loves son or daughter more than me is not worthy of me.

Ps. 37.4 (ESV) - Delight yourself in the Lord, and he will give you the desires of your heart.

Ps. 63.3 (ESV) - Because your steadfast love is better than life, my lips will praise you.

Picking Up on Different Wavelengths (continued)

Ps. 89.6 (ESV) - For who in the skies can be compared to the Lord? Who among the heavenly beings is like the Lord

Phil. 3.8 (ESV) - Indeed, I count everything as loss because of the surpassing worth of knowing Christ Jesus my Lord. For his sake I have suffered the loss of all things and count them as rubbish, in order that I may gain Christ

1 John 3.2 (ESV) - Beloved, we are God's children now, and what we will be has not yet appeared; but we know that when he appears we shall be like him, because we shall see him as he is.

Rev. 21.3 (ESV) - And I heard a loud voice from the throne saying, "Behold, the dwelling place of God is with man. He will dwell with them, and they will be his people, and God himself will be with them as their God.

Rev. 21.22-23 (ESV) - And I saw no temple in the city, for its temple is the Lord God the Almighty and the Lamb. [23] And the city has no need of sun or moon to shine on it, for the glory of God gives it light, and its lamp is the Lamb.

Ps. 115.3 (ESV) - Our God is in the heavens; he does all that he pleases.

Jer. 32.17 (ESV) - Ah, Lord God! It is you who has made the heavens and the earth by your great power and by your outstretched arm! Nothing is too hard for you.

Dan. 4.35 (ESV) - all the inhabitants of the earth are accounted as nothing, and he does according to his will among the host of heaven and among the inhabitants of the earth; and none can stay his hand or say to him, "What have you done?"

Eph. 3.20-21 (ESV) - Now to him who is able to do far more abundantly than all that we ask or think, according to the power at work within us, [21] to him be glory in the Church and in Christ Jesus throughout all generations, forever and ever. Amen.

Principles Behind Prophecy
Dr. Don L. Davis

1. Prophecy provides divinely inspired truth about God, his universe, and his will.

   - Who is God and what is the nature of the "real"?

   - What is the truth, and how can we know it?

   - Where did we come from, why are we here, and how shall we act?

2. Prophecy originates and has its source in the Holy Spirit.

   - It is his gift (Rom. 12.6; 1 Cor. 12.10; Eph. 4.8).

   - Prophet = "person of the Spirit," *pneumatikos* (1 Cor. 14.37 and Hos. 9.7)

   - The hope of Moses (Num. 11.16, 29; cf. Luke 10.1)

3. Diverse and various forms of revelation (Jer. 18.18, Law from the priest, counsel from the wise, and word from the prophet).

   - Lived in communities and guilds, some were attached to the temple, while others were priests (cf. 2 Kings 2.3ff.; Ezek. 1.3; Jer. 1.1).

   - Sages and wisdom teachers were "recipients and mediators" of the divine gift (cf. Gen. 41.38; 2 Sam. 14.20; 16.23; 1 Kings 3.9, etc.).

   - Wisdom teacher and prophet both: Daniel.

4. Prophecy not self-authenticating: it must be judged valid.

   - Conflict existed between prophets within both the Old Testament and New Testament (cf. 1 Kings 22; Jer. 23; 28 and 2 Cor. 11.4, 13; 1 John 4.1-3).

   - Prophetic claims must agree with Moses (Deut. 13.1-5) and Jesus (Matt. 7.15; 24.11; 2 Pet. 2.1).

   - If the word comes to pass, it is from the Lord (Deut. 18.15-22).

   - All prophecy is to be examined for its truth value (1 Thess. 5.19-21).

5. The testimony of Jesus is the spirit of prophecy (Rev. 19.10).

   - Prophecy speaks to Messiah's suffering and glory (Luke 24.25-27; 44).

   - The prophetic Scriptures focus on his person and work (John 5.39-40).

   - Apostolic preaching connected him to their message (Acts 3.12-18; 10.43; 13.27; Rom. 3.21-22; 1 Pet. 1.10-12; 2 Pet. 1.19-21).

APPENDIX 26

A Harmony of the Ministry of Jesus

Adapted from Walter M. Dunnett, Exploring the New Testament, p. 14.

Gospel	The Period of Preparation	The Period of Public Ministry		The Period of Suffering	The Period of Triumph
		Opening	Closing		
Matthew	1.1-4.16	4.17-16.20	16.21-26.2	26.3-27.66	28.1-20
Mark	1.1-1.13	1.14-8.30	8.31-13.37	14.1-15.47	16.1-20
Luke	1.1-4.13	4.14-9.21	9.22-21.38	22.1-23.56	24.1-53
John	1.1-34	1.35-6.71	7.1-12.50	13.1-19.42	20.1-21.25

Appearances of the Resurrected Messiah

Dr. Don L. Davis

	Appearance	Scripture
1	Appearance to Mary Magdalene	John 20.11-17; Mark 16.9-11
2	Appearance to the women	Matt. 28.9-10
3	Appearance to Peter	Luke 24.34; 1 Cor. 15.5
4	Appearance to the disciples on the road to Emmaus	Mark 16.12-13; Luke 24.13-35
5	Appearance to the ten disciples, referred to as the "Eleven" (with Thomas absent)	Mark 16.14; Luke 24.36-43; John 20.19-24
6	Appearance to the Eleven with Thomas present one week later	John 20.26-29
7	Appearance to seven disciples by the Sea of Galilee	John 21.1-23
8	Appearance to five hundred	1 Cor. 15.6
9	Appearance to James, the Lord's brother	1 Cor. 15.7
10	Appearance to the eleven disciples on the mountain in Galilee*	Matt. 28.16-20
11	Appearance to his disciples at his ascension on the Mount of Olives*	Luke 24.44-53; Acts 1.3-9
12	Appearance to Stephen prior to his death as the Church's first martyr (witness)	Acts 7.55-56
13	Appearance to Paul on the road to Damascus	Acts 9.3-6; cf. 22.6-11; 26.13-18; 1 Cor. 15.8
14	Appearance to Paul in Arabia	Acts 20.24; 26.17; Gal. 1.12,17
15	Appearance to Paul in the Temple	Acts 22.17-21; cf. 9.26-30; Gal. 1.18
16	Appearance to Paul in prison in Caesarea	Acts 23.11
17	Appearance to John during his exile in Patmos	Rev. 1.12-20

* Items 10 and 11 describe the events commonly referred to as "The Great Commission" and "The Ascension," respectively.

APPENDIX 28
General Facts Concerning the New Testament

A Comparative Chart of the Four Gospels

Robert H. Gundry. A Survey of the New Testament. Grand Rapids: Zondervan, 1981.

	Probable Date of Writing	Probable Place of Writing	First Intended Audience	Theme and Focus
Mark	50's	Rome	Gentiles in Rome	Jesus' redemptive activity
Matthew	50's or 60's	Antioch in Syria	Jews in Palestine	Jesus the Jewish Messiah, and the disciples as the new people of God
Luke	60's	Rome	Interested Gentile seekers	The historical certainty of the Gospel account
John	80's or 90's	Ephesus	General Population in Asia Minor	Believing in Jesus as the Messiah for eternal life

Old Testament Apocrypha

Walter A. Elwell and Robert W. Yarbrough. Encountering the New Testament. Grand Rapids: Baker Books, 1998.

Roman Catholics and some Eastern Orthodox churches recognize the writings listed below as Scripture. Protestants acknowledge their literary value and historical significance but do not view them as possessing spiritual authority		
Additions to Esther Baruch Bel and the Dragon Ecclesiasticus (Wisdom of Jesus Son of Sirach) 1 Esdras 2 Esdras	Judith Letter of Jeremiah 1 Maccabees 2 Maccabees 3 Maccabees 4 Maccabees Prayer of Azariah	Prayer of Mannasseh Psalm 151 Song of the Three Jews Susanna Tobit Wisdom of Solomon

General Facts Concerning the New Testament (continued)

General Facts about the New Testament

1. The NT is the testament of God's saving work in more recent times and announces the Savior that the OT awaits.

2. The NT contains 27 books, four dealing with Jesus' life and ministry called *Gospels*, one dealing with history of the Church, Acts, and 21 *Epistles* or letters, and one book of *prophecy*.

3. The collection of books in the NT comprise the *canon*, an authorized collection that came together over 3 centuries.

4. NT manuscripts were first written on papyrus (a paper made from reeds, and then on leather). Nearly 300 others are written on *uncials*, in capital letters, usually on leather. *Minuscules* represent the largest group and display a kind of cursive writing that developed in *Byzantium* around the ninth century. *Lectionaries*, books used in Church worship, include portions of Scripture as well.

5. The NT is reliable because of 1) the extensive evidence supporting it; 2) the authors wrote them within the first generation or two of Christian history, and 3) ancient versions were widely distributed.

6. The personal tone of the NT is seen in the fact that of the 27 books, 24 are personal letters, and 3 are personalized accounts of the life and work of Christ.

7. The Apocrypha includes 14 *non-canonical* books written between 200 B.C. and A.D. 100.

8. Jesus was seen as a threat by the Jews because he made controversial claims about himself and took liberties with Jewish customs.

9. Jesus appeared at a time when the traditions of Judaism dictated much of Jewish life and practice. A knowledge of these customs can greatly aid our understanding of the NT.

APPENDIX 29

Portrayals of Jesus in the New Testament Books

*Adapted from John Stott, **The Incomparable Christ***

The Thirteen Letters of Paul				
Approximate Date of Writing	Period	Group	Letters	How Messiah is Presented
48-49	End of 1st missionary journey	A polemical letter	Galatians	Christ the Liberator
50-52	During 2nd missionary journey	The early letters	1 and 2 Thessalonians	Christ the Coming Judge
53-57	During 3rd missionary journey	The major letters	Romans, 1 and 2 Corinthians	Christ the Savior
60-62	During 1st imprisonment in Rome	The prison letters	Colossians, Philemon, Ephesians, and Philippians	Christ the Supreme Lord
62-67	During release and 2nd imprisonment	The pastoral letters	1 and 2 Timothy and Titus	Christ the Head of the Church
General Epistles and Revelation				
Before 70	During the Pauline and Petrine ministry	Epistle to believing Jews	Hebrews	Christ our Great High Priest
45-50	First book of the NT to be written	General epistles	James	Christ our Teacher
64-67	Early period of persecution	General epistles	1 and 2 Peter	Christ our Exemplary Sufferer
90-100	Toward end of Apostle's ministry	General epistles	1, 2, and 3 John	Christ our Life
66-69	Threat and rise of early apostasy	General epistles	Jude	Christ our Advocate
95	Written while in exile	Prophecy	Revelation	King of kings and Lord of lords

APPENDIX 30

Readings on the New Testament's Historical Credibility

The Historical Accounts of Yeshua: Truth or Fiction?

> ➤ *Verses taken from David H. Stern, **The Complete Jewish Bible***

Luke 1.1-4 - Dear Theophilos: concerning the matters that have taken place among us, many people have undertaken to draw up accounts based on what was handed down to us by those who from the start were eyewitnesses and proclaimers of the message. Therefore, Your Excellency, since *I have carefully investigated all these things from the beginning, it seemed good to me that I too should write you an accurate and ordered narrative*, so that you might know how well-founded are the things about which you have been taught.

John 20.30-31 - In the presence of the talmidim, Yeshua performed many other miracles which have not been recorded in this book. *But these which have been recorded are here so that you may trust that Yeshua is the Messiah*, the Son of God, and that by this trust you have life because of who he is.

John 21.24-25 - This one is the talmid who is testifying about these things and who has recorded them. And *we know that his testimony is true*. But there are also many other things Yeshua did; and if they were all to be recorded, I don't think the whole world could contain the books that would have to be written!

The Modern Critical View I: What Is the Historical Credibility of the New Testament?

> ➤ *Howard Clark Kee. **Understanding the New Testament**. Englewood Cliffs, NJ: Prentice-Hall, 1983. p. 9.*

Once it is acknowledged that there are differences of outlook within the New Testament and that there are discrepancies within the narrative accounts, *many feel that the credibility of the New Testament as a historical document is compromised or even denied*. Candor requires us to acknowledge, no matter what our point of view, that the New Testament writings record events that occurred at least a generation before they were written down.

When we add to this the New Testament's own description of the disciples as illiterate (Acts 4.13), we must acknowledge that *there was a crucial stage of oral transmission of the Jesus tradition before the Gospels were produced as we have them.* The differences that are evident among them are in some cases not matters of great consequence–such as whether the family of Jesus lived originally in Bethlehem (Matt. 2) or whether they were only temporarily there, but resided in Nazareth (Luke 2). Nevertheless, a serious effort to understand the NT must come to terms with these differences and seek to account for them.

Readings on the Historical Credibility of the New Testament (continued)

The Modern Critical View II: Are the Accounts of Jesus' Passion Propaganda?

We must also call into question whether it is appropriate for us to impose our supposed standards of historical objectivity on documents like the NT. As John 20.31 puts it, he has reported the story of Jesus' spectacular acts ("signs") in order "that you may believe that Jesus is the Christ, the Son of the Living God." Clearly not all his readers are going to share his conclusions, but he is forthright in telling his readers his aims. And those aims are not objective reporting. *Using the term in its root sense, of a means of propagating a point of view or belief, the New Testament is not objective history, but propaganda.* But then history in any time and culture is always event plus interpretation; it is never merely objective, in the sense of lacking a framework of interpretation or point of view. *What is required is to be aware of the writer's assumptions, the aims of the writings, what its vocabulary, style, and conceptual language presuppose.*

◄ Howard Clark Kee. Understanding the New Testament. Englewood Cliffs, NJ: Prentice-Hall, 1983. p. 9.

The Modern Critical View III: Did Community Needs Dictate the Message?

Jesus of Nazareth is the historical base for the Christian claim to be the community of the new covenant. Yet, as we have observed, our documentary evidence about him was written long after his death, probably in the last half of the first century. *Our records are a series of responses to Jesus by those who saw in him the agent of God, not the reports of detached observers.* In the process of analyzing these documents of faith we learn about Jesus, but we also learn about *the communities in which the tradition about him was treasured and transmitted.*

◄ Howard Clark Kee. Understanding the New Testament. Englewood Cliffs, NJ: Prentice-Hall, 1983. p. 78, 121.

The death of Christ was itself identified with the Passover in *the Pauline churches* (1 Cor. 5.7); and *in Johannine circles* [that is, in the churches of John], Jesus was regarded as the Lamb of God (John 1.29; Rev. 5). . . . But just Mark was content to affirm only that the death of Jesus was necessary, without explaining why or how, so he simply states that Jesus' death is in behalf of others. This is what *the community of Mark* celebrates in the communion, while looking forward to the completion of the number of the elect in the new age.

APPENDIX 31

Suffering: The Cost of Discipleship and Servant-Leadership

Don L. Davis

To be a disciple is to bear the stigma and reproach of the one who called you into service (2 Tim. 3.12). Practically, this may mean the loss of comfort, convenience, and even life itself (John 12.24-25).

All of Christ's Apostles endured insults, rebukes, lashes, and rejections by the enemies of their Master. Each of them sealed their doctrines with their blood in exile, torture, and martyrdom. Listed below are the fates of the Apostles according to traditional accounts.

- Matthew suffered martyrdom by being slain with a sword at a distant city of Ethiopia.

- Mark expired at Alexandria, after being cruelly dragged through the streets of that city.

- Luke was hanged upon an olive tree in the classic land of Greece.

- John was put in a caldron of boiling oil, but escaped death in a miraculous manner, and was afterward branded at Patmos.

- Peter was crucified at Rome with his head downward.

- James, the Greater, was beheaded at Jerusalem.

- James, the Less, was thrown from a lofty pinnacle of the temple, and then beaten to death with a fuller's club.

- Bartholomew was flayed alive.

- Andrew was bound to a cross, whence he preached to his persecutors until he died.

- Thomas was run through the body with a lance at Coromandel in the East Indies.

- Jude was shot to death with arrows.

- Matthias was first stoned and then beheaded.

- Barnabas of the Gentiles was stoned to death at Salonica.

- Paul, after various tortures and persecutions, was at length beheaded at Rome by the Emperor Nero.

APPENDIX 32

Biblical Justification for the Resurrection of Messiah Jesus
Dr. Don L. Davis

	Reasons for His Resurrection	Scriptural Text
1	To fulfill the prophecy of Holy Scripture	Ps. 16.9-10; 22.22; 118.22-24
2	To demonstrate his true identity	Acts 2.24; Rom. 1.1-4
3	To realize the promise of the Davidic covenant	2 Sam. 7.12-16; Ps. 89.20-37; Isa. 9.6-7; Luke 1.31-33; Acts 2.25-31
4	To become the source of eternal life for all who believe in him	John 10.10-11; 11.25-26; Eph. 2.6; Col. 3.1-4; 1 John 5.11-12
5	To become the source of resurrection power to others	Matt. 28.18; Eph. 1.19-21; Phil. 4.13
6	To be exalted as head over the Church	Eph. 1.20-23
7	To demonstrate that God's imputation of our righteousness has been made complete	Rom. 4.25
8	To reign until all enemies have been placed under his feet	1 Cor. 15.20-28
9	To become the first fruits of the future resurrection	1 Cor. 15.20-23
10	To assert the authority given to him by God to take his life back again	John 10.18

APPENDIX 3 3

Toward a Hermeneutic of Critical Engagement

Rev. Dr. Don L. Davis

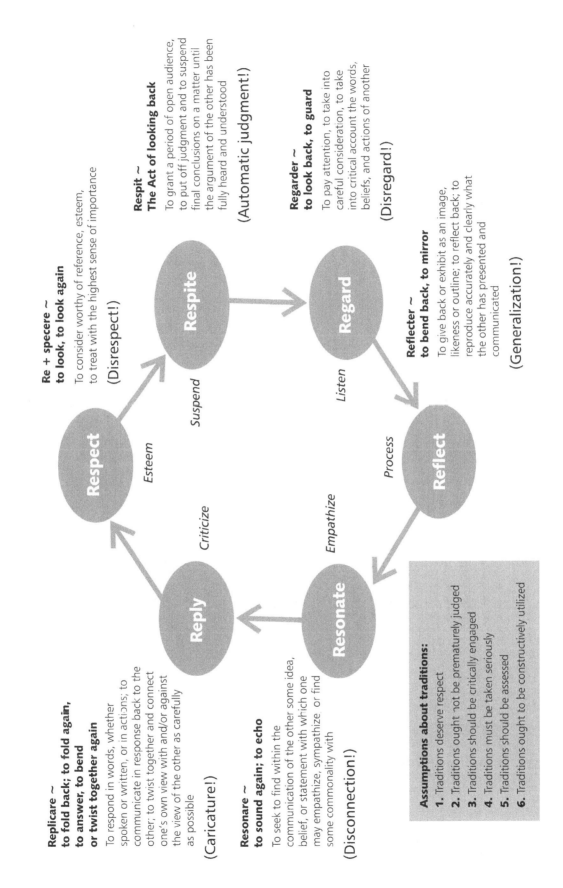

Respit ~
The Act of looking back

To grant a period of open audience, to put off judgment and to suspend final conclusions on a matter until the argument of the other has been fully heard and understood

(Automatic judgment!)

Regarder ~
to look back, to guard

To pay attention, to take into careful consideration, to take into critical account the words, beliefs, and actions of another

(Disregard!)

Re + specere ~
to look, to look again

To consider worthy of reference, esteem, to treat with the highest sense of importance

(Disrespect!)

Reflecter ~
to bend back, to mirror

To give back or exhibit as an image, likeness or outline; to reflect back; to reproduce accurately and clearly what the other has presented and communicated

(Generalization!)

Respect — Esteem — **Respite** — Suspend — **Regard** — Listen — **Reflect** — Process

Replicare ~
to fold back; to fold again,
to answer, to bend
or twist together again

To respond in words, whether spoken or written, or in actions; to communicate in response back to the other; to twist together and connect one's own view with and/or against the view of the other as carefully as possible

(Caricature!)

Resonare ~
to sound again; to echo

To seek to find within the communication of the other some idea, belief, or statement with which one may empathize, sympathize or find some commonality with

(Disconnection!)

Reply — Criticize — **Resonate** — Empathize

Assumptions about traditions:

1. Traditions deserve respect
2. Traditions ought not be prematurely judged
3. Traditions should be critically engaged
4. Traditions must be taken seriously
5. Traditions should be assessed
6. Traditions ought to be constructively utilized

APPENDIX 34

Chart of Biblical Studies

Rev. Dr. Don L. Davis

Type of Criticism	The Task in Bible Study	What is Studied	View of the Bible	Proof Level	Strengths	Weaknesses	Level of Criticism
Form Criticism	Trace the oral traditions and earliest stories associated with the texts	Oral traditions of the people of God, along with the early Church	Product of human tradition	Low	Evolving sense of the Bible's origin	Too speculative	Higher
Source Criticism	Discover the written sources used in the creation of the books	Comparing texts in various books to see similarities and contrasts	Product of human ingenuity	Low	Ability to identify key sources	No way to prove its claims	Higher
Linguistic Criticism	Study the ancient languages, words and grammar	Study of the ancient Hebrew, koine Greek, and Aramaic	Product of human culture	Mid	In-depth meaning of ancient language	Too far removed from the language	Lower
Textual Criticism	Compare the variant manuscripts to find the best reading	Focus on different manuscripts and their families of texts	Product of textual research	High	Multitude of reliable manuscripts available	Far tco extensive number	Lower
Literary Criticism	Determine the author, style, recipient, and genre	Different types of literature, background study on the books	Product of literary genius	High	Discovering what types of literature mean	We tend to read too much into it	Higher

Chart of Biblical Studies (continued)

Type of Criticism	The Task in Bible Study	What is Studied	View of the Bible	Proof Level	Strengths	Weaknesses	Level of Criticism
Canonical Criticism	Analyze the Church's acceptance, view and use of the text	History of the Bible in ancient Israel and the early Church (councils, conventions)	Product of religious community	High	Taking the community's view of the Bible seriously	Tends to make the Bible merely a group book	Higher
Redaction Criticism	Focus on the theology of the person who wrote it	Intense study of individual books to understand the meaning of the author's theme and views	Product of creative personality	Mid	Deep analysis of an author's entire collection of writings	Does not correlate the Bible with other books	Higher
Historical Criticism	Investigate the historical setting, culture, and background	Research of the ancient cultures, their customs, and their history	Product of historical forces	Mid	Firmer grasp of historical issues of the text	Too far removed from the history	Higher
Translation Studies	Provide a clear, readable translation based on the best manuscripts	Understanding of the receiving culture's language along with the meanings of the text for the best translation	Product of dynamic interpretation	Mid	Pursuing a version of the Bible in one's own tongue and thought world	Reflects our own opinions about the text's meaning	Lower

APPENDIX 35

The Life of Christ according to Seasons and Years

Adapted from Ray E. Baughman, The Life of Christ Visualized

(watermark across table: B.C. — A.D. 26 / 27)

Key Events - Spring	M	M	L	J
Birth at Bethlehem, shepherds, angels			2.1-20	1.14
Adoration of Simeon, Anna, wise men	2.1-12		2.31-38	
Bethlehem babies killed	2.16-18			
Into Egypt (Flight of Joseph, Mary, and Jesus)	2.13-15			
Egyptian exile ended, settled in Nazareth	2.19-23		2.39-40	
Search for Jesus (12 years old, visit to Jerusalem)			2.41-52	
Cana, changing water into wine (first miracle)				2.1-11
Capernaum (first sojourn at future home)				2.12
Belligerent rejection (1st), at Nazareth			4.16-31	
Large catch of fish, call of disciples (Galilee)	4.18-22	1.16-17	5.1-11	
Demoniac healed (Capernaum)	8.14-17	1.21-22	4.31-37	
Peter's mother-in-law healed (Capernaum)	4.23-25	1.29-30; 1.35-36	4.38-44	
Galilean Tour (2nd) with four disciples				
Leper healed (sent to Jerusalem)	8.2-4	1.40-41	5.12-16	
Roof opened for sick man (Capernaum)	9.1-8	2.1-2	5.17-26	
Call of Matthew, his party (Capernaum)	9.9-17	2.13-14	5.27-39	

Key Events - Summer	M	M	L	J
First Passover during ministry (Jerusalem)				2.13
First cleansing of the Temple (Jerusalem)				2.14ff.
Nicodemus' interview (Jerusalem)				3.1-21
Judean ministry of John and Jesus				3.22-26
Jesus leaves Judea as John is imprisoned (Machearus)	4.12	1.14	3.19-20	4.1-4
Impotent man at the pool (Jerusalem)				5.1-47
Disciples pluck grain (Galilee)	12.1-8	2.23ff.	6.1-5	
Man with withered hand (Capernaum)	12.9ff.	3.1-12	6.6-11	
Jesus chooses twelve apostles (Galilee)		3.13ff.	6.12ff.	
Sermon on the Mount (horns of Hattin)	5.1-8.1		6.17ff.	
Centurion's servant healed (Capernaum)	8.5-13		7.1-10	
Widow's son raised (Nain)			7.11ff.	
John's disciples inquire of Jesus (Galilee)	11.2ff.		7.18ff.	
First anointing of Jesus' feet (Capernaum)			7.36ff.	
Galilean tour (3rd) with disciples			8.1-3	
Demon possessed, blind-dumb man healed (Capernaum?)	12.22-23	3.20ff.		
Beelzebub charged against Jesus	12.46-47	3.21, 32-35		
Friends and family believe he is insane			8.18-21	

Key Events - Fall	M	M	L	J
Baptism of Jesus (Jordan River)	3.13-17	1.9-11	3.21-23	
Temptation (Wilderness of Judea)	4.1-11	1.12-13	4.1-13	
Testimony of John the Baptist				1.15-34
Jesus' first five disciples (Jordan)				1.35-31
Woman at the well (Sychar)				4.5-42
Noble man's son made well (Jesus at Cana and son at Capernaum)				4.43-54
Jesus preaches in synagogues of Galilee, is well received (first Galilean tour)		1.14-15	4.14ff.	
Kingdom of heaven parables by the sea (Capernaum)	13.1-53	4.1-34	8.4-18	
Stilling the sea and the wind	8.18ff.	4.35-41	8.22-25	
Demoniac in graveyard, swine into the sea (Gadarenes)	8.28-34	5.1-20		
Crossing back over the sea to Capernaum and four miracles: Jairus' daughter raised, woman touches Messiah's garment	9.18-26	5.21-43	8.40-56	
Two blind men and dumb demoniac healed	9.27-34			

The Life of Christ according to Seasons and Years (continued)

Key Events - Spring	M	M	L	J
- Second rejection at Nazareth	13.54-58	6.1-6		
- Twelve sent forth (4th Galilean tour)	9.35-11.1	6.6-13	9.1-6	
- John the Baptist's death (Machaerus)	14.1-12	6.14ff.	9.7-9	
- Teaching in Perea, warned about Herod			13.22-23	10.40-42
- Healing of man on Sabbath			14.1-2 14.7ff.	
- Parables on humility, rewards, excuses, discipleship			15.1ff.	
- Lost sheep, coin, son			16.19-20	
- Rich man and Lazarus				11.1-2
- Raising of Lazarus (Bethany)				11.45-54
- Conspiring to kill Jesus			17.11-12	
- Ten lepers healed (Samaria)			18.1-17	
- Answered prayer, divorce, little children, rich young ruler	19.1-15 19.16ff.	10.1-2 10.17-31	18.18-19	
- Foretold death and resurrection	20.17-18	10.32-45	18.31-32	
- Blind men of Jericho	20.29-30	10.46-52	18.35-36	
- Zacchaeus's transformation			19.1ff.	
- Last stop, 2nd anointing	26.6-7	14.3-9		11.55-12.8

Key Events - Summer	M	M	L	J
- Feeding of the 5,000 (Sea of Galilee)	14.13ff.	6.33-31	9.10-11	6.1-2
- Walking on water, Bread of Life discourse				6.16ff.
- Eating with unwashed hands (Capernaum)	15.1-2	7.1ff.		
- Daughter of Syrophonecian healed (Phonecia)	15.21ff.	7.24-25		
- Deaf and dumb man healed		7.31-32		
- Feeding of the 4,000 (Decapolis)	15.29-30	8.1-9		
- Pharisees and Sadducees seek a sign	15.39-40	8.10-11		
- Warning against false teaching	16.5-6	8.13-14 8.22ff.		
- Blind man healed at Bethsaida		8.22ff.		
- Peter's good confession (Caesarea Philippi)	16.13-14	8.27-28	9.18ff.	
- Foretelling death, resurrection, second coming	16.21-22	8.31-32	9.22ff.	
- Transfiguration (Mount Hermon)	17.1ff.	9.2-13	9.28ff.	
- Demon possessed boy healed	17.14-15	9.4ff.	9.37ff.	
- Foretells death and resurrection (to Galilee)	17.22-23	9.30ff.	9.43-44	
- Coin in fish's mouth (Capernaum)	17.24-25			
- Instructions to disciples	18.1ff.	9.33-34	9.46-47	
- Sunday - Triumphal Entry	21.1-11	11.1-11	19.29-44	12.12-19
- Monday - Second cleansing of the Temple	21.12-22	11.2-26	19.45-48	12.20-50
- Tuesday - Jesus challenged, Olivet Discourse	21.23-26.16	11.27-1.11	20.1-22.6	
- Wednesday				
- Thursday - Passover supper, Upper Room Discourse, Gethsemane, Arrest	26.17-56	14.12-52	22.7-53	13.1-18.12
- Friday - Trial, crucifixion, burial	26.57-27.66	12.53-15.47	22.54-23.56	18.12-19.42
- Saturday - in the tomb				

Key Events - Fall	M	M	L	J
- Tabernacle Feast (Jerusalem)				7.1-8.1
- Adulterous woman				8.2-11
- Light of the world				8.12-59
- Man born blind healed				9.1-41
- Good shepherd discourse				10.1-21
- Seventy sent out (Judea)			10.1-24	
- Good Samaritan			10.25-37	
- Supper at Mary and Martha's (Bethany)	10.1-42		10.38-42	
- Disciples taught to pray			11.1-13	
- Accused of tie with Beelzebub, demoniac healed			11.14-36	
- Eating with Pharisee			11.37-54	
- Hypocrisy denounced (Judea)			12.1-13.9	
- Parables on service				
- Healing of a crippled woman			13.10-21	
- Feast of Dedication (Jerusalem)				10.22-23
- Earthquake as angel rolls away the stone	28.1-4			
- Women visit tomb	28.5-8	16.1-8	24.1-8	20.1-2
- Peter and John visit tomb			24.9-12	20.2-3
- Jesus appears to Mary Magdalene (Jerusalem)		16.9-11		20.11-18
- Jesus appears to other women	28.9-10			
- Guards report to rulers	28.11-15			
- Jesus appears to disciples on road to Emmaus (& Simon)		16.12-13	24.13-35	
- Jesus appears to 10 disciples			24.36-43	20.19-25
- Jesus appears to all, w/Thomas		16.14		20.26-31
- Jesus appears to 7 disciples by the sea of Galilee (second miracle of the fish)				21.1-25
- Jesus appears to 500 disciples (cf. 1 Cor. 15.5-7)	28.16-20	16.15-18	24.44-53	
- The Ascension (Acts 1.9-12)		16.19-20		

APPENDIX 36

An Example of the Practice of Textual Criticism

Adapted from R. C. Briggs, **Interpreting the New Testament Today.**

Mark 1.1 The beginning of the Gospel of Jesus Christ, *(the Son of God)*

According to the critical apparatus, the following manuscripts (or group of manuscripts) read

Ιησοῦ Χριστοῦ υἱού θεοῦ

A (*Codex Alexandrinus*). Fifth century. Byzantine text (in the Gospels).

B (*Codex Vaticanus*). Fourth century. Alexandrian text (in the Gospels and Acts).

D (*Codex Bezae*). Fifth or sixth century. Western text.

W (*Washington Codex*). Fifth century. Western text (in Mark 1.1-5.30).

'Ω (*koine*). Group of late uncial and minuscule manuscripts dating from the seventh century. Western text.

λ (*Family 1, Lake Group*). Twelfth century and later. Akin to fourth- and fifth-century Caesarean text.

φ (*Family 13, Ferrar Group*). Twelfth century and later. Akin to Caesarean text.

it (*Itala or Old Latin*). Eleventh century and later. Text is early Western (prior to date of Vulgate).

vg (*Vulgate*). Authorized Latin translation, completed by Jerome in A. D. 405 (Gospels A. D. 385). Western text.

sy[P] (*Peshitta*). Authorized fifth-century Syriac translation. Akin to the Byzantine text (in the Gospels).

sa (*Sahidic*). Fourth-century Coptic (Egyptian) translation. Alexandrian text, with Western influence.

bo (*Bohairic*). Coptic translation, later than Sahidic. Western text. The critical apparatus also lists two significant manuscripts which preserve the shorter reading.

S also designated ~ (*Codex Sinaiticus*). Fourth century. Like B, a primary representative of the Alexandrian text.

Θ (*Codex Koridethi*). Ninth century. Text akin to third- and fourth-century Alexandrian text.

APPENDIX 37

Typology Readings

Rev. Dr. Don L. Davis

The Study of Types Critical to New Testament Mastery

➢ *Ada R. Habershon,*
***Study of the Types**.*
Grand Rapids: Kregel
Publishing, (1957) 1974.
pp. 19, 21

There are many passages in the New Testament which we cannot understand without having become in some measure familiar with the types. The epistle to the Hebrews is almost entirely made up of references to the Old Testament: as the substance, Christ, is proved to be better than the shadows–better than Moses, than Joshua, than Abraham, than Aaron, than the first Tabernacle, than the Levitical sacrifices, than the whole cloud of witnesses in the picture gallery of faith; and lastly, his blood is proved to be better than the blood of Abel.

We sometimes forget that the writers of the New Testament were *students of the Old Testament*; that it was *their Bible*, and that they would naturally allude again and again to the types and shadows, expecting their readers also to be familiar with them. *If we fail to see these allusions, we lose much of the beauty of the passage, and cannot rightly understand it. . . .*

[The study of types] gives us a sure antidote for the poison of the so-called "higher criticism." If we acknowledge the Divine intention of every detail of the types, even though we may not understand all their teaching, and if we believe there is a lesson in every incident recorded, the attacks of modern criticism will not harm us. We may not be clear enough to understand what the critics say, or to answer their criticisms; but *if our eyes have been opened to see the beauty of the types, the doubts which such writers suggest will not trouble us, and we shall have a more profitable occupation than reading their works.* When so much of this destructive criticism is about, we cannot do better than urge all–even the youngest Christians–to take up the typical study of God's Word; for though *he has hid these things from the wise and prudent, he reveals them unto babes.*

Do We Presently Study the Bible in the Same Way and with the Same Methods as the Lord and the Apostles?

➢ *James DeYoung and*
Sarah Hurty, ***Beyond***
***the Obvious**. Gresham,*
OR: Vision House
Publishing, 1995. p. 24

After more than twenty years of teaching the grammatical-historical hermeneutic, I can see only one problem with it: it doesn't appear to be the way the biblical writers always did it! When we examine how the biblical writers used previously written Scripture, we see that they seemed to "discover" meaning there that, judged by its

Typology Readings (continued)

original context, can hardly be imagined to have been in the mind of the original author. This problem is especially evident in the way the New Testament authors used Old Testament passages to prove that Jesus Christ fulfilled prophecy (or to make some theological point.)

Can or Should We Reproduce the Exegesis of the New Testament?

To the question whether we can reproduce the exegesis of the New Testament, S. L. Johnson answers: "Unhesitatingly the reply is yes, although we are not allowed to claim for our results the infallibility of the Lord and his Apostles. They are reliable teachers of biblical doctrine and they are reliable teachers of hermeneutics and exegesis. We not only can reproduce their exegetical methodology, we must if we are to be taught their understanding of the Scriptures."

*◄ James DeYoung and Sarah Hurty, **Beyond the Obvious**. p. 265*

What of Typology as a Valid, Important Method of Bible Interpretation?

[Typology] is a genuine approach widely practiced in the New Testament. For example, the furniture of the tabernacle and other matters associated with it and the temple (the altar and sacrifices, the veil, the golden cover of the ark of the covenant) are all types of Christ and of the heavenly realm (see Heb. 9). When we come to typology, we must avoid being too broad or too narrow in our interpretation. We can be too broad if we find typology everywhere. We can be too narrow if we reject typology as an exegetical method on the basis of the claim that it is not consistent with a literal meaning which embraces on meaning, found by means of grammatical-historical study. . . .

*◄ James DeYoung and Sarah Hurty, **Beyond the Obvious**. p. 74*

Yet we believe that typology is not to be divorced from exegesis, even though it cannot be fully "regulated hermeneutically, but takes place in the freedom of the Holy Spirit." It very much involves a deeper meaning and was readily practiced by the Bible in its exegetical method (see 1 Cor. 10; Rom. 5).

Diverse Usages of the Term *Typos* in the New Testament

➤ *Patrick Fairbairn,*
Typology of Scripture.
Grand Rapids: Kregel
Publishing. p. 42

The language of Scripture being essentially popular, its use of particular terms naturally partakes of the freedom and variety which are wont to appear in the current speech of a people; and it rarely if ever happens that words are employed, in respect to topics requiring theological treatment, with such precision and uniformity as to enable us, from this source alone, to attain to proper accuracy and fullness.

The word type (*typos*) forms no exception to this usage.

- Occurring once, at least, in the natural sense of *mark* or *impress* made by a hard substance on one of softer material (John 20.25)

- It commonly bears the general import of *model*, *pattern*, or *exemplar*, but with such a wide diversity of application as to comprehend a material object of worship, or idol (Acts 7.43)

- An *external framework* constructed for the service of God (Acts 7.44; Heb. 8.5)

- The *form* or *copy* of an epistle (Acts 23.25)

- A *method of doctrinal instruction* delivered by the first heralds and teachers of the Gospel (Rom. 7.17)

- A *representative character*, or, in certain respects, normal example (Rom. 5.14; 1 Cor. 10.11; Phil. 3.17; 1 Thess. 1.7; 1 Pet. 5.3)

Such in the New Testament Scriptures is the diversified use of the word *type* (disguised, however, under other terms in the authorized version).

Extreme Misuse of Typology is Very Possible

➤ *J. Sidlow Baxter,*
The Strategic Grasp
of the Bible.

We marvel with peculiar awe at the ability and agility which some well-meaning brethren display in seeing what is not there; as also we marvel, with a sense of our denseness, at the super-spirituality which they evince in aerifying the most unsuspicious details of Scripture into rare spiritual significances.

The "three white baskets" which Pharaoh's ill-fated baker dreamed were on his head are to ourselves part of a true story; but to see in those same three basket recondite

Typology Readings (continued)

bearings upon the doctrine of the Trinity makes one part of our mind laugh and another part groan. We feel the same sort of reaction when we are assured that the bride's hair in the Song of Solomon is the mass of the nations converted to Christianity.

It is an eye-opener to learn that the "two pence" which the Good Samaritan gave to the innkeeper were covertly Baptism and the Lord's Supper. We cannot but feel sorry for Matthew, Mark, Luke and John, when another ministerial victim of typomania tells us the "four barrels" of water which Elijah commanded to be poured over the altar on Mount Carmel were the four Gospel writers.

As for the clergyman who would persuade us the boat in which our Lord crossed Galilee is the Church of England, while the "other little ships" which accompanied it were the other denominations, we cannot shake off a sly idea that the novel expositor himself, like the boats, must have been all "at sea." We feel just the same about Pope Gregory the Great's exposition of Job, in which Job's verbose "friends" typify heretics; and his seven sons the twelve Apostles; his seven thousand sheep God's faithful people and his three thousand hump-backed camels the depraved Gentiles!"

The Three Errors of Typology to Avoid

There are three dangers, however, which must be avoided:

- Limiting the type, and therefore not using it

- Exaggerating the type, and therefore overusing it

- Imagining the type, and therefore misusing it

The Case Against the "Older View" of Typology

The case against typology:

- Concerned only with finding "prefigurations" of Christ all over the Old Testament

- God ordained Old Testament events, institutions, and/or persons for the primary purpose of foreshadowing Christ.

◅ J. Boyd Nicholson from the foreword to *Harvest Festivals.*

◅ Christopher J. H. Wright, *Knowing Jesus through the Old Testament.. Downers Grove: InterVarsity Press, 1992. pp. 115-116*

Two bad results of this old hermeneutic:

- No need to find much reality and meaning in the events and persons themselves (Old Testament becomes nothing more than a collection of shadows)

- Interpreted every obscure detail of Old Testament "type" as a foreshadowing of Jesus (hermeneutics becomes magic, like pulling a rabbit out of a hat)

Conclusion: typology is not *the* way of interpreting the Old Testament for itself. "But when we go back and read the whole of Psalm 2, Isaiah 42 and Genesis 22, it is equally true that they have enormous depths of truth and meaning for us to explore which are not *directly* related to Jesus himself. Typology is a way of helping us understand Jesus in the light of the Old Testament. It is not the exclusive way to understand the full meaning of the Old Testament itself" (Wright, 116).

Rebutting Wright's Claims

- Jesus used typology (e.g., the brazen serpent, manna in the wilderness, the Temple of his body, the Good Shepherd, etc.)

- The Apostles and early Christian interpreters used typology as their normal way of reading the Old Testament (e.g., Moses' striking the Rock, the wilderness journey of the nation of Israel, Jesus as the second Israel, etc.)

- The Bible refers to itself in this way (e.g., the Book of Hebrews, the Tabernacle, the priesthood, etc.)

The question: Should we use the Old Testament as Jesus and the Apostles did, with some reference to *typology*?

The Christological Hermeneutic: Messiah Jesus Connects the Testaments

➤ *Norman Geisler, To Understand the Bible Look for Jesus. (1979) 2002. p. 68*

Christ at once sums up in himself the *perfection of the Old Testament precepts*, the *substance of Old Testament shadows and types*, and the *fulfillment of Old Testament forecasts*. Those truths about him which bud forth in the Old Testament come into

Typology Readings (continued)

full bloom in the New Testament; the flashlight of prophetic truth turns into the floodlight of divine revelation.

The Old Testament foreshadows find their fulfillment in the New Testament in several ways: (1) The *moral precepts* of the Old Testament become fulfilled or perfected in the life and teachings of Christ. (2) The *ceremonial* and *typical* truths were only shadows of the true substance to be found in Christ. (3) The *Messianic prophecies* foretold in the Old Testament were finally fulfilled in the history of the New Testament. In each of these relationships it can be seen that the Testaments are inseparably connected. The New is not only supplementary to the Old but it is the necessary complement to it.

As the book of Hebrews puts it, "God had foreseen something better for us, that apart from us they [Old Testament believers] should not be made perfect" (Heb. 11.40). For what was contained in the Old Testament is fully explained only in the New Testament.

The Way Paul and the Apostles Read Scripture

As can be clearly seen, the hermeneutical procedure which Paul and the other New Testament authors use to interpret the Law in a spiritual sense is allegorical, in that a meaning other than the literal or immediate sense is perceived from the given text. The usual term which Paul employs to define the relationship between the two levels of meaning is *typos* = form, figure, symbol, or prefiguration (Rom. 5.14; 1 Cor. 10.6, etc.); but in Galatians 4.24, where he presents the sons of Hagar and Sarah as prefigurations of the Jews and Christians, he says 'Now this is an allegory (*allegoroumena*), showing that he regarded 'typos' as synonymous with 'allegory.'

In deference to Paul's terminology, modern scholars call this kind of interpretation - which, as we shall see, enjoyed immense success and became the authentic Christian way of reading the Old Testament - 'typology' or 'typological interpretation.' In antiquity [i.e., in olden times] it was called 'spiritual' or 'mystical.'

It was rooted in the firm conviction that the old Law was consistently directed towards the great Christ-event, and that, as a result, it would give up its true significance only to those who interpreted it in Christological terms.

◄ *Manlo Simonetti, Biblical Interpretation in the Early Church. p. 11-12*

APPENDIX 38
Readings on Messianic Prophecy
Rev. Dr. Don L. Davis

Rudolph Bultmann and the Predictions of Passion and Resurrection

➤ Rudolph Bultmann, *Theology of the New Testament*. Vol. 1. Trans. Kendrick Grobel. New York: Charles Scribner's Sons, 1951. pp. 29-30

And how would Jesus have conceived *the relation of his return as Son of Man to his present historical activity*? He would have had to count upon being removed from the earth and raised to heaven before the final End, the irruption of God's Reign, in order to come from there on the clouds of heaven to perform his real office. But how would he have conceived his removal from the earth?

As a *miraculous translation*? Among his sayings there is no trace of any such fantastic idea. As *departure by natural death*, then? Of that, too, his words say nothing.

By *a violent death, then*? But if so, could he count on that as an absolute certainty–as the consciousness of being raised to the dignity of the coming Son of Man would presuppose?

To be sure, *the predictions of the passion* (Mark 8.31; 9.31; 10.33-34; cf. 10.45; 14.21, 41) foretell his execution as divinely foreordained. **But can there be any doubt that they are all *vaticinia ex eventu*?** Besides, they do not speak of his parousia! And the predictions of the parousia (Mark 8.38; 13.26-27; 14.62; Matt. 24.27, 37, 44) on their part, do not speak of the death and resurrection of the Son of Man.

Clearly the predictions of the parousia originally had nothing to do with the predictions of death and resurrection; i.e., in the sayings that speak of the coming of the Son of Man there is no idea that this Son of Man is already here in person and must be removed by death before he can return from heaven.

Modern Biblical Interpretation: *Not What Happened* but What Did the Church Preach?

➤ Rudolph Bultmann, *Theology of the New Testament*. Vol. 1. p. 31

Now it is true that in the predictions of the passion the Jewish concept Messiah-Son-of-Man is re-interpreted–or better, singularly enriched–insofar as the idea of a suffering, dying, rising Messiah or Son of Man was unknown to Judaism. But this reinterpretation of the concept was done not by Jesus himself but by the Church ex eventu. Of course, the attempt is made to carry the idea of the suffering Son of Man back into Jesus' own outlook by assuming that Jesus regarded himself as Deutero-Isaiah's Servant of God who suffers and dies for the sinner, and fused

Readings on Messianic Prophecy (continued)

together the two ideas Son of Man and Servant of God into the single figure of the suffering, dying and rising Son of Man. At the very outset, the misgivings which must be raised as to the historicity of the predictions of the passion speak against this attempt. In addition, the tradition of Jesus' sayings reveals no trace of a consciousness on his part of being the Servant of God of Isaiah 53.

[To the early Church] it was all the more significant and impressive that the risen Lord was he who had previously died on the cross. Here too, formula-like expressions promptly form, as the tradition of 1 Corinthians 15.3-4 again indicates, and also the description at Romans 4.25: "who was put to death for our trespasses and raised for our justification."–a statement that had evidently existed before Paul and had been handed down to him. . . . This same thing is shown by the predictions put into Jesus mouth in Mark (and also in Matthew and Luke) carrying back the Hellenistic kerygma into the preaching of Jesus.

◆ *Rudolph Bultmann, Theology of the New Testament. Vol. 1. pp. 82-83*

Messianic Prophecy: Something More Sure

2 Peter 1.19-21 (ESV) - And we have something more sure, the prophetic word, to which *you will do well to pay attention as to a lamp shining in a dark place, until the day dawns and the morning star rises in your hearts,* [20] knowing this first of all, that no prophecy of Scripture comes from someone's own interpretation. [21] For no prophecy was ever produced by the will of man, but men spoke from God as they were carried along by the Holy Spirit.

Questions about Messianic prophecy

1. What does the prophecy *say exactly*?

2. How does Jesus' life and ministry *make it plain*?

3. How does it shine on my understanding of . . .

   What *God's master plan* for reestablishing his kingdom rule?

   What *the enemy's schemes* are to undermine it?

   What we can expect as God fulfills his Word?

APPENDIX 39
New Testament Readings

The Problem: Who Precisely Was Jesus of Nazareth?

> C. S. Lewis, *Mere Christianity*. New York: Touchstone by Simon and Schuster, (1943) 1996. p. 52

A man who was merely a man and said the sort of things Jesus said wouldn't be a great moral teacher. He would either be a lunatic–on a level with a man who says he is a poached egg–or else he'd be the devil of hell. You must make your choice. Either this man was, and is, the Son of God, or else a madman or something worse.

Tell Us Plainly: Are You the Messiah, or Not?

> Archibald M. Hunter, *The Work and Words of Jesus*. Philadelphia: The Westminster Press, (1950) 1973. p. 134

Always at the center of the Jews' concern is the question of questions, "Can this Galilean possibly be the Messiah?" On his part, Jesus does not give them the unequivocal answer which they desire, but in a simple parable "drawn from ancient Palestinian tradition," John 10.1-5, he does make a veiled Messianic claim. "I am no interloper," he says in effect, "but the rightful shepherd of God's flock. I need no signs to prove my authority which is self-authenticating: it lies in the fact that my sheep follow my leadership because they recognize in me the accents and actions of Israel's true shepherd" (see Ezekiel 34).

Why Didn't Jesus Embrace More Publicly His Identity as Messiah, and Therefore Silence His Adversaries?

> Archibald M. Hunter, *The Work and Words of Jesus*. p. 103

Jesus knew himself to be the Messiah, albeit in his own terms, during his ministry. What does this mean? That he was the person through whom God's rule was being realized and the ancient prophecies fulfilled. Yet when Peter or Caiaphas sought to apply the title to him, Jesus seemed to shy away from it and talk instead of the Son of Man. Why?

The only convincing answer is that Jesus conceived his Messiahship in spiritual and eschatological terms, not in nationalist and political ones. One indication of what it means to him comes in his reply to John the Baptist's questions. "I am," he replies in effect, "the fulfiller of the great Isaianic prophecies (Isa. 29.18-19; 35.5-6; and 61.1), and come to bring healing, life, and good news to God's needy children." Another clue he gives in his mode of entry into the holy city recalls Zechariah's prince of peace (Zech. 9.9-10). Not the Psalms of Solomon but Servant Songs of Isaiah and the Psalms of the Righteous Sufferer (22, 69, etc.) shaped his thought of the Messiah."

Documenting Your Work
A Guide to Help You Give Credit Where Credit Is Due
The Urban Ministry Institute

Plagiarism is using another person's ideas as if they belonged to you without giving them proper credit. In academic work it is just as wrong to steal a person's ideas as it is to steal a person's property. These ideas may come from the author of a book, an article you have read, or from a fellow student. The way to avoid plagiarism is to carefully use "notes" (textnotes, footnotes, endnotes, etc.) and a "Works Cited" section to help people who read your work know when an idea is one you thought of, and when you are borrowing an idea from another person.

Avoiding Plagiarism

A citation reference is required in a paper whenever you use ideas or information that came from another person's work.

Using Citation References

All citation references involve two parts:

- Notes in the body of your paper placed next to each quotation which came from an outside source.

- A "Works Cited" page at the end of your paper or project which gives information about the sources you have used

There are three basic kinds of notes: parenthetical notes, footnotes, and endnotes. At The Urban Ministry Institute, we recommend that students use parenthetical notes. These notes give the author's last name(s), the date the book was published, and the page number(s) on which you found the information. Example:

Using Notes in Your Paper

> In trying to understand the meaning of Genesis 14.1-24, it is important to recognize that in biblical stories "the place where dialogue is first introduced will be an important moment in revealing the character of the speaker . . ." (Kaiser and Silva 1994, 73). This is certainly true of the character of Melchizedek who speaks words of blessing. This identification of Melchizedek as a positive spiritual influence is reinforced by the fact that he is the King of Salem, since Salem means "safe, at peace" (Wiseman 1996, 1045).

Documenting Your Work (continued)

Creating a Works Cited Page

A "Works Cited" page should be placed at the end of your paper. This page:

- lists every source you quoted in your paper

- is in alphabetical order by author's last name

- includes the date of publication and information about the publisher

The following formatting rules should be followed:

1. Title

The title "Works Cited" should be used and centered on the first line of the page following the top margin.

2. Content

Each reference should list:

- the author's full name (last name first)

- the date of publication

- the title and any special information (Revised edition, 2nd edition, reprint) taken from the cover or title page should be noted

- the city where the publisher is headquartered followed by a colon and the name of the publisher

3. Basic form

- Each piece of information should be separated by a period.

- The second line of a reference (and all following lines) should be indented.

- Book titles should be underlined (or italicized).

- Article titles should be placed in quotes.

Example:

Fee, Gordon D. 1991. *Gospel and Spirit: Issues in New Testament Hermeneutics.* Peabody, MA: Hendrickson Publishers.

Documenting Your Work (continued)

4. Special Forms

A book with multiple authors:

> Kaiser, Walter C., and Moisés Silva. 1994. *An Introduction to Biblical Hermeneutics: The Search for Meaning.* Grand Rapids: Zondervan Publishing House.

An edited book:

> Greenway, Roger S., ed. 1992. *Discipling the City: A Comprehensive Approach to Urban Mission.* 2nd ed. Grand Rapids: Baker Book House.

A book that is part of a series:

> Morris, Leon. 1971. *The Gospel According to John.* Grand Rapids: Wm. B. Eerdmans Publishing Co. The New International Commentary on the New Testament. Gen. ed. F. F. Bruce.

An article in a reference book:

> Wiseman, D. J. "Salem." 1982. In *New Bible Dictionary.* Leicester, England - Downers Grove, IL: InterVarsity Press. Eds. I. H. Marshall and others.

(An example of a "Works Cited" page is located on the next page.)

Standard guides to documenting academic work in the areas of philosophy, religion, theology, and ethics include:

For Further Research

> Atchert, Walter S., and Joseph Gibaldi. 1985. *The MLA Style Manual.* New York: Modern Language Association.

> *The Chicago Manual of Style.* 1993. 14th ed. Chicago: The University of Chicago Press.

> Turabian, Kate L. 1987. *A Manual for Writers of Term Papers, Theses, and Dissertations.* 5th edition. Bonnie Bertwistle Honigsblum, ed. Chicago: The University of Chicago Press.

Documenting Your Work (continued)

Works Cited

Fee, Gordon D. 1991. *Gospel and Spirit: Issues in New Testament Hermeneutics*. Peabody, MA: Hendrickson Publishers.

Greenway, Roger S., ed. 1992. *Discipling the City: A Comprehensive Approach to Urban Mission*. 2nd ed. Grand Rapids: Baker Book House.

Kaiser, Walter C., and Moisés Silva. 1994. *An Introduction to Biblical Hermeneutics: The Search for Meaning*. Grand Rapids: Zondervan Publishing House.

Morris, Leon. 1971. *The Gospel According to John*. Grand Rapids: Wm. B. Eerdmans Publishing Co. *The New International Commentary on the New Testament*. Gen. ed. F. F. Bruce.

Wiseman, D. J. "Salem." 1982. In *New Bible Dictionary*. Leicester, England-Downers Grove, IL: InterVarsity Press. Eds. I. H. Marshall and others.

Mentoring
The Capstone Curriculum

Before the Course Begins

- First, read carefully the Introduction of the Module found on page 5, and browse through the Mentor's Guide in order to gain an understanding of the content that will be covered in the course. The Student's Workbook is identical to your Mentor's Guide. Your guide, however, also contains a section of additional material and resources for each lesson, called *Mentor's Notes*. References to these instructions are indicated by a symbol in the margin: 📖. The Quizzes, Final Exam, and Answer Keys can all be found on the TUMI Satellite Gateway. (This is available to all approved satellites.)

- Second, you are strongly encouraged to view the teaching on both DVDs prior to the beginning of the course.

- Third, you should read any assigned readings associated with the curriculum, whether textbooks, articles or appendices.

- Fourth, it may be helpful to review the key theological themes associated with the course by using Bible dictionaries, theological dictionaries, and commentaries to refresh your familiarity with major topics covered in the curriculum.

- Fifth, please know that the students *are not tested on the reading assignments*. These are given to help the students get a fuller understanding of what the module is teaching, but it is not required that your students be excellent readers to understand what is being taught. For those of you who are receiving this module in any translation other than English, the required reading might not be available in your language. Please select a book or two that is available in your language - one that you think best represents what is being taught in this module - and assign that to your students instead.

- Finally, begin to think about key questions and areas of ministry training that you would like to explore with students in light of the content that is being covered.

Before Each Lesson

Prior to each lesson, you should once again watch the teaching content that is found on the DVD for that class session, and then create a *Contact* and *Connection* section for this lesson.

Review the Mentor's Guide to understand the lesson objectives and gather ideas for possible Contact activities. (Two to three Contacts are provided which you may use, or feel free to create your own, if that is more appropriate.)

Then, create a Contact section that introduces the students to the lesson content and captures their interest. As a rule, Contact methods fall into three general categories.

Attention Focusers capture student attention and introduce them to the lesson topic. Attention focusers can be used by themselves with motivated learners or combined with one of the other methods described below. Examples:

- Singing an opening song related to the lesson theme.

- Showing a cartoon or telling a joke that relates to an issue addressed by the lesson.

- Asking students to stand on the left side of the room if they believe that it is easier to teach people how to be saved from the Gospels and to stand on the right side if they believe it is easier to teach people from the Epistles.

Story-telling methods either have the instructor tell a story that illustrates the importance of the lesson content or ask students to share their experiences (stories) about the topic that will be discussed. Examples:

- In a lesson on the role of the pastor, a Mentor may tell the story of conducting a funeral and share the questions and challenges that were part of the experience.

- In a lesson about evangelism, the Mentor may ask students to describe an experience they have had of sharing the Gospel.

Problem-posing activities raise challenging questions for students to answer and lead them toward the lesson content as a source for answering those questions, or they may ask students to list the unanswered questions that they have about the topic that will be discussed. Examples:

- Presenting case studies from ministry situations that call for a leadership decision and having students discuss what the best response would be.

Preparing the Contact Section

- Problems framed as questions such as "When preaching at a funeral, is it more important for a minister to be truthful or compassionate? Why?"

Regardless of what method is chosen, the key to a successful Contact section is making a transition from the Contact to the Content of the lesson. When planning the Contact section, Mentors should write out a transition statement that builds a bridge from the Contact to the lesson content. For example, if the lesson content was on the truth that the Holy Spirit is a divine Person who is a full member of the Godhead, the Contact activity might be to have students quickly draw a symbol that best represents the Holy Spirit to them. After having them share their drawings and discuss why they chose what they did, the Mentor might make a transition statement along the following lines:

> *Because the Holy Spirit is often represented by symbols like fire or oil in Scripture rather than with a human image like the Father or the Son, it is sometimes difficult to help people understand that the Spirit is a full person within the Godhead who thinks, acts, and speaks as personally as God the Father or Jesus Christ. In this lesson, we want to establish the scriptural basis for understanding that the Spirit is more than just a symbol for "God's power" and think about ways that we can make this plain to people in our congregations.*

This is a helpful transition statement because it directs the students to what they can expect from the lesson content and also prepares them for some of the things that might be discussed in the Connection section that comes later. Although you may adapt your transition statement based on student responses during the Contact section, it is important, during the planning time, to think about what will be said.

Three useful questions for evaluating the Contact section you have created are:

- Is it creative and interesting?

- Does it take into account the needs and interests of this particular group?

- Does it focus people toward the lesson content and arouse their interest in it?

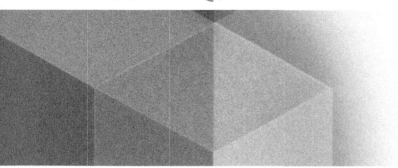

Again, review the Mentor's Guide to understand the lesson objectives and gather ideas for possible Connection activities.

Then, create a Connection section that helps students form new associations between truth and their lives (implications) and discuss specific changes in their beliefs, attitudes, or actions that should occur as a result (applications). As you plan, be a little wary of making the Connection section overly specific. Generally this lesson section should come to students as an invitation to discover, rather than as a finished product with all the specific outcomes predetermined.

At the heart of every good Connection section is a question (or series of questions) that asks students how knowing the truth will change their thinking, attitudes, and behaviors. (We have included some Connection questions in order to "prime the pump" of your students, to spur their thinking, and help them generate their own questions arising from their life experience.) Because this is theological and ministry training, the changes we are most concerned with are those associated with the way in which the students train and lead others in their ministry context. Try and focus in on helping students think about this area of application in the questions you develop.

The Connection section can utilize a number of different formats. Students can discuss the implications and applications together in a large Mentor-led group or in small groups with other students (either open discussion or following a pre-written set of questions). Case studies, also, are often good discussion starters. Regardless of the method, in this section both the Mentor and the learning group itself should be seen as a source of wisdom. Since your students are themselves already Christian leaders, there is often a wealth of experience and knowledge that can be drawn on from the students themselves. Students should be encouraged to learn from each other as well as from the Mentor.

Several principles should guide the Connection discussions that you lead:

- First, the primary goal in this section is to bring to the surface the questions that students have. In other words, the questions that occur to students during the lesson take priority over any questions that the Mentor prepares in advance–although the questions raised by an experienced Mentor will

still be a useful learning tool. A corollary to this is to assume that the question raised by one student is very often the unspoken question present among the entire group.

- Second, try and focus the discussion on the concrete and the specific rather than the purely theoretical or hypothetical. This part of the lesson is meant to focus on the actual situations that are being faced by the specific students in your classroom.

- Third, do not be afraid to share the wisdom that you have gained through your own ministry experience. You are a key resource to students and they should expect that you will make lessons you have learned available to them. However, always keep in mind that variables of culture, context, and personality may mean that what has worked for you may not always work for everyone. Make suggestions, but dialogue with students about whether your experience seems workable in their context, and if not, what adaptations might be made to make it so.

Three useful questions for evaluating the Connection section you have created are:

- Have I anticipated in advance what the general areas of implication and application are likely to be for the teaching that is given in the lesson?

- Have I created a way to bring student questions to the surface and give them priority?

- Will this help a student leave the classroom knowing what to do with the truth they have learned?

Finally, because the Ministry Project is the structured application project for the entire course, it will be helpful to set aside part of the Connection section to have students discuss what they might choose for their project and to evaluate progress and/or report to the class following completion of the assignment.

Steps in Leading a Lesson

- Take attendance.

Opening Activities

- Lead the devotion.

- Say or sing the Nicene Creed and pray.

- Administer the quiz.

- Check Scripture memorization assignment.

- Collect any assignments that are due.

- Use a Contact provided in the Mentor's Guide, or create your own.

Teach the
Contact Section

- Present the Content of the lesson using the video teaching.

Oversee the
Content Section

Using the Video Segments
Each lesson has two video teaching segments, each approximately 25 minutes in length. After teaching the Contact section (including the transition statement), play the first video segment for the students. Students can follow this presentation using their Student Workbook which contains a general outline of the material presented and Scripture references and other supplementary materials referenced by the speaker. Once the first segment is viewed, work with the students to confirm that the content was understood.

Ensuring that the Content is Understood
Segue
Using the Mentor's Guide, check for comprehension by asking the questions listed in the "Student Questions and Response" section. Clarify any incomplete understandings that students may demonstrate in their answers.

Ask students if there are any questions that they have about the content and discuss them together as a class. NOTE - The questions here should focus on

understanding the content itself rather than on how to apply the learning. Application questions will be the focus of the upcoming Connection section.

Take a short class break and then repeat this process with the second video segment.

Teach the Connection Section

- Summary of Key Concepts

- Student Application and Implications

- Case Studies

- Restatement of Lesson's Thesis

- Resources and Bibliographies

- Ministry Connections

- Counseling and Prayer

Remind Students of Upcoming Assignments

- Scripture Memorization

- Assigned Readings

- Other Assignments

Close Lesson

- Close with prayer

- Be available for any individual student's questions or needs following the class

Please see the next page for an actual "Module Lesson Outline."

The quizzes, the final exam, and their answer keys are located at the back of this book.

Module Lesson Outline

Lesson Title   Introduction

Lesson Objectives

Devotion

Nicene Creed and Prayer

Quiz

Scripture Memorization Review

Assignments Due

Contact (1-3)   Contact

Video Segment 1 Outline   Content

Segue 1 (Student Questions and Response)

Video Segment 2 Outline

Segue 2 (Student Questions and Response)

Summary of Key Concepts   Connection

Student Application and Implications

Case Studies

Restatement of Lesson's Thesis

Resources and Bibliographies

Ministry Connections

Counseling and Prayer

Scripture Memorization   Assignments

Reading Assignment

Other Assignments

Looking Forward to the Next Lesson

The Messiah Announced

📖 **1**

Page 13
Lesson Introduction

Welcome to the Mentor's Guide for Lesson 1, *The Messiah Announced*. The overall focus of *The New Testament Witness to Christ and His Kingdom* module is to provide the students with a biblical overview of the life of Jesus, based largely on a topical outline of the Gospels, and the first chapter of Acts. In a real sense, this study covers the concepts usually covered in a survey of the life of Christ course, and the appendices largely cover different aspects of this approach.

What will be important for you to do in this course is to concentrate on providing your students with an overview of the issues. Because of the nature of the course, there simply will not be time to do an in-depth analysis of the materials. (You may have greater flexibility, of course, depending on how you actually use your time in this module.) What is of critical weight is that you keep focused on the broad issues of Jesus' identity as Messiah: his announcement, opposition, revelation, and vindication.

Please notice in the objectives section of the module that these aims represent the sum of the content covered in the segment, and are a handy list to know what's ahead, both for you and the students. They are clearly stated, and you ought to emphasize them throughout the lesson, during the discussions and interaction with the students. The more you can highlight the objectives throughout the class period, the better the chances are that they will understand and grasp the magnitude of these objectives.

📖 **2**

Page 13
Lesson Objectives

Do not hesitate to discuss these objectives briefly before you enter into the class period. Draw the students' attention to the objectives, for, in a real sense, this is the heart of your educational aim for the class period in this lesson. Everything discussed and done ought to point back to these objectives. Find ways to highlight these at every turn, to reinforce them and reiterate them as you go.

Your decision to focus on the objectives of the segment and lesson is critical, for only by committing to a particular objective will you know precisely what you will want to include, emphasize, and cover in your teaching, both for the segment and lesson. So, always keep them in mind and emphasize them as often as possible in the actual presentation and discussion of the material.

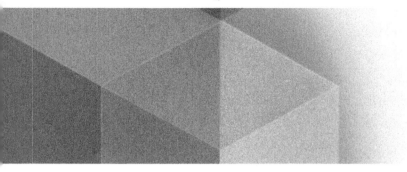

3
Page 13
Devotion

This devotion focuses on the importance of joy in understanding the revelation of Jesus as Messiah to the world. Often times the purpose of theology is largely intellectual and conceptual, and students, eager to wrestle with the theological implications of the coming of Christ, miss its most obvious and important emphasis. Jesus' coming into the world ought to produce unashamed and unabashed joy in our lives. His coming represents the fulfillment of God's ancient promise to save us, and many of the texts associated with his coming have to do with the comfort and joy of the Lord associated with the coming of Messiah for his own. See an example below:

Isa. 40.1-5 - Comfort, comfort my people, says your God. [2] Speak tenderly to Jerusalem, and cry to her that her warfare is ended, that her iniquity is pardoned, that she has received from the Lord's hand double for all her sins. [3] A voice cries: "In the wilderness prepare the way of the Lord; make straight in the desert a highway for our God. [4] Every valley shall be lifted up, and every mountain and hill be made low; the uneven ground shall become level, and the rough places a plain. [5] And the glory of the Lord shall be revealed, and all flesh shall see it together, for the mouth of the Lord has spoken."

Isa. 49.13-16 - Sing for joy, O heavens, and exult, O earth; break forth, O mountains, into singing! For the Lord has comforted his people and will have compassion on his afflicted. [14] But Zion said, "The Lord has forsaken me; my Lord has forgotten me." [15] "Can a woman forget her nursing child, that she should have no compassion on the son of her womb? Even these may forget, yet I will not forget you. [16] Behold, I have engraved you on the palms of my hands; your walls are continually before me."

Isa. 51.3 - For the Lord comforts Zion; he comforts all her waste places and makes her wilderness like Eden, her desert like the garden of the Lord; joy and gladness will be found in her, thanksgiving and the voice of song.

Isa. 51.12 - I, I am he who comforts you; who are you that you are afraid of man who dies, of the son of man who is made like grass.

Isa. 61.1-3 - The Spirit of the Lord God is upon me, because the Lord has anointed me to bring good news to the poor; he has sent me to bind up the brokenhearted, to proclaim liberty to the captives, and the opening of the prison to those who are bound; [2] to proclaim the year of the Lord's favor, and the day of vengeance of our God; to comfort all who mourn; [3] to grant to those who mourn in Zion—to give them a beautiful headdress instead of ashes, the oil of gladness instead of mourning, the garment of praise instead of a faint spirit; that they may be called oaks of righteousness, the planting of the Lord, that he may be glorified.

The purpose of the theological truth regarding the coming of the Messiah is to produce comfort, joy, purpose, and direction in the hearts and souls of humankind, and give the whole of creation hope that God has not abandoned his world to sin and chaos. Help them understand this pulse of joy that underlies God's revelation about Messiah in Scripture.

📖 **4**

Page 15
Contact

These contacts all highlight aspects related to the identity of the Messiah, and the provability of the case for him. In other words, many, many others have claimed down through the years of history to be the Messiah, and all of these claims must be weighed. Indeed, even the claim of Jesus of Nazareth must likewise be weighed for its validity and accuracy. Awaken in the students a need to critically engage in this debate, and to play the role of exegetical judges to discover if there is truly biblical warrant for the belief that Jesus is the Messiah.

📖 **5**

Page 19
Outline Point II-F

Emphasize the need for *preparation* when it comes to a profitable study of Christ. These demands go further than having the right translation of the Bible and the appropriate exegetical and theological dictionary tools. More importantly, a level of spiritual readiness to respond to his authority underlies all real profitable study of the Lord Jesus.

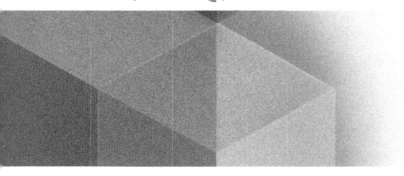

John 8.31-32 - So Jesus said to the Jews who had believed in him, "If you abide in my word, you are truly my disciples, [32] and you will know the truth, and the truth will set you free."

John 15.4-9 - Abide in me, and I in you. As the branch cannot bear fruit by itself, unless it abides in the vine, neither can you, unless you abide in me. [5] I am the vine; you are the branches. Whoever abides in me and I in him, he it is that bears much fruit, for apart from me you can do nothing. [6] If anyone does not abide in me he is thrown away like a branch and withers; and the branches are gathered, thrown into the fire, and burned. [7] If you abide in me, and my words abide in you, ask whatever you wish, and it will be done for you. [8] By this my Father is glorified, that you bear much fruit and so prove to be my disciples. [9] As the Father has loved me, so have I loved you. Abide in my love.

The questions connected with these lesson transitions are specifically designed to ensure that the students review and discuss the critical aims and facts presented in the first video segment. Depending on how you actually have scheduled your class meeting, it will be important for you to gauge your time well, especially if your students are intrigued with the concepts, and want to discuss their implications at length. Allow for the proper time to focus in on the main points, and still have enough time for a break before the next video segment is started.

What is important in this segment is to show the ways in which the biblical materials introduce the idea of Jesus of Nazareth in the context of the Roman occupation of Israel, and to verify his actual, historical place. Notice carefully the many allusions to the Old Testament in the birth narratives associated with the person of Jesus. Right from the beginning, the Apostles want us to understand the *continuity and fulfillment* themes associated with Jesus and the promised Messiah. Highlight this theme especially in your discussion of the segment with the students.

📖 **6**

Page 24
Student Questions
and Response

📖 **7**

Page 25
Summary of
Segment 2

John the Baptist was the son of Zechariah, the priest, and Elizabeth (also of priestly descent and a relative of Mary the mother of Jesus). Born in the hill country of Judah, his birth having been foretold by an angel (Luke 1.11ff.), he spent his early years in the wilderness of Judea (Luke 1.80). His public ministry began in the fifteenth year of the emperor Tiberius (A.D. 27) when he suddenly appeared out of the wilderness. John represents the fulfillment of the Elijah expectation, for Jesus (Mark 9.11-13) and the announcing angel (Luke 1.17). His person and importance cannot be underestimated for our understanding of Jesus and his announcement of his Messiahship. In every way, John shows similarities with Elijah (e.g., a "garment of camel's hair, and a leather girdle around his waist") (Matt. 3.4) was similar to the dress of Elijah (2 Kings 1.8). Although John refused to identify himself as Elijah (John 1.21-25), he did suggest his identification with Isaiah's "voice in the wilderness" (John 1.23).

Note carefully as you speak with the students John's twofold message emphasis: (1) the imminent appearance of the Messianic Kingdom, and (2) the immediate need for Israel to repent in preparation for the Messiah's appearing (Matt. 3.2). This message was especially directed to the people of God, the Jews, because of God's salvific purpose to prepare Israel for the Messiah's coming (Matt. 3.7-12). John's testimony is critical in affirming and announcing the identity of Jesus as Messiah (John 1.29).

It is a popular interpretation to associate John with the Essenes, a group we will consider in later lessons, especially because of his ascetic habits and his location near the chief settlement of the sect. The discovery of the Dead Sea Scroll (Qumran) sect, an Essenish group which dwelt on the northwest shore of the Dead Sea, has lent more credibility to this opinion, although it has not been proven.

John was beheaded for his prophetic judgment upon Herod Antipas for his marriage to his brother's wife (Matt. 14.1-12). Jesus testifies of John's critical importance in the realm of prophetic ministry, I believe, largely because of his role in announcing the coming of the Messiah himself.

Matt. 11.1-15 (ESV) - When Jesus had finished instructing his twelve disciples, he went on from there to teach and preach in their cities.[2] Now when John heard in prison about the deeds of the Christ, he sent word by his

disciples [3] and said to him, "Are you the one who is to come, or shall we look for another?" [4] And Jesus answered them, "Go and tell John what you hear and see: [5] the blind receive their sight and the lame walk, lepers are cleansed and the deaf hear, and the dead are raised up, and the poor have good news preached to them. [6] And blessed is the one who is not offended by me." [7] As they went away, Jesus began to speak to the crowds concerning John: "What did you go out into the wilderness to see? A reed shaken by the wind? [8] What then did you go out to see? A man dressed in soft clothing? Behold, those who wear soft clothing are in kings' houses. [9] What then did you go out to see? A prophet? Yes, I tell you, and more than a prophet. [10] This is he of whom it is written, 'Behold, I send my messenger before your face, who will prepare your way before you.' [11] Truly, I say to you, among those born of women there has arisen no one greater than John the Baptist. Yet the one who is least in the kingdom of heaven is greater than he. [12] From the days of John the Baptist until now the kingdom of heaven has suffered violence, and the violent take it by force. [13] For all the Prophets and the Law prophesied until John, [14] and if you are willing to accept it, he is Elijah who is to come. [15] He who has ears to hear, let him hear.

This section of the module is a handy snapshot of the critical concepts discussed in both segments of the lesson. This is usable for a number of reasons (e.g., to summarize the truths of the lesson, to hone in on the big ideas the lesson is designed to communicate, to define the critical issues which will serve as the basis for the case studies, etc.). Listed below are the fundamental truths written in sentence form which the students should have received from this lesson, that is, from the videos and your guided discussion with them. Make sure that these concepts are clearly defined and carefully considered, for their quiz work and exams will be taken from these items directly.

📖 **8**

Page 36
Summary of
Key Concepts

📖 **9**

Page 37
Student Application
and Implications

One of the critical tools your students must master is not merely the ability to discern the truths in a presentation, but to explore the implications of the truths for their personal lives as well as for those whom they serve.

In helping your students think through their own situations, you might want to design some questions or use those provided below as water to "prime the pump" of their interests, so to speak. What is significant here is not the questions written below, but for you, in conversation with your students, to settle on a cadre of issues, concerns, questions, and ideas that flow directly from their experience, and relate to their lives and ministries. Do not hesitate to spend the majority of time on some question that arose from the video, or some special concern that is especially relevant in their ministry context right now.

What is most important here is to empower your students to have the courage and boldness to explore the ramifications of the truth. Therefore, the goal of this section is for you to enable them to think critically and theologically in regards to their own lives and ministry contexts. Again, the questions below are provided as guides and primers, and ought not to be seen as absolute necessities. Pick and choose among them, or come up with your own. The key is relevance now, to their context and to their questions.

📖 **10**

Page 41
Assignments

In covering the material for the lesson, make sure that you review all the assignments, materials, questions, and responsibilities that the students are responsible for in the next class session. Do not take anything for granted here; sometimes, students will avoid asking what they think are "stupid" questions, even though they do not personally understand some item on the agenda or in the assignment. Create an atmosphere where your students feel the freedom to ask anything about anything required, and encourage even the most so-called "elementary" questions. You can never set a goal to become too clear with your students regarding their assignments, for it is a rule of classroom management: *if something can be misunderstood, it probably will be.*

Make it your aim, then, to do all you can to help the students understand the assignment for next week, especially the written piece. This is not difficult; the goal is that they would read the material as best as they can and write a few sentences on what they take them to mean. This is a critical intellectual skill for your students to learn, so make sure that you encourage them in this process. Of course, for those students who might find this difficult, assure them of the intent behind this assignment, and emphasize their understanding of the material being the key, not their writing skills. We want to improve their skills, but not at the expense of their encouragement and edification. Nor, however, do we want to sell them short. Strike to find the midpoint between challenge and encouragement here.

The Messiah Opposed

MENTOR'S NOTES
2

📖 1

Page 45
Lesson Introduction

Welcome to the Mentor's Guide for Lesson 2, *The Messiah Opposed*. The overall focus of this lesson is to highlight and detail the kind of social and spiritual opposition that Jesus faced as he fleshed out his Messianic ministry in Israel. What is critical for the students to comprehend is the intrinsic nature of conflict to the ministry of Jesus. This focus on the warrior nature of Jesus' ministry should be a key theme emphasized throughout this lesson. The fact that Jesus came to engage the powers is clear in the Scriptures, and should be the notable emphasis in your overall guidance of the class. The texts below can be helpful to you in leading your students in discussing the nature of the spiritual conflict that Jesus encountered.

Social Conflict

Isa. 53.3 - He was despised and rejected by men; a man of sorrows, and acquainted with grief; and as one from whom men hide their faces he was despised, and we esteemed him not.

Matt. 5.11 - Blessed are you when others revile you and persecute you and utter all kinds of evil against you falsely on my account.

Matt. 10.34-36 - Do not think that I have come to bring peace to the earth. I have not come to bring peace, but a sword. [35] For I have come to set a man against his father, and a daughter against her mother, and a daughter-in-law against her mother-in-law. [36] And a person's enemies will be those of his own household.

Matt. 10.21 - Brother will deliver brother over to death, and the father his child, and children will rise against parents and have them put to death.

Matt. 24.10 - And then many will fall away and betray one another and hate one another.

Mark 13.12 - And brother will deliver brother over to death, and the father his child, and children will rise against parents and have them put to death.

Luke 21.16 - You will be delivered up even by parents and brothers and relatives and friends, and some of you they will put to death.

Matt. 10.22 - and you will be hated by all for my name's sake. But the one who endures to the end will be saved.

Matt. 24.9 - Then they will deliver you up to tribulation and put you to death, and you will be hated by all nations for my name's sake.

Mark 13.13 - And you will be hated by all for my name's sake. But the one who endures to the end will be saved.

Luke 6.22 - Blessed are you when people hate you and when they exclude you and revile you and spurn your name as evil, on account of the Son of Man!

John 3.20 - For everyone who does wicked things hates the light and does not come to the light, lest his deeds should be exposed.

John 7.7 - The world cannot hate you, but it hates me because I testify about it that its works are evil.

John 15.18-25 - If the world hates you, know that it has hated me before it hated you. [19] If you were of the world, the world would love you as its own; but because you are not of the world, but I chose you out of the world, therefore the world hates you. [20] Remember the word that I said to you: "A servant is not greater than his master." If they persecuted me, they will also persecute you. If they kept my word, they will also keep yours. [21] But all these things they will do to you on account of my name, because they do not know him who sent me. [22] If I had not come and spoken to them, they would not have been guilty of sin, but now they have no excuse for their sin. [23] Whoever hates me hates my Father also. [24] If I had not done among them the works that no one else did, they would not be guilty of sin, but now they have seen and hated both me and my Father. [25] But the word that is written in their Law must be fulfilled: "They hated me without a cause."

Heb. 12.2 - looking to Jesus, the founder and perfecter of our faith, who for the joy that was set before him endured the cross, despising the shame, and is seated at the right hand of the throne of God.

James 4.4 - You adulterous people! Do you not know that friendship with the world is enmity with God? Therefore whoever wishes to be a friend of the world makes himself an enemy of God.

1 John 3.1 - See what kind of love the Father has given to us, that we should be called children of God; and so we are. The reason why the world does not know us is that it did not know him.

1 John 3.13 - Do not be surprised, brothers, that the world hates you.

Spiritual Conflict

1 John 3.8 - Whoever makes a practice of sinning is of the devil, for the devil has been sinning from the beginning. The reason the Son of God appeared was to destroy the works of the devil.

Gen. 3.15 - I will put enmity between you and the woman, and between your offspring and her offspring; he shall bruise your head, and you shall bruise his heel.

Isa. 27.1 - In that day the Lord with his hard and great and strong sword will punish Leviathan the fleeing serpent, Leviathan the twisting serpent, and he will slay the dragon that is in the sea.

Mark 1.24 - "What have you to do with us, Jesus of Nazareth? Have you come to destroy us? I know who you are— the Holy One of God."

Luke 10.18 - And he said to them, "I saw Satan fall like lightning from heaven."

John 12.31 - Now is the judgment of this world; now will the ruler of this world be cast out.

John 16.11 - concerning judgment, because the ruler of this world is judged.

Rom. 16.20 - The God of peace will soon crush Satan under your feet. The grace of our Lord Jesus Christ be with you.

Col. 2.15 - He disarmed the rulers and authorities and put them to open shame, by triumphing over them in him.

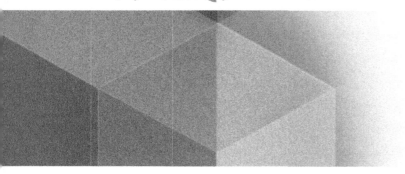

Heb. 2.14 - Since therefore the children share in flesh and blood, he himself likewise partook of the same things, that through death he might destroy the one who has the power of death, that is, the devil.

1 John 3.5 - You know that he appeared to take away sins, and in him there is no sin.

Rev. 20.2-3 - And he seized the dragon, that ancient serpent, who is the devil and Satan, and bound him for a thousand years, [3] and threw him into the pit, and shut it and sealed it over him, so that he might not deceive the nations any longer, until the thousand years were ended. After that he must be released for a little while.

Rev. 20.10 - and the devil who had deceived them was thrown into the lake of fire and sulfur where the beast and the false prophet were, and they will be tormented day and night forever and ever.

Please notice again in the objectives that these truths are clearly stated. As usual, your responsibility as Mentor is to emphasize these concepts throughout the lesson, especially during the discussions and interaction with the students. The more you can highlight the objectives throughout the class period, the better the chances are that they will understand and grasp the magnitude of these objectives.

📖 2
Page 45
Lesson Objectives

In order to understand the nature of conflict, a disciple must embrace this as a part of their normal, spiritual journey. Because our Lord suffered at the hands of those who neither knew God nor him, and because we are united to Christ by faith (Rom. 6.1-6), no believer or Christian leader need be shocked at persecution, as though something is happening to them that was unexpected or unplanned. This devotion focuses on the inevitability of persecution on the lives of those who follow in the footsteps of Jesus. And the testimony of the Word of God bears this out:

📖 3
Page 45
Devotion

1 Pet. 4.12-14 - Beloved, do not be surprised at the fiery trial when it comes upon you to test you, as though something strange were happening to you. [13] But rejoice insofar as you share Christ's sufferings, that you may also rejoice and be glad when his glory is revealed. [14] If you are insulted for the name of Christ, you are blessed, because the Spirit of glory and of God rests upon you.

1 Cor. 10.13 - No temptation has overtaken you that is not common to man. God is faithful, and he will not let you be tempted beyond your ability, but with the temptation he will also provide the way of escape, that you may be able to endure it.

1 Thess. 3.2-4 - and we sent Timothy, our brother and God's coworker in the gospel of Christ, to establish and exhort you in your faith, [3] that no one be moved by these afflictions. For you yourselves know that we are destined for this. [4] For when we were with you, we kept telling you beforehand that we were to suffer affliction, just as it has come to pass, and just as you know.

1 Pet. 5.9 - Resist him, firm in your faith, knowing that the same kinds of suffering are being experienced by your brotherhood throughout the world.

Acts 14.22 - strengthening the souls of the disciples, encouraging them to continue in the faith, and saying that through many tribulations we must enter the kingdom of God.

Rom. 8.35-37 - Who shall separate us from the love of Christ? Shall tribulation, or distress, or persecution, or famine, or nakedness, or danger, or sword? [36] As it is written, "For your sake we are being killed all the day long; we are regarded as sheep to be slaughtered." [37] No, in all these things we are more than conquerors through him who loved us.

1 Cor. 4.9 - For I think that God has exhibited us apostles as last of all, like men sentenced to death, because we have become a spectacle to the world, to angels, and to men.

2 Tim. 3.11-12 - my persecutions and sufferings that happened to me at Antioch, at Iconium, and at Lystra—which persecutions I endured; yet from them all the Lord rescued me. [12] Indeed, all who desire to live a godly life in Christ Jesus will be persecuted.

1 Pet. 2.21 - For to this you have been called, because Christ also suffered for you, leaving you an example, so that you might follow in his steps.

Highlight this significant spiritual truth as you discuss with the students their reaction to the devotional.

It should not surprise you if you get a great variation of responses and opinion from your students concerning the inevitability of suffering and opposition in the Christian life. Depending upon the spiritual diet they are accustomed to, students may respond, on the one hand, to this as a no-brainer, a clearly articulated truth that lies at the very center of the Word of God's testimony about any who affiliate with the Messiah. On the other hand, if the diet of the students tend toward "health-wealth" cuisine, then such teaching will not be seen as helpful. It may even be seen as mildly dismissive of the victory won for us by Christ, and at worst even heretical. Regardless of the initial reaction, it is important to make certain that the students understand the central role that this teaching plays in Jesus' teaching, as well as the clear model he provides in his own life. The opposition that believers must endure is intrinsic to their allegiance to Messiah. All those who hate him will instantly hate them as well, and they must be prepared for this onslaught and rejection from those who do not know him.

📖 **4**

Page 47
Contact

For a thorough and comprehensive treatment on these groups and others that made up the milieu and social environment of Jesus, the following texts may be helpful.

Elwell, Walter A. and Robert W. Yarbrough. *Encountering the New Testament*. Grand Rapids: Baker Books, 1998.

📖 **5**

Page 51
Outline Point II

Meeks, Wayne. A., ed. *The New Testament in its Social Environment.* Philadelphia: Westminster Press, 1986.

Lohse, Eduard. *The New Testament Environment.* trans. by John E. Steely. Nashville: Abingdon Press, 1971.

Tenney, Merrill C. *New Testament Times.* Grand Rapids: Eerdmans Publishing, 1965.

📖 **6**
Page 60
Student Questions and Response

Take the time to carefully monitor and distinguish the various responses of the different groups to Jesus in his original *Sitz im Leben* (literally "situation-in-life"). This attention will pay off dramatically for a student of the Gospels, for if one understands the various responses of the key players in the Gospel drama they will be better able to discern larger issues and meanings which may go unnoticed without this particular knowledge.

In the questions below you will find the focus is upon mastering the data and the facts associated with the claims made in the first video segment. Concentrate on ensuring that the students understand the answers in light of the lesson aims of the first segment. Make certain that you watch the clock here, covering the questions below and those posed by your students, being cautious of any tangents which may lead you from rehearsing the critical facts and main points.

📖 **7**
Page 61
Summary of Segment 2

Here again it is critical to track carefully not merely the social conflict which Jesus encountered with his contemporaries in Israel, but perhaps most importantly to track his constant and ongoing battle with the spiritual forces which sought to undermine his ministry. Satan and his minions play a dramatic role in the Gospel drama, and no full understanding of the life and ministry of Jesus is possible that underestimates or overlooks these critical dimensions.

The Nature of Demons in Scripture

In order to understand Jesus' ongoing conflict with the powers of evil in this age, you should introduce to the students briefly and carefully the subject of demons. I

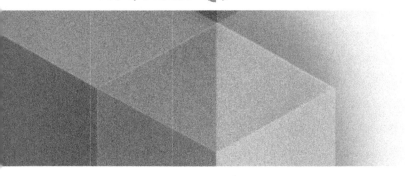

say briefly and carefully because we are not exhorted in the New Testament to become experts on the ways of the "dark side." Rather, we are told not to become ignorant of his schemes (e.g., 2 Cor. 2.11 - "so that we would not be outwitted by Satan; *for we are not ignorant of his designs*"), and to be alert to his machinations at all times because of his desire to devour anyone he can (e.g., 1 Pet. 5.8-9 - "Be sober-minded; be watchful. Your adversary the devil prowls around like a roaring lion, seeking someone to devour. [9] Resist him, firm in your faith, knowing that the same kinds of suffering are being experienced by your brotherhood throughout the world").

Although the Old Testament does not seek to speculate much on the subject of dark spirituality, it is clear that some links are connected with the work of the enemy and the practices of idolatry, magic, and witchcraft forces (Deut. 32.17; Ps. 96.5). These practices were against the Law and will of God, they were strictly forbidden to God's community (Deut. 18.10-14; 1 Sam. 15.23). As one scholar suggests, demonic activity in the Old Testament is largely to be understood as an "opposing force to God and his own personal intermediary beings, the *malakim* (angels)."

In the New Testament, the terms associated with these spirits are *daimon* and *daimonion*, the actual presence of these beings is defined as "unclean" (*akatharton*, Mark 1.24-27; 5.2-3; 7.26; 9.25; Acts 5.16; 8.7; Rev. 16.13) and "evil" (*ponera*, Acts 19.12-16) spirits. The majority of texts in reference to the activity of these spirits connect them to the possession of individuals. While the New Testament does not seek to give a systematic answer as to where these beings originated, there is no question that they exist in the mind of the New Testament writers, and that they operate against the affairs of Christ and his work.

There is a strong connection to the activity associated with these beings and idolatry (cf. Paul's understanding of the link to idols and demons in 1 Corinthians 10.20-21; 12.2; cf. Rev. 9.20). Paul and John indicate that demonic activity will increase as the end draws near, with very powerful effects of deception and seduction of others (1 Tim. 4.1; Rev. 16.13-14). Christians are to be engaged with these powers, even as our Lord was, as detailed in Ephesians 6.10-18. The Christian must be prepared to combat "rulers . . . authorities . . . powers, this dark world and the spiritual forces of evil in the heavenly realms."

What is crucial to emphasize here is that the coming of Messiah was directly related to overcoming the forces of evil, including those effects of the curse and powers of evil which sought to interfere with God's reassertion of his rule over his creation.

📖 8

Page 75
Case Studies

These case studies are designed to evoke open dialogues and conversations about some of the implications associated with modern views of suffering, opposition, conflict, and triumph in the Christian life. What is important to note here is that these issues are some of the most common and pervasive in the Church, especially in the American church which tends to think of the Christ victory in terms of health, wealth, and blessing. This view of the Christian life is so common that many take it to be the only credible reading and interpretation of the meaning of Christ's life and death for us today. To revisit this question is critical, especially for those planting churches and making disciples in neighborhoods amidst populations which are poor, disenfranchised, broke, and dangerous. Encourage your students to wrestle with these concepts, for they lie at the base of an entire cadre of related issues that arise from the different frameworks of Christian spirituality which believers adhere to today.

📖 9

Page 77
Counseling
and Prayer

In this lesson, which highlights the issues of suffering, opposition, and conflict, it should be plain that an emphasis on prayer is appropriate. If you can, seek to spend a good amount of time in this lesson on prayer, especially since this was Jesus' surest and most common way to receive from the Father the grace, instruction, and leading he needed in order to endure the constant onslaught of his worldly foes and invisible enemies. In this, we ought to model the example of Christ and the Apostles, who made prayer a significant ongoing discipline in their lives.

> Luke 6.12-13 - In these days he went out to the mountain to pray, and all night he continued in prayer to God. [13] And when day came, he called his disciples and chose from them twelve, whom he named Apostles.

> Matt. 14.23-25 - And after he had dismissed the crowds, he went up on the mountain by himself to pray. When evening came, he was there alone, [24]

but the boat by this time was a long way from the land, beaten by the waves, for the wind was against them. [25] And in the fourth watch of the night he came to them, walking on the sea.

Mark 6.46 - And after he had taken leave of them, he went up on the mountain to pray.

Col. 4.2 - Continue steadfastly in prayer, being watchful in it with thanksgiving.

Also, do not consider it an overly familiar or unnecessary thing to ask the students if they need prayer for someone or something connected to the ideas and truths presented in the lesson. Prayer is a wonderfully practical and helpful way to apply truth; by taking specific needs to God in light of a truth, the students can solidify those ideas in their soul, and receive back from the Lord the answers they need in order to be sustained in the midst of their ministries. Of course, everything is somehow dependent on the amount of time you have in your session, and how you have organized it. Still, prayer is a forceful and potent part of any spiritual encounter and teaching, and if you can, it should always have its place, even if it is a short summary prayer of what God has taught us, and a determination to live out its implications as the Holy Spirit teaches us.

The Messiah Revealed

 1

Page 81
Lesson Introduction

Welcome to the Mentor's Guide for Lesson 3, *The Messiah Revealed*. The central focus of this lesson is to grapple with the character of Jesus' works and words, and how they actually reveal concretely and definitively the legitimacy of his claim to Messiahship. It is hard to estimate the power of Jesus' character, which is incomparable and magnificent, and its significance for making the case for his role as Messiah. Jesus is the Suffering Servant of the Old Testament, concealed there but revealed in the New Testament, and made plain to all who are interested in him. While our current study focuses on the New Testament Gospel's witness to Jesus' Messianic identity, the same majestic character is seen in the epistles.

Jesus as the Servant of the LORD

The term "servant of the Lord," or the Hebraic expression *'ebed yhwh*, "servant of Jehovah," was applied to worshipers of God such as Abraham (Ps. 105.6), or others fulfilling God's purposes, like Nebuchadnezzar (Jer. 25.9). The most important use of the term appears as the "servant of Jehovah" when Isaiah prophesies his encouragements and comforts while Sennacherib sought to ravage Israel around 701 B.C. The term, "servant of the Lord" is referred to some twenty times in Isaiah 40-53.

While the identification of the servant tends to vary, it appears as if the name refers primarily to an individual to come, the Messiah of God. The reference to Israel, "Israel, my servant" (41.8) is present, but in Isaiah's "servant songs" (42.1-7; 49.1-9; 50.4-9; 52.13-53; and probably 61.1-3), this terms refers to a person to come who would be the Lord's own holy servant, who would bring Jacob back to the Lord (49.5). This personage is not Isaiah himself (42.1), and the majesty of his future work and sinless character suggest that this servant (53.9) is not merely an outstanding character of Israel to come (42.4).

In the New Testament (John 12.38, 41; Acts 8.32-35), we see that Jesus of Nazareth meets the full criteria for being the Servant of the Lord, the one who embodies Israel and who himself will restore to God his own righteous remnant (Isa. 49.6).

In a very real way, the contours of Jesus' life demonstrate that he is the Servant of the Lord. Look at the various elements associated with the Servant.

1. He will be a prophet of God (49.1-2; cf. Jer. 1.5) filled and strengthened by the power of the Holy Spirit (Isa. 42.1; 61.1; Luke 4.21).

2. He will do the will of God, without asserting his own desires or rights (Isa. 42.2-3; Matt. 12.18-21).

3. He will suffer on behalf of others bearing their sin, diseases, and guilt (Isa. 53.4; Matt. 8.17).

4. He will not be believed, but will be opposed and become a subject of reproach (Isa. 53.1; 49.7; 50.6; Matt. 26.67; 27.26).

5. He will be condemned as a guilty criminal, and will give up his life as a punishment for the sins of others (Isa. 53.5-8; 1 Pet. 2.22-25).

6. His soul will be made by God to be a priestly *asam*, "guilt offering" (Isa. 53.10), through whom God will "sprinkle many nations" (52.15; Heb. 12.24; 1 Pet. 1.2).

7. He will be buried with the rich (Isa. 53.9-10; Matt. 27.57).

8. He will be resurrected in glory (Isa. 53.10, 12).

9. He will justify many through his sacrifice (Isa. 53.11), including Gentiles (42.6; Luke 2.32).

10. He will establish the justice of God in the earth (Isa. 42.4; Rom. 15.21).

11. He himself will be the one through whom God establishes a new covenant (Isa. 42.6; 49.8).

It is right in my mind to equate the servant songs of Isaiah to the Davidic Messiah (the one mentioned in Gen. 3.15). Both the Servant and the Messiah are chosen by God and are righteous (Isa. 42.1, 6; 9.6-7; cf. Ps. 89.3-4). The Messiah would be humbled at his appearing (Isa. 7.15; Dan. 9.25-26; Zech. 9.9) which aligns with the Servant's humble status (49.6; 55.4). Further, the Holy Spirit fills both the Davidic "branch" (11.1-4) and the Servant of God (42.1). Both would ultimately be exalted by God (49.5, 7; 52.15). While John the Baptist associated Jesus as Messiah and Lamb of God (John 1.29-30), those to whom he preached did not see it (12.34). Above all,

however, Jesus did in fact display his identity, both as the Davidic Messiah (4.25-26) and as Suffering Servant of the LORD (Luke 22.37).

Now, why is this so important, again? The life and character of Jesus identify him as the Suffering Servant of the Lord, and, if the Servant and the Messiah *are one and the same*, then Jesus of Nazareth is the Messiah. A careful analysis, then, of Jesus' life, character, mindset, and behavior can give us clues into his true identity, which we believe to be the Messiah of Israel.

Highlight this truth as you focus on the objectives in this lesson. These aims are clearly stated, and you ought to emphasize them throughout the lesson with this connection of Jesus to the Servant of Yahweh in mind. Help them to make the connection between the characteristics of Jesus' life and his claim regarding Messiahship. This was a critical part of Jesus' own evidence for who he was, cf. John 14.7ff.

📖 **2**

Page 81
Devotion

This devotion focuses on the humility of Jesus. Christ's lowliness is the subject matter for the disciple of Christ (cf. Matt. 11.29-30 - Take my yoke upon you, and learn from me, for I am gentle and lowly in heart, and you will find rest for your souls. [30] For my yoke is easy, and my burden is light).

Perhaps no virtue of Jesus is more transparent and remarkable than his meekness and gentleness. Look at some of the representative texts:

Zech. 9.9 - Rejoice greatly, O daughter of Zion! Shout aloud, O daughter of Jerusalem! behold, your king is coming to you; righteous and having salvation is he, humble and mounted on a donkey, on a colt, the foal of a donkey.

Matt. 12.19-20 - He will not quarrel or cry aloud, nor will anyone hear his voice in the streets; [20] a bruised reed he will not break, and a smoldering wick he will not quench, until he brings justice to victory

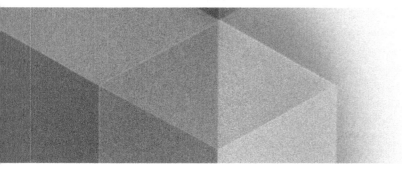

2 Cor. 10.1 - I, Paul, myself entreat you, by the meekness and gentleness of Christ - I who am humble when face to face with you, but bold toward you when I am away!

Phil. 2.5-8 - Have this mind among yourselves, which is yours in Christ Jesus, [6] who, though he was in the form of God, did not count equality with God a thing to be grasped, [7] but made himself nothing, taking the form of a servant, being born in the likeness of men. And being found in human form, [8] he humbled himself by becoming obedient to the point of death, even death on a cross.

1 Pet. 2.21-23 - For to this you have been called, because Christ also suffered for you, leaving you an example, so that you might follow in his steps. [22] He committed no sin, neither was deceit found in his mouth. [23] When he was reviled, he did not revile in return; when he suffered, he did not threaten, but continued entrusting himself to him who judges justly.

Perhaps no trait displayed in our lives gives greater claim of Jesus' presence within us than the simple lowliness that he displayed in every facet of his life. We ought to follow in his steps.

Again, it is important to note the context of this lesson content to be what was emphasized in a previous note before. If Jesus is the Suffering Servant of the LORD, and if his teaching, ministry, and conduct coincide with the figure, we have great confidence to also believe that he is in fact the Davidic Messiah to come, the one whom God would appoint to reign and rule over his people. Pay careful attention to these objectives in this light, that is, the light of how Jesus' character reveals his identification with the Servant of the Lord. Remember, Jesus introduces his Messianic call with a quotation of the Song of the Servant in Isaiah 61.1-3.

Luke 4.16-21 - And he came to Nazareth, where he had been brought up. And as was his custom, he went to the synagogue on the Sabbath day, and he stood up to read. [17] And the scroll of the prophet Isaiah was given to him. He unrolled the scroll and found the place where it was written, [18] "The

📖 **3**

Page 84
Summary of
Segment 1

Spirit of the Lord is upon me, because he has anointed me to proclaim good news to the poor. He has sent me to proclaim liberty to the captives and recovering of sight to the blind, to set at liberty those who are oppressed, [19] to proclaim the year of the Lord's favor." [20] And he rolled up the scroll and gave it back to the attendant and sat down. And the eyes of all in the synagogue were fixed on him. [21] And he began to say to them, "Today this Scripture has been fulfilled in your hearing."

📖 **4**

Page 95
Student Questions
and Response

Make sure that your students are seeing the central role that the righteousness of Jesus Christ played in his claim to be the Messiah. His matchless life and character add weighty evidence to the case being made for Jesus' Messiahship revealed in the nature of his life, as well as his teaching and works.

Make sure that you highlight this important fact as you lead the students in reviewing the material and Scriptures contained in the first video segment. Let your dialogue ensure that they are tracking with the lesson aims of the first segment, and that they are comprehending the richness of the case being made in the Gospels for the association of Jesus with the Messiah.

📖 **5**

Page 96
Summary of
Segment 2

While the heart of our aim is to concentrate on the materials which support Jesus as the Messiah contained in the Gospels, there is an abundance of materials referring to the Messiahship of Jesus in the books of Acts through Revelation. This data *confirms the historicity* of the materials in the Gospels. A brief and concise listing of this information includes the following data:

1. Jesus was born a Jew (Gal. 4.4).

2. Jesus is a descendant of David (Rom. 1.3).

3. The character of Jesus is dramatically meek and gentle (2 Cor. 10.1), righteous (1 Pet. 3.18), sinless (2 Cor. 5.21), and profoundly humble (Phil. 2.6).

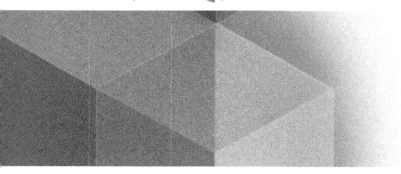

4. Jesus was tempted in the same way other human beings are (Heb. 2.18; 4.15).

5. Jesus commanded that we keep his Supper (1 Cor. 11.23-26).

6. According to Peter's eyewitness testimony, Jesus' person was transfigured in the mount (2 Pet. 1.17-18).

7. Jesus was betrayed and crucified (1 Cor. 11.23; 1 Cor. 1.23).

8. He was buried and rose again from the dead on the third day (1 Cor. 15.3ff).

9. Jesus, risen and glorified, ascended into heaven (Eph. 4.8).

10. Certain specific sayings of Jesus are known (cf. 1 Cor. 7.10; 9.14; Acts 20.35), and possible allusions to his sayings are also found (e.g., Rom. 12.14, 17; 13.7, 8-10; 14.10).

In other words, the testimony of the Gospels are confirmed and underscored in the preaching, writing, and prophecy of the rest of the New Testament.

As you emphasize the centrality of Jesus' death, it may be helpful for you to be aware of the some of the central texts whereby Jesus demonstrates that his death is part and parcel of his reason for coming into the world. This awareness of the necessity of his own death controls much of Jesus' actions and dialogue.

📖 **6**

Page 107
Student Questions
and Response

Isa. 53.8 - By oppression and judgment he was taken away; and as for his generation, who considered that he was cut off out of the land of the living, stricken for the transgression of my people?

Isa. 53.12 - Therefore I will divide him a portion with the many, and he shall divide the spoil with the strong, because he poured out his soul to death and was numbered with the transgressors; yet he bore the sin of many, and makes intercession for the transgressors.

Dan. 9.26 - And after the sixty-two weeks, an anointed one shall be cut off and shall have nothing. And the people of the prince who is to come shall

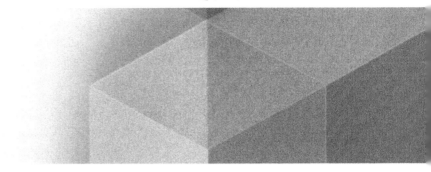

destroy the city and the sanctuary. Its end shall come with a flood, and to the end there shall be war. Desolations are decreed.

Mark 8.31 - And he began to teach them that the Son of Man must suffer many things and be rejected by the elders and the chief priests and the scribes and be killed, and after three days rise again.

Mark 9.31 - for he was teaching his disciples, saying to them, "The Son of Man is going to be delivered into the hands of men, and they will kill him. And when he is killed, after three days he will rise."

Mark 10.45 - For even the Son of Man came not to be served but to serve, and to give his life as a ransom for many.

Luke 9.22 - saying, "The Son of Man must suffer many things and be rejected by the elders and chief priests and scribes, and be killed, and on the third day be raised."

Luke 9.31 - who appeared in glory and spoke of his departure, which he was about to accomplish at Jerusalem.

John 10.11 - I am the good shepherd. The good shepherd lays down his life for the sheep.

John 11.51 - He did not say this of his own accord, but being high priest that year he prophesied that Jesus would die for the nation.

John 12.23-24 - And Jesus answered them, "The hour has come for the Son of Man to be glorified. [24] Truly, truly, I say to you, unless a grain of wheat falls into the earth and dies, it remains alone; but if it dies, it bears much fruit."

📖 7

Page 110
Case Studies

The heart of the following case studies is getting at the meaning of the idea that Jesus is the *Suffering Servant of the Lord*. In a sense, many congregations and Christian leaders have all but eclipsed the meaning of opposition and conflict from their understanding of the Christian faith. Pay careful attention to the ideas and concepts

your students share regarding the nature of discipleship, leadership, and the Christian faith. Make sure that you reemphasize the objectives of the lesson here. As mentor, you will want to help them "unpack" these ideas carefully, for they will carry great weight and implication for every dimension of their lives and ministries as they progress. *A bloodless, non-suffering Messiah is not a biblical one.*

By the end of the second class session, you ought to have made clear to the students their need to have done all the mind work, leg work, and planning necessary to carry out their Ministry Project. Also, by this time, the end of the third session, you should have also emphasized the need for them to select their biblical text for their Exegetical Project. Both the Ministry Project and the Exegetical Project, in order to be done excellently and thoroughly, require ample time and good planning. The earlier they can think through these assignments, the better they will carry them out. Please, do not fail to emphasize to them the need to plan ahead. The end of any course is usually its most difficult season, when a number of assignments become due and the exam looms on the horizon. Often times, when students do not plan ahead and prepare for the sudden rush of assignments, they suffer greatly. Too many things become due, and the added pressure of time interferes with the quality of their work. Any way that you can remind them of the need for advanced planning will be wonderfully helpful for them, whether they realize it immediately or not.

Because of this, we advocate that you consider docking a modest amount of points for late papers, exams, and projects. While the amount may be nominal, your enforcement of your rules will help them to learn to be efficient and on time as they continue in their studies.

📖 **8**

Page 112
Assignments

The Messiah Vindicated

MENTOR'S NOTES
4

📖 **1**

Page 117
Lesson Introduction

Welcome to the Mentor's Guide for Lesson 4, The Messiah Vindicated. This lesson centers on the vindication of Jesus' claim of Messiahship, primarily based on the mystery and veracity (truthfulness) of the resurrection. One could make an argument that a mastery of the data regarding the resurrection of Jesus is essential for every person claiming to be a disciple of Christ, and an absolute necessity for those who represent him in ministry. In light of this importance, it will be key for you to spend the requisite amount of time mastering this material yourself. In other words, set as a personal goal to understand the appearances of Jesus, from the first appearance at the tomb till the morning beach meal with the Apostles at the Sea of Galilee. This is not done merely to impress others, or to demonstrate a mastery of mere facts. Rather, this learning is critical both for the defense of the Gospel, as well as a source of great encouragement in your own personal life.

Here in this final lesson, note for the last time the objectives section below. Many ideas, facts, and assertions are mentioned in this lesson, and it will be important for you to know what you need to concentrate upon in your presentations and review with the students. The idea of vindication runs throughout this lesson, which is an idea of validation, of being proven right, or having your position verified. Jesus is in fact the Suffering Servant of God, the Messiah of Israel, and the overwhelmingly important supporting fact underwriting that claim is his resurrection from the dead. Make this simple but clear assertion the central claim and objective in this lesson.

📖 **2**

Page 117
Devotion

As you can tell, this devotional does a kind of running experiment to trace the possible inner thought reactions of the women at the tomb on the third day after our Lord's sufferings. What this experiment is intended to do is simple: to challenge the students to empathize with the range of emotion, wonder, and astonishment that the apostolic party must have experienced in those three short days. To go from the pits of despair and fear to the untold heights of wonder and mystery with the resurrection of the Lord from the dead–what a remarkable experience that must have been for them, and now for us, through their word.

What is truly astonishing today is how the pale fog of familiarity has caused us to lose sight of the wonder and mystery associated with our Lord's resurrection. We

must seek to capture and sustain the same level of wonder and devotion that turned that scared little group into world-changing Apostles and messengers of God. They were transformed, in a radically revolutionary way. The experience that catapulted them into the volumes of history was their experience of the risen Lord. The encounters they had with the Lord Jesus, and then with the Holy Spirit after his ascension changed them in every way, from head to toe. The power of faith in Messiah to transform and radicalize our lives is critical to everything we are doing, both in our own discipleship and in our service for Christ. What should be encouraging to all of us is that a single encounter with the risen Savior is enough to make world-changers out of a scared, timid, little band of Jesus' followers. May God so touch us as to make us world-changers, too, through the same powerful encounter with the glory of the risen Christ.

One of the primary aims of this lesson is to emphasize the importance of the apostolic deposit of faith, the Apostles' doctrine regarding Jesus as the Messiah. In our day, which has tended to downplay doctrine as a kind of old-fashioned, abstract, and uninteresting relic of past theological wars, it is important to rediscover the power and wonder of the theology, especially in its most central and fundamental form (i.e., the teaching regarding the resurrection of Jesus Christ). Emphasize throughout this lesson the central role that doctrine plays in the Christian life and ministry, and do not hesitate to exhort your students to new levels of committed, firsthand study of the scriptural evidence for Jesus as the Messiah of God. Below are some texts to aid you in your exhortations and challenges:

📖 **3**

Page 121
Summary of
Segment 1

> Jude 1.3 - Beloved, although I was very eager to write to you about our common salvation, I found it necessary to write appealing to you to contend for the faith that was once for all delivered to the saints.

> Acts 28.28 - Therefore let it be known to you that this salvation of God has been sent to the Gentiles; they will listen.

> Gal. 3.28 - There is neither Jew nor Greek, there is neither slave nor free, there is neither male nor female, for you are all one in Christ Jesus.

Titus 1.4 - To Titus, my true child in a common faith: Grace and peace from God the Father and Christ Jesus our Savior.

2 Pet. 1.1 - Simon Peter, a servant and apostle of Jesus Christ, to those who have obtained a faith of equal standing with ours by the righteousness of our God and Savior Jesus Christ.

Acts 20.27 - for I did not shrink from declaring to you the whole counsel of God.

1 Cor. 15.3 - For I delivered to you as of first importance what I also received: that Christ died for our sins in accordance with the Scriptures, [4] that he was buried, that he was raised on the third day in accordance with the Scriptures.

Gal. 2.5 - to them we did not yield in submission even for a moment, so that the truth of the gospel might be preserved for you.

2 Pet. 3.2 - that you should remember the predictions of the holy prophets and the commandment of the Lord and Savior through your apostles.

Phil. 1.27 - Only let your manner of life be worthy of the gospel of Christ, so that whether I come and see you or am absent, I may hear of you that you are standing firm in one spirit, with one mind striving side by side for the faith of the gospel.

1 Thess. 2.2 - But though we had already suffered and been shamefully treated at Philippi, as you know, we had boldness in our God to declare to you the gospel of God in the midst of much conflict.

1 Tim. 1.18 - This charge I entrust to you, Timothy, my child, in accordance with the prophecies previously made about you, that by them you may wage the good warfare.

1 Tim. 6.12 - Fight the good fight of the faith. Take hold of the eternal life to which you were called and about which you made the good confession in the presence of many witnesses.

2 Tim. 1.13 - Follow the pattern of the sound words that you have heard from me, in the faith and love that are in Christ Jesus.

2 Tim. 4.7-8 - I have fought the good fight, I have finished the race, I have kept the faith. [8] Henceforth there is laid up for me the crown of righteousness, which the Lord, the righteous judge, will award to me on that Day, and not only to me but also to all who have loved his appearing.

Rev. 12.11 - And they have conquered him by the blood of the Lamb and by the word of their testimony, for they loved not their lives even unto death.

While this present segment concentrates mainly on Paul's extended argument in 1 Corinthians 15 about the nature and importance of Jesus' resurrection, he teaches about the centrality of the resurrection in other passages in his other writings, as well. For instance, in Romans 1.3-4, considered by many scholars to be an ancient creedal statement of the Church, Paul provides the Romans with a concise but important summary statement on the doctrine of Christ, suggesting that Jesus through his resurrection has proven himself to be the Son of God, the Davidic Messiah and Lord (cf. Rom. 14.9). The resurrection of Jesus is the event which, according to Paul, provides salvation (Rom. 10.9-10) and guarantees that all who believe in Jesus Christ will also rise, even as he did (1 Cor. 15.20; 2 Cor. 4.14; 1 Thess. 4.14).

Moreover, we find in the writings of Luke some key citations about the resurrection. Jesus declared in his teaching to the Apostles, after his resurrection, that the sufferings and glory of the Messiah, including his rising from the dead, was in fact a key and central theme of the Old Testament (Luke 24.25-27). Peter, in his great Pentecost sermon, proclaimed that the great acts and miracles that Jesus did, especially the resurrection, were key indicators and signs that the Father accepted his actions and approved of his message (Acts 2.22-32). Likewise, the preaching of Paul in his sermons throughout his missionary tours constantly emphasized the centrality of Jesus' rising from the dead, treating it as the central foundation and basis of his evangelistic message (cf. Acts 13.29-39; 17.30-31).

📖 **4**

Page 128
Conclusion

Truly, the entire New Testament underscores what this segment suggests about the centrality of Jesus' resurrection to faith. The hope of the New Testament is a single, seamless, and eternal hope. Jesus suggested that his resurrection would be the confirming sign of both the authority and accuracy of his teachings about himself and the Kingdom of God (Matt. 12.38-40). It is the resurrection of Jesus that not only guarantees the salvation of all those who cling to Jesus by faith (1 Pet. 1.3), but also establishes the means whereby our Lord, as exalted and ascended High Priest, can carry out his priestly intercession on behalf of his Church (Heb. 7.23-25).

What all of this suggests is that this segment on both the centrality of the resurrection, and the validity of its history is central to faith, to hope, to service, and to ministry. Ensure that the students comprehend the significance of this doctrine before you go on to other matters.

📖 **5**

Page 128
Student Questions
and Response

Make sure that the students understand the basic terms, definitions, and concepts associated with the resurrection of Jesus. This is the place in the Capstone curriculum where these issues are considered largely from a historical vantage point, although the same are considered in the *God the Son* module from a more theological and Christological view. What is important here is your confidence that the students understand the actual facts and the ramification of those facts as they relate to the historical events surrounding the resurrection of Christ. Ask carefully worded questions designed to test their knowledge of the facts, and their understanding of the significance of those facts for the purpose of verifying the identity of Jesus as Messiah.

📖 **6**

Page 129
Summary of
Segment 2

The Great Commission is one of the central post-resurrection injunctions of the risen Lord. In it, Jesus commands his Apostles to go into all the world and make disciples, carrying the message of the Messiah and the Kingdom of God to all nations, to the very ends of the earth. This is the continuation of a basic message associated with the salvation of God, first alluded to in the Old Testament (e.g., Isa. 45.22; cf. Gen. 12.3) and fulfilled and instituted formally for the Church in the New Testament (Matt. 9.35-38; 28.19; Acts 1.8). Jesus, as risen and living Messiah,

commanded his Apostles to make disciples through preaching and teaching the good news of Jesus of Nazareth as Savior and Lord, with baptism and obedience as confirming emblems of its reception (2 Tim. 4.2; Matt. 28.20). This proclamation would be accompanied with signs and wonders confirming his Word (Heb. 2.2-4; Mark 16.17-18) and good works which testify of the power of its declaration (Acts 9.36; Gal. 6.9-10; Eph. 2.10).

What are the contents of the message to be given through the commission? This message is to concentrate on God's love and mercy shown in the person of Jesus of Nazareth, and include the historical events of his life, especially his death on the cross (1 Cor. 15.3; Col. 2.14-15). It is to also include testimony regarding his resurrection from the dead, his ascension to the Father (Luke 24.46-48; Rom. 4.25; 1 Cor. 15.3-4; Eph.1.20-23), and the hope of his second appearing (Acts 3.19-21).

As shown from a careful study of the texts surrounding the commission, it is God's love in Jesus Christ demonstrated in his death and resurrection (2 Cor. 5.14-21) that serves as the controlling power and sustaining motive for making disciples worldwide. It is founded, however, on the absolute authority of the risen Messiah himself, who both as the Lord of glory (1 Cor. 2.8) and the Author of life (Acts 3.15) commands his followers to make disciples. Because he possesses all authority and power in heaven and earth, our risen Lord can anticipate, acknowledge, and answer every conceivable contingency in the world that might seek to dissuade him from his task. Nothing can stop his own from this commission, for all authority belongs to him, and him alone (Matt. 28.18-19).

This commission itself is patterned on the Messiah's own faithful service to his Father, and his own obedient fulfillment of his Father's commission (John 20.21 [RSV] Jesus said to them again, "Peace be with you. As the Father has sent me, even so I send you"). Our Lord went about doing good, releasing men and women from the power of the evil one (Acts 10.38). He proclaimed the message of the Kingdom of God and his salvation, and declared his mission to come and seek and save the lost (Mark 10.45; Luke 19.10). In the same way our Lord, as Messiah and Servant of the Lord, preached the good news of God's in-breaking Kingdom (Matt. 4.23), so his disciples are now commissioned to go into the world and declare Jesus as Lord, the risen Savior and Messiah of God (Acts 4.2).

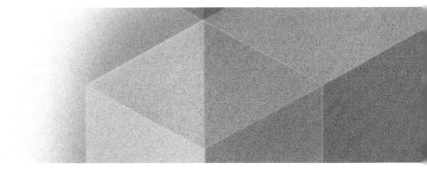

The elements of the commission ought to be covered carefully for the students so they can understand its breadth and power. For instance, it is a universal message, to go to the entire world beginning in Jerusalem and Judea, then in neighboring Samaria, and expanding to the very ends of the earth (Luke 24.47-48; Acts 1.8). It is for all people, Jews (Acts 2.5-11) and Gentiles (Acts 13.46; Rom.1.16). In one sense, this Gospel is the single message of salvation, starting in God's first telling of the Gospel in the Garden of Eden (Gen. 3.15-17), going through the period of the cross of Jesus (Rom. 3.25; Gal.3.8-9), all the way through this present age, to the very coming of Jesus at his return (Matt. 24.14).

Jesus was clear that no work of Gospel proclamation was to occur until the Holy Spirit was poured out on his disciples. Only the Holy Spirit's indwelling wisdom, leading, and power are sufficient for the work of evangelism, mission, and the spreading of the Good News (Luke 24.49; Acts 1.8). Merely the telling of the Good News will never suffice for salvation, for it is only through the convicting and redeeming power of the Holy Spirit that a person can be convicted of their sin, regenerated through his power, and empowered to confess our Lord Jesus as Lord of all (John 16.8; Titus 3.5; 1 Cor. 12.3).

📖 7

Page 135
Outline Point III

The promise of the Holy Spirit is a message directly connected with the coming of the Messiah, the end of time, and the ushering in of God's Kingdom reign upon the earth. From the very beginning of his ministry Jesus identified himself as the Lord, the Messiah King who also is the Suffering Servant figure of Old Testament prophecy (Isa.42.1ff.; cf. Mark 10.45). In one sense, this entire module has sought to show that Jesus combined these two concepts, which historical Judaism had traditionally interpreted as separate ideas. Jesus understood himself to be the Messiah of God, the one anointed by God to deliver the captives, preach good news to the poor, to proclaim the favor of God, and to reassert God's rulership in this in-breaking Kingdom. The promise of the Holy Spirit was directly associated with these motifs, and Jesus' asking the disciples to tarry until the Holy Spirit was given undeniably asserts that in himself the New Age had dawned. This is the very heart of his message at his inaugural sermon at the synagogue in Nazareth (Luke 4.16ff.). Our Lord, in quoting the Messianic promise, stopped short of reading the words of

judgment, focusing instead on the comfort and salvation of the Servant Song of Isaiah 61. Jesus emphasized in this age the blessing and power of the Spirit; Jesus himself was filled with the Spirit without measure (John 3.36), and now baptizes with the Spirit, and at the Second Coming, with fire. This clearly is the emphasis of John the Baptist when he questions whether Jesus is indeed the Messiah, the one who was to come (Luke 7.18-23). In this age, Jesus baptizes with the Holy Spirit, and at his coming, the judgment of the nations and the earth, he will baptize with fire (cf. Luke 3.15ff.). Jesus' promise of the coming Holy Spirit was a focus on the salvation promise of the Messiah associated with God's in-breaking Kingdom, and as such, concentrated upon the positive, saving aspect of the New Age, an age known for the outpouring of the Holy Spirit upon all who believe (Acts 1.5; 11.16).

The crucial place of the ascension in theology is shown by its prominent place in theology in the Gospels and Epistles. In John, the ascension is alluded to on at least three occasions (John 3.13; 6.62; 20.17). Paul relates that the ascension of Jesus resulted in his exaltation far above all the heavens in order that he might fill the entire heavens with his glory (Eph. 4.10). Much of the Apostles' writings include key phrases such as "received up in glory" (1 Tim. 3.16), "gone into the heavens" (1 Pet. 3.22), and "passed through the heavens" (Heb. 4.14), all of which point to this same event. Our very spirituality is anchored in the Pauline assertion that the believers are to ". . . seek the things that are above, where Christ is, seated at the right hand of God" (Col. 3.1b). Many citations in the New Testament refer to the work that Jesus is doing on behalf of the redeemed as a result of his ascension in glory to the Father's right hand.

The teaching of the ascension is linked inseparably to the Apostles' teaching about the resurrection. For instance, in Ephesians 1.15-23 the Apostle Paul links his teaching regarding the resurrection directly to the exaltation of Jesus to the place of supreme authority and headship over the Church. Texts such as Romans 8.34 and Colossians 3.1 also link the resurrection and ascension, as a single movement of God's verification of Jesus' Messiahship (resurrection), and the corresponding exaltation to the place of glory and authority (ascension). What is key to emphasize in your lesson instruction here is that the same Lord whose Messiahship was

📖 **8**

Page 138
Outline Point IV

confirmed through his resurrection, was exalted to a position of authority, power, and glory in the ascension.

📖 **9**

Page 143
Case Studies

What is emphasized in these case studies is the importance of understanding that the testimony of the resurrection and ascension are anchored on the experience and testimony of the Apostles, not the shrewdness and cogency of our logical arguments. In an age of missions science and church growth principles, it pays to remind your students of the helpful place these things have, but they can never be decisive. Only the truth of the Apostles' testimony, mixed with the illumination and conviction provided by the Holy Spirit, will suffice in helping individuals come to a full and compelling understanding of Jesus as the Messiah. Without the Spirit, the natural man cannot by any means understand the things of God (1 Cor. 2.9-16).

Does this mean that we ought not present these truths with a clear, logical, and appropriate presentation geared to the culture of those who receive it? Absolutely not! Paul is unequivocal in suggesting that he strove to become all things to all people in order that he might win some (1 Cor. 9.23ff.). He was equally aware, however, that he was merely a planter, or one who watered. Only God himself could provide the actual growth of the seed and plant (1 Cor. 3.6-7).

📖 **10**

Page 147
Assignments

Make sure that you pay the price at this time to cover all of your bases as a mentor or professor. You must be as organized as your students, paying careful attention to every dimension of the course, and ensuring your own well-organized and disciplined approach to your student's assignments and grades.

At this point in the module, attention must be given to tracking the various assignments of your students, and recording their grades carefully and accurately. Your work as an instructor and grader begins in earnest now. Make sure that you have commitments for the ministry projects, exegetical projects, and other data together as this will be important for you to determine the student's overall grade. Again, your discretion regarding late work can easily determine whether you dock students of points, resulting in letter grade changes, or give students an

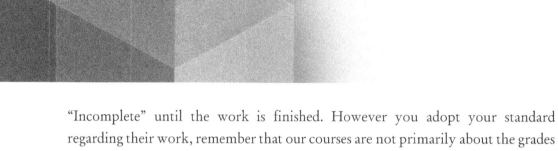

"Incomplete" until the work is finished. However you adopt your standard regarding their work, remember that our courses are not primarily about the grades that students receive, but the spiritual nourishment and training these courses provide. Also, however, remember that helping our students strive for excellence is an integral part of our instruction.

Made in United States
Orlando, FL
09 March 2023

30874202R00154